THE APOSTLES AFTER JESUS

A History of the Apostles

(Separating Tradition and History)

David Criswell

FORTRESS

ADONAI
PRESS

Dallas, TX

THE APOSTLES AFTER JESUS

A History of the Apostles

(Separating Tradition and History)

David Criswell

ISBN NUMBER 0-61575-778-2

Cover Design by David Criswell
Art by Henryk Siemiradzki, "Christian Dirce" 1897

FORTRESS

ADONAI
PRESS

Dallas, TX

Printed in the United States of America

Dedication

For those who believed in me when no else did.

"We conquer in dying.
We go forth victorious at the very time we are subdued."
- Tertullian on Martyrdom.[1]

Preface

This book evolved out of an appendix for my last book in the Controversies series, *Controversies in the Acts and Epistles*. I wanted to write an appendix dealing with the lives of the apostles after the close of the book of Acts. What did the apostles do which is not recorded in the Bible? How did they die? To what countries did they travel? To whom did they bring the gospel?

As I was writing the appendix I soon found that it was not a mere appendix, but a book. I had outlined nearly fifty pages without having written a single paragraph. Obviously the subject was more than could be adequately placed in an appendix.

As a result, I began to write the book you have before you now. However, it is fair to ask how this book differs from others. In fact, although many have come out over the years, there are few in print today. How then does this book differ from those few?

First, I lay out all the ancient ante-Nicene (before Constantine's day) historical records and traditions separately from my evaluation and conclusions. Each chapter is divided into these three sections so as to allow the reader to make his own judgments. Second, I rely more strongly on early records and traditions and less so upon post-Nicene traditions. Although the famous "martyrology of Jerome" and Bede are of importance, the more ancient traditions are of more value to genuine historical research. The reasons for this should become apparent. Third, I have reached some different conclusions than some others, based largely on the second point. Fourth, I include, wherever possible, original citations from the ante-Nicene fathers, whereas others too often quote secondary sources, if at all. Fifth, many neglect the apostle Paul, because he is not counted among the twelve. I, however, include him since he is certainly the most influential apostle, whether he be rightly considered the thirteen apostle or the twelfth. Sixth, I include, wherever possible, in the final chapter, brief biographies and martyrologies of the apostles' companions. Finally, I neither accept Catholic tradition at face value, nor reject it out of hand. The traditions of different churches, whether Catholic, Orthodox, Nestorian, or Syrian, are only of value as they relate to specific times, places, and incidences which they would have observed or had reported to them at the time the original tradition developed. Every tradition must be weighed against the facts, and most importantly, against the Bible.

It is my hope that the history of the apostles after the Biblical records will be recognized as more than mere traditions and legends. Every child is taught in Sunday school that the apostles all died a martyr's death, save the Beloved John. How do we know this? How did they die? Where did they preach the gospel? These are the questions I hope to answer.

David Criswell, January 2013

Table of Contents

✝   ✝   ✝

1

Introduction

"The blood of the martyrs is the seed of the church." This famous paraphrase of the ancient church father Tertullian[2] has echoed throughout the centuries. Although all religions have been persecuted, most all resist, and some even view dying in war as "martyrdom," but alone among the religions of the world has Christianity blossomed amid the most savage persecutions, while her children walk quietly and passively to meet the most cruel and savage of fates. The pagan historian records that Christians were "covered with the skins of beasts, they were torn by dogs and perished, or were nailed to crosses, or were doomed to the flames and burnt, to serve as a nightly illumination, when daylight had expired."[3]

These were but a few of the atrocities and crimes committed against the servants of our Lord Jesus, but because we surrendered peacefully, without resistance, this actually created a unique problem for the emperors' thrist for blood. In ancient Rome the gladiatorial games were composed entirely of criminals under the death penalty. They fought because it gave them a chance at life; a slim one, but a chance. Christians, however, were unique in that we refused to fight, even though it meant certain cruel deaths. For that very reason Nero invented such barbaric tortures for the enjoyment of audiences that even pagan historians shirked at the barbarities.

Now this book is not truly a martyology, for there are far better martyrologies in existence, such as the unabridged 6000 pages of John Foxe's *Acts and Monuments*, better known as the *Book of Martyrs* in its grotesquely abbreviated form. I have also relied on Thieleman Van Braght's *Martyr's Mirror*. However, both of these were written in the days of the Reformation, and hence 1500 years removed from the original martyrs. My goal here is not to repeat what others have said, or what traditions may yield, but to discover the true history of the apostles after the record of the Bible ends in Acts 28. What happened to the apostles? Where did they minister? To what contries did they travel? How did they die?

Obviously this is similar to a martyology of the apostles, but it differs in two fundamental ways. First, I seek to understand the lives as well as the deaths of the apostles. Their ministries are as important as their martyrdoms, for without their ministries, they martydoms would be meaningless. Thus Tertullian's famed remark should be revised. The blood was not the seeds, but the water. The seeds were the apostles' ministries. The blood is the water which nourished the seeds and made them grow.

The second difference is that I seek to separate the true history of the apostles from the tradition of the apostles. Before the days of revisionist history, this was the goal of all historians. It was not to tear down what we don't like as the lawyer does in court, but to be like the police detective who seeks to unearth the truth. How then can this be done?

Many people do not understand that there is a different criteria for the historical research of antiquity than that of modern history. Before the invention of the printing press documents were fewer in number and not as well preserved. Additionally, as more time elapses and new kingdoms rise and fall, often destroying many of the documents left behind by those who came before them, only a handful of original documents survive, if any. How then can we know that Raamses was not the Pharaoh of Egypt? For that matter, how do we know that Julius Caesar was really killed by all the Senators of Rome? The answer to this fills volumes of books in itself, but I will summarize the answer as follows.

The people of antiquity were not stupid. They made copies of documents and passed those down through the centuries. If someone made a change to a document, someone somewhere would notice and object to the change. There is even a famous anecdote of a fight which erupted when an ancient bishop got into a verbal spar over a priest who substituted the then modern word for "bed" or "pallet" for the antiquated Biblical word found in John 5:8.[4] This illustrates that even minor changes were subjected to scrutiny and objections.

But what happens when first and second hand accounts fail us? Since we are talking about post-Biblical history, first hand accounts do not exist, and second hand accounts are few in number. What do we make of the traditions which followed?

Separating Tradition and History

History is reality. What really happened is history. Tradition is like gossip. The closer the gossip is to the event, the more accurate it is. The further it is from the event, the closer it is to legend. One might say that what you say to your wife is history, what she tells her best friend is tradition, and what her best friend tells your best friend is legend.

So how can we determine what is history, what is tradition, and what is legend? The answer is not unlike a police detective investigating a crime scene. Criminals do not like to leave evidence, and take great care not to leave any, so the police must piece together the events by talking to eyewitnesses, many of whom often contradict one another, and then compare their testimony to the bits of information and trace evidence which the criminal may inadvertently have left behind.

Now missionaries are not politicians. We would not expect ancient historians to pen first hand accounts of simple missionaries. For this very reason it is surprising that we have so much historical data outside of the Bible as we do. This is itself a testament to the impact which Chrisitanity had on the world, and still has. Consider, for example, that when missionaries arrived in India in the second century, expecting to be the first to bring the gospel, they not only found a thriving Christian community,[5] but archaeology has unearthed evidence that one of the kings of ancient second century Kerala, decades before their arrival, was a Christian![6] Their tradition said that it was Thomas who brought them the gospel. Missionaries also found in other parts of India that the people already had copies of the book of Matthew, but only Matthew.[7] These facts lend credibility to otherwise unconfirmed traditions of Thomas and Bartholomew in India. Is this evidence sufficient? That is one of the questions I will examine in this volume, but in order to do this it is necessary to lay out a few rough guide lines to understand my approach.

Unlike Jesus, where even pagan historians record his trial and death under Pontius Pilate, there is very little "secular" history mentioning the apostles. This is not surprising as they were missionaries and not politicians. Some evidence, such as the Talmud, does exist, but this is limited in its value. What we are left with are four primary sources. The value of these sources decreases with time, and some are of more value than other. If all things were equal (as we shall see, *they are not*), then we could break down the *relative* reliability and value of these sources as follows:

	Apostolic Age	Sub-apostolic Age	Ante-Nicene	Nicene	Post-Nicene
Epistemological	A-	A-	B-	C	D+
Historical	A-	B+	B	B-	C+
Apocryphal	B+	B-	C+	D+	D-
Legendary (oral)	C+	C-	D	D-	F

The reader may notice several peculiarities in my list. Epistemology, for example, *may* be of higher value than historical references in the sub-apostolic age, but of less value in the Nicene era? Why? Let us look at these sources individually to ascertain why.

Epistomological References

By epistemological references I refer to matter-of-fact references in letters addressed by the church fathers to various churches. The earliest of these epistles are of great historical value for the generation which lived in the apostolic age, and the generation immediately following it, would obviously know whether or not an apostle had truly visited their country or church. If, for example, an epistle is written to the church of Ephesus and speaks of John in Ephesus in a matter-of-fact non-controversial manner then we might expect that the Ephesians would know whether this was true or not. Thus the apostolic and sub-apostolic epistles are of great value, whereas later epistles written centuries after the fact may begin to merely mimic traditions and legends, and are thus of less value. These sort of references are also limited in both number and substance. They are therefore limited in their overall value.

Historical References

Ideally historical references would be of the most value, except that most count Eusebius as the first "true" church historian. Since Eusebius wrote over two hundred and fifty years after the apostles, his research is valuable, but not without flaws. Nevertheless, this is not the limit of our historical references, for although they may not have been true historians, the early church fathers were obviously interested in history. Consequently, men like Hippolytus, and others, wrote brief histories of the apostles. Others discuss the history of a country's evangelism or similar topics which may embrace part of the history of the apostles. Historical references are therefore of the most overall value, and yet, as aforementioned, the lack of full church history before the time of Eusebius make these references limited in number and content. They are pieces of an incomplete puzzle.

Apocryphal References

Apocrypha has become a term referring to ancient books about Biblical figures which is not a part of the canon of Scripture. These writings range from historical, but flawed, to historical fiction to pure legends. They may be compared to Hollywood movies about historical figures. Depending on the author, the time it was made, and its target audience, it may be largely historical with some revisions to pure absurbities. Likewise the target audience may effect the credibility of the document. The so-called *Gospel of Thomas*, for example, although very ancient, it is a well known forgery of zero historical value written by gnostic cult members to promote their heresies. It is of no value, whereas the *Acts of Thomas*, although also bearing some gnostic influences and heresies, appears to be a work of historical fiction, which has some underlying historical basis.

Apocryphal writings can therefore be a double edged sword. Like trying to learn history from watching a Hollywood movie, it is not always easy. When we know the political agenda of the filmmaker, we can more easily decipher what elements of the film are fiction, and which parts are loosely based on history. So it is with apocryphal books. They are of little value in determining the specifics of events, but there are ways to decipher whether or not the works bear the marks of history or fiction. Historical accuracy, for example, is the easiest. If an apocryphal work gets the name of a king or city wrong, then the entire work is suspect. If, however, it demonstrates knowledge of geography, history, and the politics of the region, we may assume some first hand knowledge, such as in the *Acts of Barnabas*. Apocrypha is therefore useful, but used with extreme caution.

Legendary or Oral Traditions

Such traditions are of the least value. Sometimes early traditions and legends are useful, when supported by secondary evidence, but when a tradition is passed on orally through generations it quite literally becomes like gossip. Once the gossip has gotten around the table, there is no telling how much of it, if any, is true.

Now having determined the relative value of our sources does not really answer the question. Just because we have these sources does not automatically make them credible. What criteria then can be used to determine the truth of a source?

Historical Criteria

Using the police analogy, we can say that gaining eyewitness testimony is the most valuable information (more so than forensic evidence) a police officer can have, but this does *not* mean that all testimony is equal. A witness may be mistaken, only have seen part of the incident, or even be lying for various reasons. Therefore, although the relative value of eyewitnesses are very strong, not all eyewitnesses are equally reliable. How then can we determine if the sources are reliable outside of its relative value? There are several factors which I take into account.

Is it consistent with the Biblical record?

Although the Bible obviously does not record what happened to the apostles in post-Biblical times, it is still important because a tradition which conflicts with what we know from the Bible cannot be trusted. For example, some late traditions claim that James the Greater traveled to Spain after Pentecost and returned before his execution described in Acts 12:2.[8] This tradition is not consistent with the Biblical record, for it is clear, as will be discussed later, that Paul was the first to venture beyond the Middle East. The apostles had stayed in

Judea to witness the gospel until they were driven away, and James's execution was one of those pivotal events. We, therefore, cannot accept the tradition as being consistent with the Biblical record.

Is the secondary information historically accurate?

A good policeman will ask an eyewitness seemingly irrelevant questions. There are several reasons for this. One of those purposes is to see if he was really an eyewitness at all. Simple facts, such as whether there was a Burger King across the street, help to establish whether the individual was really present at all. So also apocryhal works are often filled with factual errors, such as the names of kings or cities. If an apocryphal work cannot get these details correct, then it cast suspicion upon its credibility. Conversely, a work such as the *Acts of Barnabas*, which goes into detail in local geography, show a knowledge of the region and area. It does not prove that the story is true, but it does show knowledge of the region in which the story took place, and thus elevates its credibility.

Is it consistent with other histories?

If one witness describes something different from other witnesses, we may suspect that there is something wrong. So also when we see traditions which say Simon the Zealot died in the Middle East, while others say he died in Britain, we may suspect that one or the other tradition is not accurate.

Is the Source Conflated?

In the above example, Simon the Zealot is shown in two far away places. Some traditions attempt to reconcile conflicting traditions by conflating them. As the reader will see, the most difficult issues found in this book are easily resolved when we see that the traditions are conflating various people or events.

When we examine these criteria combined with the relative value of its antiquity and source, we have some knowledge of its general history. Obviously the more credible evidence, the more likely we are to believe the stories, or at least the underlying tradition behind it. Still each must be evaluated on its own merit.

Chapter Structure

I organize my book the same way I would have wished other books I have read to be organized. I want the reader to be able to come to his own conclusions rather than simply accept my own. Therefore each chapter is structured the same. I will present a brief summary of all known apostolic traditions with little or no commentary, *regardless* of whether there is any historical merit to the tradition. *Then* I will present a second section which will examine the evidence and compare the traditions. In this section I will weigh and evaluate all the evidence. Finally, I will summarize what I believe to be the true and accurate known history of the apostle in question. Additionally, I provide a map, where necessary, to illustrate where the apostles traveled in their missionary activities.

Summary

The history of antiquity uses a different criteria than that of modern history. Most of the documents and records of antiquity are long gone. Archaeology does not unearth new information, but *old* lost information, and rarely does it uncover paper documents which comprise the majority of ancient records. Consequently, we are often left with second hand histories of those who had seen documents which are no longer in existence. Jesus Christ is one of those rare exceptions wherein we have a wealth of information, both first and second hand. This is not the case with the post-Biblical history of the apostles, however.

When first and second hand information fails us we are left with traditions of varying value. The more ancient the tradition, the better its worth, but this leads to a conflict. Catholic tradition is often elevated above the tradition of antiquity. This is an irony which will effect some of our decisions. To the Catholic I will state here in full disclosure that I am a Protestant who holds late Catholic traditions of far less value and credibility than the traditions of the apostolic age.

Jesus Himself often criticized his fellow Jews for elevating tradition above the Scriptures (Matthew 15:3, 6; Mark 7:8-13). The apostles did not reject all tradition (1 Corinthians 11:2; 2 Thessalonians 2:15, 3:6), but neither did they venerate tradition (Colossians 2:8). So also I accept tradition when it is in accordance with the Bible and history, but I reject it when it contradicts the Bible, history, or itself.

Let me further say in full disclosure that some Protestants will object as much as Catholics, for I base my critique upon the merit of history and the Bible, not upon Catholic tradition, nor upon a reactionary rejection of it. This issue will be most prevalent in the history of Peter, so it is appropriate Peter is the first disciple of whom we will speak.

2

Simon Peter

The last thing we read of Peter in the book of Acts is at the Council of Jerusalem (chapter 15) where the apostles decreed that there should be no stumbling blocks to gentiles in the evangelization of the gospel. The importance of the council is beyond the scope of this book, save that it signaled the beginnings of a shift from evangelizing the Jews to the evangelization of gentiles.

The apostle Paul was the first to reach out to the gentiles, but we do know that Peter eventually left Judea himself. At least one of his epistles alludes to his being in "Babylon" (1 Peter 5:13). The question is, what happened after the Council of Jerusalem? Why did Peter leave Judea? Where did he go? Was he truly the first pope? Did he die in Rome?

It is no secret that Protestants and Catholics are more bitterly divided over Peter than any other apostle. This is because of the debate over whether or not Peter was ever a pope or pontiff. Catholics make Peter out to be the first bishop of Rome whereas some reactionary Protestants deny Peter was ever even in Rome! Both are groundless in history. The early histories do indeed record Peter (and Paul) as the founder of the Roman church but none make him out to be bishop, instead giving the first episcopate to Linus (2 Timothy 4:21).[9] Furthermore, both Catholics and Protestants may be surprised to hear what the early traditions do record of Peter. Traditions, for example, that Peter was crucified next to his wife, and leaving behind a daughter.

Can these traditions be trusted? As I will do in each chapter, I will first lay out the various traditions (even if they be contradictory to one another) and histories with little commentary. Then I will debate the validity of the traditions in light of history, the Bible, and common sense.

Rembrandt – The Apostle Peter Kneeling – 1631

Background

Peter was not his real name. His name was Simon, or Simeon, which was very common among the Jews, as Simeon was one of the twelve tribes of Israel. He was a humble fisherman when he and his brother, Andrew, (Matthew 4:18) met a carpenter name Joshua (better know by the Greek form of his name, Jesus).[10] This same Jesus gave Simon the nickname "Peter" (Mark 3:16; John 1:42) to distinguish him from Simon the Zealot.

Simon was the son of man named Jonah (Matthew 16:17) and his mother's name was allegedly (according to one tradition) Joanna.[11] Both he and Andrew were followers of John the Baptist before having met Jesus. That is how Andrew first saw Jesus when He was baptized by John (John 1:40-41). Andrew immediately went and told Peter about the Messiah, whom they followed thereafter. Based on Mark 1:16 and other passages, many believe that Peter and Andrew were the first called by Jesus, or at least the first mentioned in the gospels. Peter soon became one of Jesus's most loyal apostles.

Peter was a member of Jesus's inner circle along with James and John (Matthew 17:1), and one of the first to see the risen Christ. He appears to have been the spokesperson for the apostles (Acts 1 & 2) and was one of the most respected. Often considered impulsive and rash for his actions, such as attacking the priest in Gethsemane, no one has ever questioned Peter's love and zeal for Jesus. Though he sometimes spoke and acted before thinking (as many do), he was always motivated by his love and zeal of Christ. He became among the most important of the apostles, and their most controversial.

So what happened to Peter after the Council of Jerusalem? The Bible gives some clues, but other evidence lays in the historical records and traditions of antiquity.

History and Traditions

The Biblical Record

The first part of Peter's ministry is recorded in the first fifteen chapters of Acts. Peter was a member of Jesus's inner circle and was the apparent spokesperson for the apostles. He helped proclaim the gospel message across Judea, but met with heavy resistance. Eventually, disputes among Christians as to what to do with gentile converts arose, leading to the Council of Jerusalem. After being challenged by the apostle Paul, Peter eventually conceded and deferred to Paul at the Council of Jerusalem, forbidding Christians from requiring the circumcision of new gentile believers.

The Biblical record after the time of the Council of Jerusalem is restricted to his own comments in his first epistle "to those who reside as aliens, scattered throughout Pontus,

Galatia, Cappadocia, Asia, and Bithynia, who are chosen" (1 Peter 1:1). He also mentions companions in "Babylon" (1 Peter 5:13). Beyond this we must look to extra-Biblical records and traditions for clues as to what happened to him after the Council of Jerusalem.

Extra-Biblical Records and Traditions

Here I will list the primary ancient ante-Nicene records and traditions with little or no commentary. Instead, I will discuss their validity under the next section : "Evaluation."

Clement of Rome was listed as the third overseer (or bishop) of the church of Rome according to the earliest sources.[12] He resided in that office from approximately 91 to 101 A.D.[13] He is sometimes believed to have been the same Clement mentioned in Philippians 4:3. He said very little about Peter, except in giving the earliest confirmation that Peter died a martyr. He said, "There was Peter who by reason of unrighteous jealousy endured not one not one but many labors, and thus having borne his testimony went to his appointed place of glory" (1 Clement 5:4).[14]

Dionysius, an overseer (or bishop) of the church at Corinth, wrote to the Roman church sometime before his death in 170 A.D.[15] In that letter he said, "Therefore you also have by such admonition joined in close union the churches that were planted by Peter and Paul, that of the Romans and that of the Corinthians: for both of them went to our Corinth, and taught us in the same way as they taught you when they went to Italy; and having taught you, they suffered martyrdom at the same time."[16]

Irenaeus lived from 130 to 202 A.D.[17] He was among the most important of the early church fathers, having been taught by Polycarp, who was in turn the disciple of the apostle John himself. Irenaeus was then a second generation disciple who served as the overseer (or bishop) of Lyons in Gaul (modern France). He stated that the Roman church was "founded and organized at Rome by the two most glorious apostles, Peter and Paul."[18] Further, he said, "the blessed apostles, then, having founded and built up the Church, committed into the hands of Linus the office of the episcopate. Of this Linus, Paul makes mention in the Epistles to Timothy"[19] (2 Timothy 4:21).

Next we come to Clement of Alexandria who lived from approximately 150 to 211 A.D. He is another important early church father of some esteem. He related the tradition that, "the blessed Peter, on seeing his wife led to death, rejoiced on account of her call and conveyance home, and called very encouragingly and comfortingly, addressing her by name, 'Remember thou the Lord.' Such was the marriage of the blessed and their perfect disposition towards those dearest to them."[20] He also related that Peter had at least one child, saying, "Peter and Philip had children, and Philip gave his daughters in marriage."[21]

Hippolytus was an overseer (by now called "bishop") of the then divided church of Rome in the earliest part of the third century. He had been taught by Irenaeus, and lived from 170 to 235 A.D. when he was martyred. He recorded that "Peter preached the Gospel in Pontus, and Galatia, and Cappadocia, and Bithynia, and Italy, and Asia, and was afterwards crucified by Nero in Rome with his head downward, as he had himself desired to suffer in that manner."[22]

The *Acts of Peter* is an apocryphal work which has been described as a work of historical fiction.[23] This is an accurate depiction, for it is filled with wild embellishments and fanciful tales. Nevertheless, historical fiction is, in theory, based on historical incidents. Furthermore, it is dated to the second century, which makes the traditions underlying the imaginative story among the oldest. In the *Acts of Peter* Simon Magus is said to arrive in Rome after Paul had departed following his first trial and acquittal. Having no one to confront Simon, the church sent for Peter who promptly came to Rome. There he engaged in a battle of miracles with Simon including resurrecting a fish and even making a dog speak. Finally, in a battle of magic versus prayer Simon levitated himself in the air, but when Peter prayed, Simon fell and broke his leg.[24]

More significant is that this early second century document is the first to relate the following story.

> "And as he went forth of the city, he saw the Lord entering into Rome. And when he saw him, he said: Lord, where are you going? And the Lord said unto him: I go into Rome to be crucified. And Peter said unto him: Lord, are you being crucified again? He said

unto him: Yea, Peter, I am being crucified again. And Peter came to himself: and having beheld the Lord ascending up into heaven, he returned to Rome, rejoicing, and glorifying the Lord, for that he said: I am being crucified: that which was about to befall Peter."[25]

Peter is then taken to be crucified, but he begs to be crucified upside down in deference to Christ of whom he is unworthy.[26] Later Nero is said to be enraged, because he desired to torture Peter more before allowing him to die. Some manuscripts also include the story of Peter's daughter, named Petronilla, who was born after Christ, and crippled in childhood.[27]

Among historical writings Gaius (or Caius) of Rome (circa 200 A.D.), who died a martyr,[28] claimed that both Peter and Paul were the founders of the church of Rome.[29] The famed church father Tertullian (160-225 A.D.) stated that Peter was crucified under Nero[30] and that it was in Rome "where Peter endures a passion like his Lord's."[31]

The so-called *Teachings of the Apostle*, dating to around 230 A.D., claims that "Antioch, and Syria, and Cilicia, and Galatia, even to Pontus, received the apostles' ordination to the priesthood from Simon Cephas, who himself laid the foundation of the church there, and was priest and ministered there up to the time when he went up from thence to Rome on account of Simon the sorcerer, who was deluding the people of Rome with his sorceries ... The city of Rome, and all Italy, and Spain, and Britain, and Gaul, together with all the rest of the countries round about them, received the apostles' ordination to the priesthood from Simon Cephas, who went up from Antioch; and he was ruler and guide there, in the church which he had built there, and in the places round about it."[32]

Later in the early third century, Cyprian, the famed bishop of Carthage, rejected that Peter ever claimed supremacy or a succession of an apostolic see,[33] which is also an admission that the doctrine of papal succession was beginning to rise to prominence at that time, or else there would have been no need to refute it. Some lists were now beginning to call Peter the first bishop of Rome, rather than Linus.

Later, Lactantius (240-320 A.D.), the famous church father who befriended the new Christian emperor Constantine before his death, said, "it was (Nero) who first persecuted the servants of God; he crucified Peter, and slew Paul."[34]

Finally, Eusebius (263-339 A.D.), considered the father of church history, repeated the story that Peter came to Rome to combat Simon Magus but without the wild embellishments.[35] He also affirmed the tradition of both Peter and his wife having died under Nero in Rome, and of requesting to be crucified upside down.[36]

In addition to these sources, there are two other important documents of unknown, and suspect origin, that give important information on the ancient traditions of Peter. The first of these is *the Apostolic Constitutions* which was originally dated to the third century,[37] but later scholia and scribes said it was found in the "most ancient" manuscripts[38] which no longer exist. It is, therefore, assumed to date to the second century. In it, the story of Simon the Magician being confronted by Peter is related including the legend that Simon fell to the ground after levitating and broke his hip and ankle.[39]

The final document is another apocryphal story based in part on the *Acts of Peter*. It is called the *Acts of the Holy Apostles Peter and Paul* and is of an unknown date. However, it clearly borrows from early sources, such as the *Acts of Peter*, save that it expounds upon those legends and traditions. According to *Acts of the Holy Apostles Peter and Paul* the apostle Paul had sought an audience with the emperor Nero, but he refused, fearing Paul would stir up the people. He then ordered Paul banned from all of Italy. Consequently, Paul then landed in Sicily and snuck into Italy with the help of Peter's disciples. Reaching Rome he found Simon Magus conspiring with the Jewish enemies of Peter and Paul. While they preached the gospel in Rome it is claimed that Nero's wife Libia became a convert and fled the palace. Thus Peter, Paul, and Simon Magus were brought before an irate Nero for a hearing. After hearing each of their accounts the following is related :

> "Then both Peter and Paul were led away from the presence of Nero. And Paul was beheaded on the Ostesian road.

17

"And Peter, having come to the cross, said: Since my Lord Jesus Christ, who came down from the heaven upon the earth, was raised upon the cross upright, and He has deigned to call to heaven me, who am of the earth, my cross ought to be fixed head down most, so as to direct my feet towards heaven; for I am not worthy to be crucified like my Lord. Then, having reversed the cross, they nailed his feet up."[40]

Furthermore it is said that Peter urged the Christians not to riot against Caesar, saying:

"Peter restrained them, saying: A few days ago, being exhorted by the brethren, I was going away; and my Lord Jesus Christ met me, and having adored Him, I said, Lord, whither are You going? And He said to me, I am going to Rome to be crucified. And I said to Him, Lord, were You not crucified once for all? And the Lord answering, said, I saw you fleeing from death, and I wish to be crucified instead of you. And I said, Lord, I go; I fulfill Your command. And He said to me, Fear not, for I am with you. On this account, then, children, do not hinder my going; for already my feet are going on the road to heaven. Do not grieve, therefore, but rather rejoice with me, for today I receive the fruit of my labours. And thus speaking, he said: I thank You, good Shepherd, that the sheep which You have entrusted to me, sympathize with me; I ask, then, that with me they may have a part in Your kingdom. And having thus spoken, he gave up the ghost."[41]

These are the primary histories, traditions, and legends from the first three hundred years of Christianity. There are others as well, but these are the primary ones which I quote. Most other traditions and histories simply echo what is said in these sources. It is best, therefore, to examine these existing documents and weigh them against the Bible and known history.

Evaluation

Because of the importance of Peter, and particularly his esteem in the Catholic tradition, it is best to look at the individual aspects of the history and traditions of Peter separately. Too often the traditions are lumped together and many people react for or against a tradition based on their own biases or backgrounds. Catholics, for example, insist that Peter was the first bishop of Rome whereas some reactionary Protestants go so far as to insist that Peter never even stepped foot in Rome. By looking at each aspect of the records separately it is easier to distinguish between which traditions are true, which ones are suspect, and which ones are false.

Missionary Travels

Aside from the question of Rome, there are few records or even traditions of Peter's missionary travels beyond what is spoken of in the Bible. One tradition claims that Peter traveled to Gaul (modern day France and Germany) and Britain.[42] One scholar even argues that 2 Peter was written from Britain.[43] However, the *Teachings of the Apostles* is the only ancient source with this claim. There are two possibilities. One is that our medieval manuscript was corrupted and that the original had no such reference.[44] Another is that the reference to "the apostles' ordination" implies not that Peter had actually been to Gaul and Britain, but that his disciples, having received his ordination, took the gospel to those regions. This seems the best solution, for a strict reading of the verse never actually says that Peter went to Gaul or Britain; only that they received "the apostles' ordination to the priesthood from Simon Cephas."[45] This would also explain why later medieval traditions erroneously claimed that Peter had been to France. It arose from a misunderstanding of the *Teachings of the Apostles*.

What then can we say of Peter's travels? Beginning with the Bible itself we know that Peter remained in Judea until the persecutions of Herod Agrippa (Acts 12). At that time the apostles lived in and worked from Antioch (Acts 11:27; 13:1, 14; 14:21; 15:22; etc.) which is in modern day Syria. Pope Gregory the Great (590-604 A.D.) believed that Peter lived in Antioch for seven years.[46] However long he resided there, 1 Peter 1:1 implies that Peter did work with Jews living in Pontus, Galatia, Cappadocia, Bithynia, and the country called Asia, which are all in modern day Turkey.

It was in Turkey and Greece where the majority of the apostles worked. Ephesus, Galatia, and Colossae were all in Turkey, while Corinth, Philippi, and Thessalonia were in Greece. All were under the domain of the Roman empire.

Bernard Ruffin believes Peter had been to Corinth "some time prior to A.D. 54"[47] based on 1 Corinthians 1:12 where Paul speaks about the various divisions. How could there be "followers of Peter" if Peter had never been there? This is a sound theory, particularly since the epistles of Peter had not yet been written. Dionysius also recorded that Peter had visited Corinth.[48] Thus it is clear that Peter was working in the region of Asia Minor for many years, as did several other apostles.

Did Peter then spend the rest of his life in the region of modern Syria, Turkey, and Greece? No. Peter appears to have written his letter, not from Jerusalem or Antioch, but from "Babylon" (1 Peter 5:13) where John Mark was as well. Some Protestants have argued that this must refer to ancient Babylon which is in modern day Iraq and was a part of the ancient Parthian empire which was at enmity with Rome. At first glance, this seems the most logical view, but when we examine the Bible and history it is becomes impossible for eight reasons.

1. Babylon Was Not in Peter's Dominion

The apostles were each given a particular region to which they were to take the gospel. When we examine the apostle's missionary activities it becomes obvious, for practical reasons alone, that they followed a pattern. The apostles who ministered in the west remained in the west. The apostles who headed east, remained in the east. It would be impractical and illogical for Peter have mission fields in western Turkey and Greece and then head to the Parthian empire to minister in Babylon. The apostles who ventured into Parthia had no mission fields west of Syria. Why would they? Logically, it would be waste of time given the difficulties with travel and the time required for travel in those days.

2. Parthia and Rome Were Enemies

Upon the same line of reasoning, it would be impractical to maintain mission fields crossing two enemy countries. A missionary might choose one or the other, but if he were traveling back and forth between enemy countries he would surely be singled out as a spy. One can imagine the difficulties of traveling to a country with which our own country is at enmity. Consider me visiting Iran toady? They would probably not even allow me to travel there, and if I did, I would quite possibly be arrested as a spy, as has happened to American reporters and mountain climbers in the last decade. In Peter's day the problems were even more pronounced as citizens had few rights.

3. Babylon's Prophesied Fall Had Already Taken Place

Isaiah 13:19-20 prophesied that "Babylon, the beauty of kingdoms, the glory of the Chaldeans' pride, will be as when God overthrew Sodom and Gomorrah. It will never be inhabited or lived in from generation to generation." An even longer prophesy recorded in Jeremiah 50:1 - 51:64 predicts the exact manner of Babylon's fall. 51:64 states that "Babylon shall sink down and *not rise again*." Despite these prophesies there are a number of scholars who believe that Babylon *shall* rise again.

I have written extensively on this subject in both *Controversies in the Prophets* and *Controversies in Revelation*. I will, therefore, offer only a brief summary. Both Isaiah and Jeremiah declared that Babylon would "sink down" (Jeremiah 51:64), not in a single moment (as with *Mystery* Babylon in the book of Revelation), but slowly over ages until it becomes a desert which "will never be inhabited or lived in from generation to generation" (Isaiah 13:20). History has proven this. Beginning with Cyrus's capture of Babylon in the sixth century B.C. the city would be sacked countless times, and torn down little by little over the centuries.

History records no fewer than ten conquests of Babylon since Alexander the Great took the city in 331 B.C. Perdiccas was the first regent until he was killed by Seleucus in 321 B.C.[49] Seleucus, however, lost the city to Antigonus in 316 B.C.[50] only to retake the city four years later.[51] Historian Georges Roux speaks about the "half-ruined city"[52] of this time, noting that "it was already partly deserted, a great number of its inhabitants having been transferred to Seleucia."[53] In the wars that would ensue between the Parthians and the Greeks, and later the Parthians and Romans, Babylon would again trade hands many times. In 126 B.C. the Parthians took control of Babylon[54] but they would also have trouble keeping the city. Crassus of Rome was the first to threaten the Parthians in Babylon, and under Roman conquests Babylon would again change hands several times.

At the time of Christ Babylon was a minor city under Parthian rule. The city lay largely deserted and had no significant population or presumably Jewish community. There is no reason to believe that it would be of any missionary significance to Peter.

4. "Babylon" Was a Known Byword for the Decadence of Rome

Babylon was the first nation to conquer Israel and send its people into exile. Although the city had long since fallen into the spectre of history, it had become a byword for Jewish oppression. Just as we often speak of "Sin City" in Las Vegas, as a reference to "Sodom," or of Hollywood as "Gomorrah," the Jews had become accustomed to speak of Rome as "Babylon" because of its oppression. At the time that Peter was writing his epistle war with Rome was already brewing, and was to result in their second exile. Evidence of this I have presented in *Controversies in Revelation* and will not repeat here except to say that the evidence of antiquity shows this was a common phrase. Consequently, many use this very verse as proof that Peter was writing from Rome. The real proof, however, is in the mention of John Mark as being in "Babylon."

5. Mark Was in Rome

In 1 Peter 5:13 Mark is said to send greetings from "Babylon." 1 Peter is believed by almost all scholars to have been written either shortly before or during the early persecution of Nero. Thus Peter is referring to Mark as being in "Babylon" shortly before or after the persecutions of Rome.[55] However, in 2 Timothy 4:11 Paul was awaiting his execution in Rome after having been arrested a second time (see chapter 14). In this passage he ask Timothy (who was in Ephesus[56]) to bring Mark with him to Rome. This places Mark in Rome, not Babylon, at the time of Nero's persecutions. Remembering the distance, travel, and political turmoil of the day, it is unrealistic to see Mark traveling back and forth from Greece to Iraq and then to Italy in a few short years. If Mark was in Rome during the persecutions, then Peter's reference to Mark being in "Babylon" must be seen as a euphemism, for Mark could not be in both places at the same time.

6. Not a Single Ancient Historian Records Peter in Parthia

As cited above, not a single ancient historian, tradition, or even legend depicts Peter as having traveled to Parthia. The same can be said of John Mark (see Chapter 15 : The Apostles' Companions), whom Peter speaks of being present with him in "Babylon" (1 Peter 5:13). All the ancient histories, dating to the earliest of the church fathers, record Peter traveling to Rome. This makes sense. Peter had already traveled to many churches established by Paul. The Bible itself seems to place Peter in Asia Minor and probably Greece. There is no reason to believe that he did not eventually go to Rome as well.

7. Nero Had No Juristiction Over Parthia

If we place any stock in the universal ancient traditions of Peter's crucifixion then we cannot accept that it took place in Parthia. Crucifixion was a favorite Roman execution. Although it was not unheard of in Parthian, crucifixion was primarily practiced, and refined, in Rome. Moreover, the earliest traditions record that it was Nero who sent Peter to his death,[57] and Nero could do nothing in Parthia. If Peter died by crucifixion under Nero, then it had to be in the Roman empire, not the Parthian empire over which Nero had no dominion.

8. Why Not Choose Paul as the First Pope?

This final argument is a question I ask of all my Protestant colleagues who reject Peter's death in Rome. Since we all agree that proper exegesis of Mark 16:18 does not truly establish a papacy, we cannot accept that Mark 16:18 is the reason Peter is called the first pope. So my question is, "if Peter had never been to Rome, why would not the Catholic church have simply made Paul the first pope?" This is a question they cannot answer, for Paul would actually have made a better "pope." Consider that the apostle Paul has been called the "apostle to the gentiles" (1 Timothy 2:7), whereas Peter has been called an "apostle of circumcision."[58] Would not the "apostle to the gentiles" be a better "pope" for the pagan city of Rome?

Every ancient Christian country has its patron saints. This is human nature. Of course, they chose their patron saint from among the apostles who actually visited their country. It would be absurd if a country named its patron saint after someone who had never been there! This is why the Indians revere Saint Thomas, the Armenians revere Saint Bartholomew, and the Egyptians revere Saint Mark. So the mere fact that the Catholic church erroneously attempts to make Peter the first pope, in *contrast* to the statements of the apostolic fathers, is indirect evidence that Peter had at least been to Rome.

So both Biblically and historically, we can rule out the dead city of Babylon in ancient Parthia. Peter's mission field was in the west; in countries like Pontus, Galatia, Cappadocia, Asia, Bithynia, and Achaia. It is only logical then that Italy might also be a part of Peter's plans. Lest anyone believe that this is but Catholic tradition removed by hundreds of years, then I will remind him that such great Protestant martyrologists as John Foxe[59] and Thieleman J. van Braght[60] accepted that Peter went to Rome.

If we accept the massive historical and traditional support (as well as Biblical) for Peter traveling to Rome, then we must still ask "why"?

The Legends of Simon Magus

As early as the second century the legends of Simon Magus in Rome had appeared. Even Eusebius appears to have believed the stories based on the testimony of Justin Martyr, one of the most famous and reliable of the ancient church fathers, who was born just over three decades after Peter died. Justin Martyr, so named because he was martyred under Marcus Aurelius, recorded the following:

> "In Claudius's time ... [Simon Magus] was deemed a god at Rome and honored as a god with a statue in the river Tiber between the two bridges, and bore this inscription, in the language of Rome : - '*Simoni Deo Sancto*' meaning 'To Simon the holy God.' And almost all the Samaritans, and a few even of other nations, worship him, and acknowledge him as the first god."[61]

Now the evidence sounds firm at this point and was even substantiated to a point by the discovery of a statue in 1574 whose inscription read "*Semoni Sancto Deo*."[62] The problem is that "*Semoni*", as opposed to "*Simoni*", was a Sabine deity. It is thus assumed by most modern scholars that Justin made a mistake in reading the inscription and that no such statue to Simon Magus ever existed. Nevertheless, at least one scholar believes that "this has always seemed to us very slight evidence on which to reject so precise a statement as Justin here makes : a statement which he would scarcely have hazarded in an apology addressed to Rome, where every person had the means of ascertaining its accuracy. If, as is supposed, he made a mistake, it must have been at once exposed, and other writers would not have so frequently repeated the story as they done."[63]

I will leave the reader to judge for himself whether or not Simon Magus did indeed leave his imprint upon Rome, but whether Simon Magus was there or not, there can be little doubt that the fanciful legends surrounding Simon Magus vs. Simon Peter are mere personifications of the struggle between gnosticism and Biblical Christianity.

From the earliest of days Simon Magus had been associated with the religious cult know as gnosticism. That religious perversion of Christianity is even refuted by Paul in his epistle to the Galatians. Gnosticism forms the assumptions and conspiracies which Hollywood has promoted to this very day in films like the *DaVinci Code*. Thus, based on the assumption that Simon Magus had visited Rome, the works of historical fiction like the *Acts of Peter* and the *Acts of Peter and Paul* personified the cult of gnosticism in the person of Simon Magus. It is safe to reject the stories themselves as just this; historical fiction. Were Simon to have intervened against Christians and sought Nero's aid, as in and the *Acts of Peter and Paul*, we would expect independent verification elsewhere. Moreover, the *Acts of Peter* contradicts the *Acts of Peter and Paul*, saying that Simon Magus dies and thus never meets Nero at all!

Consequently, it is best to conclude that if Simon Magus ever visited Rome, he was not the reason for Peter's journey and no such confrontations with Simon Magus took place after what is recorded in Acts 8. Why then did Peter go to

Rome? Perhaps, as many ancient traditions say, he was a co-founder of Rome? Let us examine that argument.

Co-Founder of the Church of Rome?

As early as the second century, not even a hundred years after the church of Rome was founded, we see numerous claims that both Peter and Paul were the founders of the Roman church. Some even claim that the ancient graves of the two may be found there. The traditions apparently predate its advocates by at least two or three decades, taking us back to the late first century.

The earliest citations are by Irenaeus, the second generation disciple of John (taught by Polycarp),[64] Dionysius of Corinth,[65] and Gaius of Rome.[66] Is this evidence sufficient? Not necessarily, but we can certainly agree that such evidence indicates that Peter had indeed been in Rome, as aforementioned. Lest anyone argue that this is made up to support the Catholic doctrine of the papacy, I will remind the reader that none of these early sources make Peter out to be the first bishop of Rome, and that if the church were merely inventing a tie to an early apostle then it would have been far easier to create a tie via the apostle Paul whom the Scriptures record as having been to Rome! Indeed, Paul is stated in these same traditions to be one of the two founders of Rome. So this takes us back to our original query. Why not accept the traditions at face value?

Let us consider the facts. Christopher Coxe thinks that "if St. Peter had been at Rome, St. Paul would not have come there (2 Cor. x.16). The two apostles had each his jurisdiction, and they kept to their own ... How, then, came St. Peter to visit Rome? The answer is clear : unless he came involuntarily, as a prisoner, he came to look after the Church of the *Circumcision*."[67] 2 Corinthians 10:16 clearly infers that Paul did not want to build on anything or any church established by another. He strove to go where no one else had gone before. The book of Acts makes this very clear.

Paul was a trailblazer who established churches where none had existed before. In the book of Acts Paul's desire to go to Rome was based on this very desire. Nonetheless, the book of Romans also implies that Paul had not yet visited the church

26

(Romans 1:11), meaning that the church of Rome was already in existence before Paul's arrival. How then was Rome established? Ruffin argues that Peter had temporarily left Rome when Paul wrote his epistle to the Romans in 57 A.D., hence the reason he doesn't mention Peter.[68] However, there is no evidence for this, and much evidence against it. Note, for example, that in Romans 1:11 Paul speak of "establishing you", meaning establishing the church. Why? Was the church not already established?

I attend what is called a "Bible Church." Bible Churches have something called "Church planting." What they do is to train young ministers whom they then send out to a new city where there is no Bible Church and tell them to start a Bible Church up locally in that area. This is "planting." I believe that this is what Paul did. His epistle to the Romans makes it clear that Aquila and Priscilla were in Rome (Romans 16:3). This is the same Aquila and Priscilla whom Paul had met in Corinth after they had been evicted from Rome (Acts 18:2). They became Paul's disciples and had been living in Rome before the disturbances there. It is logical that they returned to Rome with the gospel soon after Jews were permitted to return. They took with them the gospel which Paul had imparted to them, but Paul longed to see Rome himself (Acts 19:21; 23:11; Romans 1:15).

Thus in the most literal sense of the word Aquila and Priscilla were the founders of Rome, but in the larger sense of the word it was clearly Paul who was its founder and sought to "impart some spiritual gift to you, that you may be established" (Romans 1:11).

This once again brings us back to our original question. When and why did Peter come to Rome? Contrary to the opinions of some, I do not believe Peter ever came to Rome until the very end. I even believe it is likely that he arrived in Rome not long before his arrest, as I will demonstrate. One thing is certain. Paul was the first apostle to arrive in Rome, and he did so in chains. He also stated in 2 Timothy 4:16 that no one came to his defense when he first stood trial before Nero. Obviously, this means that Peter was not there at the time. The conclusion must therefore be that Peter never went to Rome until sometime after Paul's first acquittal.

Interestingly enough, the apocryphal *Acts of Peter* claims that Peter came to Rome to combat Simon Magus only because the apostle Paul had left for Spain.[69] While a work of pure historical fiction, there may a glint of truth in this. After Paul's initial acquittal he had left to check up on his other churches. It is most probably shortly before the fire in Rome that Peter arrived to shore up the Jewish Christian community. It is estimated that there were between 30 to 40,000 Jews in Rome.[70] Even if but a tiny handful had converted to Christ Jesus, then it would be a significant number for a fledgling church in the capital of the world. Thus, assuming Paul's acquittal was in either 62 or 63 A.D. Peter then arrived probably as late as 63 or even 64 A.D. The infamous fire in Rome broke out on July 19, 64 A.D. As we shall see, Peter never left Rome.

Bishop of Rome?

The first tradition that Peter served as a bishop of Rome occurs either in the late second century or possibly the early third. Cyprian, writing in the early third century, expressly rejects the doctrine of apostolic succession and supremacy.[71] It also indicates, however, that the argument was first coming to light. Nevertheless, the earliest church fathers all recorded that it was Linus who was the first bishop (or overseer) of Rome. Irenaeus, who was born some sixty years after Peter's death, states that "the blessed apostles, then, having founded and built up the Church, committed into the hands of Linus the office of the episcopate. Of this Linus, Paul makes mention in the Epistles to Timothy."[72]

Here then are two conflicting traditions, and where traditions conflict it is always best to take the earliest tradition. Moreover, there is a logical flaw with the idea that Peter served as bishop of Rome. Peter, like the other apostles, was a missionary, not a bishop. The apostles founded many churches. In all the records of the apostles only James the Just (assuming he was the apostles – see chapter 10) is recorded as having served as overseer of a particular church. All the other apostles worked as missionaries, rather than overseers (or bishops).

This also seems apparent from the Bible, for in 1 Corinthians 12:28 Paul appears to place apostles higher than bishops, overseers, elders, and other church offices. Why would

Peter then remain at Rome as a mere bishop rather than assisting all the churches of Europe? It is only because of the later Roman doctrine of the primacy of the papacy, that the Roman church was elevated above the other churches. It is natural then that they would want to make Peter the head of Rome, when Rome was, in fact, one of but many churches in the Roman empire.

Finally, note that Irenaeus stated that Peter and Paul made Linus the bishop of Rome. In current papal lists, Linus is a successor Peter which in turn means that Peter would have already been dead. One might argue that Peter had stated his desire to be succeeded but this is not what the early church fathers said. One might be inclined to argue that Aquila was the first bishop (or overseer) of Rome and that Linus was the first to succeed him (see chapter 15 - The Apostles' Companions for more on Linus), but this requires that we understand the exact offices and government used by the early church. This issue is one which is argued and debated to this very day even among like minded people. It is sufficient to say that all the earliest church fathers agree that Peter was never the bishop or overseer of Rome. He was an apostle; not a bishop.

Wife and Children
Before addressing the martyrdom of Peter it is worthy to note that the traditions of Peter's martyrdom are coupled with something else often ignored by modern books : his wife and daughter. That Peter was married is affirmed in the Bible (cf. Matthew 8:14; Mark 1:30; Luke 4:38; 1 Corinthians 9:5) and supported by the early church fathers. Some call her name Perpetua, which Bernard Ruffin believes was her adopted name when they were living among Romans as it is not a Jewish name.[73] Clement of Alexandria, in the late second century, said that Peter also had at least one child.[74] The fanciful *Acts of Peter* makes Peter's daughter, named Petronilla, crippled from childhood. Some copies also have a short story involving the death of Perpetua, although in the *Acts of Peter* she is not apparently Peter's wife.

What we can say with relative certainty is that Peter's wife was executed shortly before he was. Nero may have wanted Peter to watch his wife die as a manner of extra cruelty.

According to Clement of Alexandria, "Peter, on seeing his wife led to death, rejoiced on account of her call and conveyance home, and called very encouragingly and comfortingly, addressing her by name, 'Remember thou the Lord.' Such was the marriage of the blessed and their perfect disposition towards those dearest to them."[75]

Luca Giordano – The Crucifixion of St. Peter – 1660

Martyrdom

Now we come to the events surrounding Peter's martyrdom. That Peter was martyred was prophesied by the Lord Jesus Himself (John 21:18-19). That it was Nero who ordered the death of Peter is attested by all church historians as passed down from the earliest of church fathers. The method of execution is also agreed to have been crucifixion. However, there is some debate as to the detail; especially the timing and the events which preceded his martyrdom.

Some traditions say that Peter died June 29, 67 A.D.[76] Others say that Peter was executed "at the same time" as Paul,[77] but many believe that this would probably have been a year or two earlier. Moreover, I have argued that Peter came to Rome when Paul was absent. To make matters worse, some misdate some historical events, making their dates for Peter's death equally amiss. An examination of the facts of history may allow us to fit the pieces of this puzzle together.

In the first century Clement of Rome said that Peter suffered "not one but many labors" before meeting his death.[78] One tradition holds that Peter was held in a dungeon for nine months, chained to a column.[79] This makes sense for several reasons. Tacitus tells us that Nero tortured several Christians into confessing to the fire in Rome.[80] All agree that Nero sought to deflect suspicion from himself for the fire in Rome. If Nero knew that he had an apostle prisoner, it only makes sense that he would have tried to torture Peter into "confessing" to the fire in Rome. It would surely have been a boon to have a leader of the church renounce Jesus, and it is only logical to assume that Nero spent at least nine months attempting to do just this.

Furthermore, many believe that 1 Peter was written in anticipation of coming persecution.[81] Merrill Unger states "the Epistle is probably to be dated around 65 A.D. and the Neronian persecutions apparently furnish the background."[82] Most concur with the Neronian backdrop, which further indicates that the "Babylon" of which Peter spoke was indeed Rome, since Nero had no authority over the Parthian empire. This all, once again, fits with the fact that Peter knew he was going to die and that Nero would soon begin to persecute Christians in a way never before known at that time. Like Paul's epistles to Timothy, probably written around the same time, he knew his death was impending.

How then did Peter and Paul come to be prisoners? At least one tradition says that the church tried to smuggle Peter out of Rome to escape capture, but while leaving he saw a vision of Jesus carrying the cross toward Rome. He asked the Lord where He was going,[83] and the Lord replied, "I am going to be crucified again."[84] Peter then returned to Rome where he was immediately arrested.

Regardless of whether the story is true or not, it makes sense that Peter was arrested shortly after the fire in Rome, sometime in the Fall or Winter of 64 A.D. Nine months later would, of course, be in 65 A.D. which some hold to be the correct date for Peter's death.[85] Others place his death much later, closer to the traditional June 29, 67 A.D. date.[86]

31

Interestingly enough, the famed chronologer Archbishop Ussher, who advocated the traditional 67 A.D. date, inexplicably argued that Paul was acquitted by Nero *a second time after* the fire in Rome and after the writing of 1 and 2 Timothy when Paul clearly states his belief that he would die (2 Timothy 4:7-8)![87] However, he correctly places this second trial in 65 A.D.

Now it is hard to tell the story of Peter's execution without that of Paul's. If both Peter and Paul were held in prison for a time, then Clement's belief that Peter and Paul were executed at the same time fits. If not, then they obviously died at different times. There will, therefore, be more said of this under "Chapter 14 : Paul." Nonetheless, one question remains in regard to Peter. Was he crucified upside down as tradition decrees?

The tradition that Peter asked to be crucified upside down in deference to Christ is ancient. All agree that Peter was crucified. That he was crucified upside down is found in early traditions dating to at least the early second century, not five decades from Peter's death.[88] It appears to be accepted as fact by all the early church fathers and historians, although some only say that he was crucified with no explicit mention of the method of crucifixion.[89] In answer to this, it should be noted that there was no single manner of crucifixion as often assumed. Various different methods of crucifixion were common throughout the Roman empire.[90] Andrew's crucifixion, for example, included tying him up with ropes, so as to leave him exposed to wild animals (see Chapter 5 : Andrew). Consequently, we have no reason to reject the ancient tradition that has never been challenged by any historian or scholar of antiquity. Whether we choose to accept the story of "*quo vadis*" (Peter's vision of Jesus), there seems no doubt that Peter was sentenced to die by crucifixion and, at his own request, was hung upside down.

In short, the fire in Rome broke out on July 19, 64 A.D. Within a month or two Nero was circulating rumors that the Christians were responsible for the fire. Peter may have tried to escape Rome, but for whatever reasons he either returned (as per the *quo vadis* vision) or was discovered and arrested. This probably took place in September. Nine months later, after failing to extract a "confession" from Peter, Nero decided to make an example of the great apostles Peter and Paul (who I believe was already in prison by this time), ordering Paul beheaded (as was the law for a Roman citizen) and Peter crucified. At his request, the soldiers inverted the cross, knowing it would cause much agony. The traditional date of Peter's death is June 29, 67 A.D. but if we allow for the faulty chronology of some of the ancient historians (of which we have aplenty) then June 29, 65 A.D. appears to fit in with the known facts much better (see chapter 14 for more on this debate). In fact, it fits in perfectly.

Summary

The evidence indicates that some years after the Council of Jerusalem Peter followed the trail blazed by Paul, but concentrating upon the Jewish believers and communities in those regions reached by Paul. He was well acquainted with the churches in Pontus, Galatia, Cappadocia, Asia, and Bithynia, which all lay within the boundaries of modern day Turkey. Furthermore, he appears to have traveled to Corinth and assisted the church there. During this time Peter restricted his mission work to strengthening and edifying the churches of Asia Minor, in modern day Turkey, and Greece.

Peter did not travel to Rome until after Paul's first trial and acquittal. As he had done before, Peter soon traveled to the young church in Paul's absence to strengthen the community of Jewish believers and edify them. He arrived in Rome for the first time probably in 63 or even 64 A.D.

Nero, the despotic emperor despised even by his own people, had been content to let the esteemed statesman and philosopher Seneca govern the country in his name, but in 62 A.D., Seneca was forced to step down,[91] probably not long after Paul's acquittal. The unrestrained and power hungry Nero soon became among the most hated emperors in history. It was on July 19, 64 A.D., not long after Peter's arrival, that the infamous fire in Rome ravaged the city. The people suspected that Nero was behind it for good reason, but whether the suspicion was true or not, he deflected the suspicion by blaming Christians whom he accused of everything from cannibalism to atheism and homosexuality.[92]   Christians were arrested and some "confessed" under torture to trying to end the world by setting Rome afire.

Within a month Peter was most probably arrested himself and imprisoned. There Peter was probably tortured in an attempt to get the famous church leader to "confess" to the crimes of the Christians. After nine months or more, Nero was no longer content to wait.   The persecutions of Christians increased in severity and cruelty, and both Peter and Paul were to be made examples.   Peter's wife was executed (possibly before his very own eyes) and he was taken away to be crucified, and at his request, in deference to the Lord, of whom he was not worthy, Peter requested to be crucified upside down. This probably took place on June 29, 65 A.D.

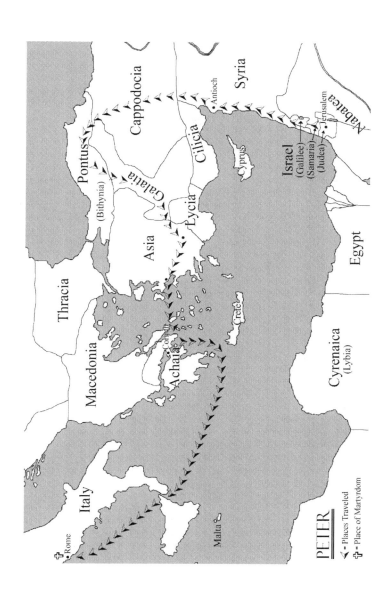

PETER

✔ = Places Traveled
✝ = Place of Martyrdom

35

3

James "the Greater"

James "the Greater" was the first apostle to be martyred, having been executed by Herod Agrippa. There is, therefore, no question as to his life after the book of Acts, for he was already with the Lord. However, there are some interesting traditions regarding the events surrounding his martyrdom not recorded in the Bible.

What we know about James from the Bible is that he was the brother of John, and surnamed one of the "sons of Thunder." Wild speculation has abounded as to exactly what this meant. Was it a comment on their personality? Did it mean "voice of God" as Philip Schaff believed?[93] Were they zealous of the Lord? The Bible doesn't say, but like all surnames, it was given with love, and so we should not read anything negative into it.

James was one of two groups of brothers explicitly defined among the twelve. Simon and Andrew were brothers, as were James and John. Nonetheless, a disease among some writers over the centuries has been to attempt to make almost all the apostles related to one another. Conjecture as to the relationships of some of the other apostles range from possible to absurd. One such absurd theory seems to be that James the Greater was actually the father of James the Less.[94] Others try to make them brothers or cousins. Some of these theories stem from speculative conflation of the various women named at the cross. Mark 15:40 names "Mary Magdalene, and Mary the mother of James the Less and Joses, and Salome." Matthew 27:56 names "Mary Magdalene, and Mary the mother of James and Joseph, and the mother of the sons of Zebedee." It is then assumed that the unnamed "mother of the sons of Zebedee" was the same as either Salome or Mary the mother of James the Less. In fact, Matthew 27:55 explicitly says, "Many women were there" and verse 56 begins by saying "among them were ..." In other words, there were many more than three women present. These verses are important in identifying James the Less, who is mentioned in Mark 15:40, but to go beyond this with wild conjecture is poor exegesis.

Perhaps more poor than this exegesis is the fanciful legend (for it cannot even be properly called a tradition) that James, beckoned by a vision of the virgin Mary, traveled to Spain sometime between Pentecost and his death in Judea.[95] Now critics have been quick to point out that Mary was still living at this time, which in itself nullifies the majority of the story. Morever, the apostle Paul is clearly depicted as the first to truly reach out to gentiles. It was he who was first called the "apostle to the gentiles" (1 Timothy 2:7), but even if we accepted that James was the first, why would James leave the eleven apostles, bypass Asia Minor, Greece, and Italy for Hispania? If he were going to evangelize the gentiles, as Paul first did, then why start with Hispania rather than Asia Minor or Italy? Finally, the legend itself is of a late date. No early church father even mentions the legend. Those who point out that Spain is among the nations said to have been evangelized by the apostles forget that the early traditions credit this evangelization to Paul (see chapter 14), not James.

In any case, James was among the inner circle of Jesus's followers. He, along with Peter and John, was alone taken to some of Jesus's most intimate meetings and events (cf. Matthew 17:1; Mark 5:37, 14:13; Luke 8:51, 9:28). The very fact that he was executed by Herod Agrippa suggest that he was one of the leaders. Herod sought to strike at the church by hitting the apostles. First he had James executed, and then he arrested Peter. Although we cannot draw too much from this, we might infer that Herod considered James more important a leader than Peter or John.

Now concerning James's execution the Bible says only "he had James the brother of John put to death with a sword." Based on the historical events spoken of in Acts, this event is usually dated to 44 A.D.,[96] although some, like John Foxe, date it much earlier in 36 A.D.[97] Which of these dates, if either, is correct?

According to Galatians 1:18 Paul first went up to Jerusalem three years after his conversion. Acts 9:26 could obviously be no earlier than this. Assuming Paul was converted the year following Pentecost, this would place the events of Acts

9 in 37 A.D. at the earliest. Acts 11:26 further indicates that Paul spent a year in Antioch, meaning that Acts 12:2 (the death of James), could have taken place no earlier than 38 A.D. Conversely, Acts 11:28 speaks of a prophet who forewarned of coming famine. That famine took place during the reign of Claudius who first took the throne in 41 A.D. Merrill Unger said that the famine took place in the fourth year of Claudius,[98] which would be sometime in 44 A.D. However, Agabus was obviously making his prophecy *before* the famine took place. But based on Acts 11:29 and the relief efforts, it seems that some time had already passed between Agabus's prophecy (11:28) and its commencement as the famine had already begun (11:29). A final clue, based on Acts 12:21, is the story of Herod's death, which is dated to 44 A.D. Acts 12:19 implies that some time had passed since James's execution, but not an extended period of time. We should therefore agree with Archbishop Ussher's date of 44 A.D., shortly before Passover (Acts 12:3).

One interesting tradition surrounding the execution is found in the works of the second century church father Clement of Alexandria. This quotation, known only through Eusebius, says:

> "And of this James, Clement also relates an anecdote worthy of remembrance in the seventh book of the Hypotyposes, from a tradition of his predecessors. He says that the man who brought him to trial, on seeing him bear his testimony, was moved, and confessed that he was a Christian himself. Accordingly, he says, they were both led away together, and on the way the other asked James to forgive him. And he, considering a little, said, 'Peace be to thee' and kissed him. And so both were beheaded together."[99]

Although we cannot know if the story is true, there is nothing about it which rings untrue. And so James the Greater became the first apostle to be martyred around March 44, A.D., not long before Passover.

4

John

The "beloved" apostle is the only apostle who did not die a martyr's death, although he did not escape torture. He is also the apostle of whom we know the most. Perhaps there is only Peter of whom more has been written concerning his post-Acts life, but unlike Peter, most the records of John are history rather than traditions, and what traditions exist have surprisingly few embellishments. Consequently, the life and death of the apostle John is one of which we can speak in almost certainties.

History and Traditions

The Biblical Record

John was the brother of James the Great, a "son of Zebedee" and a "pillar of the church" (Galatians 2:9). A member of Jesus's inner circle (cf. Matthew 17:1; Mark 5:37, 14:13; Luke 8:51, 9:28), John was also called the "disciple whom the Lord loved" (John 21:7, 20). Behind only the apostle Paul, John wrote more books of the New Testament than anyone. He wrote the Gospel of John, the three epistles of John, and is most certainly the author of the Book of Revelation, which he wrote while in exile on Patmos.[100]

John was only apostle who stood by Jesus at the cross. The other apostles were in hiding, for fear of their life. Even Peter, who had swore to fight to the death for Jesus, had denied him and fled. It was to John that Jesus, on his deathbed, entrusted his mother Mary (John 19:26-27). All of this, along with John's emphasis upon love in both his gospel and epistles, is why John has been given the affectionate name "the apostle of love."

One interesting item in John's gospel is a curious anecdote which plays into later traditions about John, for after Jesus said to Peter, "If I want him to remain until I come, what is that to you? You follow Me" (John 21:22), John makes this remark:

> "Therefore this saying went out among the brethren that that disciple would not die; yet Jesus did not say to him that he would not die, but *only,* 'If I want him to remain until I come, what *is that* to you?'" (John 21:23).

There are many different interpretations to this passage, all of which I discuss in depth in *Controversies in the Gospels.* However, some of those interpretations do play into the various traditions of John. Moreover, the very comment in John is an indication that John lived to a very old age, for why else would he have wanted to refute those who were saying that he would not die? When we examine John's history, we shall see why this rumor began to flourish.

Extra-Biblical Records and Traditions

Irenaeus, who was the pupil of John's disciple Polycarp, said that the "church in Ephesus, founded by Paul, and having John remaining among them permanently until the times of Trajan, is a true witness of the traditions of the apostles."[101]

Tertullian said that it was in Rome "where the Apostle John was first plunged, unhurt, into boiling oil, and thence remitted to his island exile."[102] Although Tertullian does not mention the emperor's name, this exile is *universally* accepted by every church father as taking place under Domitian.

Hippolytus said, "John, again, in Asia, was banished by Domitian the king to the isle of Patmos, in which also he wrote his Gospel and saw the apocalyptic vision; and in Trajan's time he fell asleep at Ephesus, where his remains were sought for, but could not be found."[103]

The co-called *Teaching of the Apostles* calls the apostle "John from Ephesus"[104] and declares that "Ephesus, and Thessalonica, and all Asia, and all the country of the Corinthians, and of all Achaia and the parts round about it, received the apostles' ordination to the priesthood from John the evangelist, who had leaned upon the bosom of our Lord; who himself built a church there, and ministered in his office of Guide which he held there."[105]

Clement of Alexandria commented that "the Apostle John ... on the tyrant's death, returned to Ephesus from the isle of Patmos [and then] went away, being invited, to the contiguous territories of the nations, here to appoint bishops, there to set in order whole Churches, there to ordain such as were marked out by the Spirit."[106]

Eusebius said that John was alotted Asia as a missionary field and that he stayed in Ephesus until his death[107] with the exception of his exile to Patmos under Domitian's reign.[108]

Among the apocryphal writings John is also featured prominently. The most important, and oldest, of these is the *Acts of the Holy Apostle and Evangelist John the Theologian* (hereafter called the *Acts of John*). With rather mild embellishments (in comparison to most apocrypha of this time) it states that "it came to the ears of Domitian that there was a certain Hebrew in Ephesus, John by name, who spread a report about the seat of empire of the Romans, saying that it would quickly be rooted out, and that the kingdom of the Romans would be given over to another" (which is the kingdom of God), and so he sent soldiers to arrest John in Ephesus and bring him to Rome. So John was dragged before Domitian and ordered to drink poison, which he did, but no harm befell him (cf. Mark 16:18). According to the custom then he could not be sentenced to die as he had been found favored by the gods, so John was then sent to Patmos where he wrote the book of Revelation. John was then returned to Ephesus under Trajan where he is said to have ascended to heaven like Elijah without having died.[109]

Additionally, John is briefly mentioned in the apocryphal *Acts of Philip* as the man who rescued Bartholomew from martyrdom in Hierapolis of modern day Turkey.[110] He is supposed to be the author of the apocryphal *Book of John Concerning the Falling Asleep of Mary* (or the *Assumption of Mary*) which says that Mary died in Jerusalem.[111]

Many other traditions and writings have been passed down through the ages, but all merely repeat what has been said in one form or another here among the ante-Nicene histories and traditions.

Evaluation

John's Travels

There seems no doubt that John went to Asia minor and nursed all the churches therein. He resided at Ephesus, which he made his home (probably with Jesus's mother Mary – see below), and traveled to the nearby churches in Asia minor to oversee their care and instruction. Some have credited John with the founding of the churches in Smyrna, Pergamos, Sardis, Philadelphia, Laodicea, and Thyratira,[112] but others say he merely took over the "orphaned" churches that Paul had established.[113] That latter assumes that Paul had died before John moved to Ephesus, the former that John had preceded Paul to those cities. The truth is probably in between the two. Paul had established mission works among the gentiles long before the Council of Jerusalem. The other twelve apostles only moved out of Israel after the council. It appears, as will be discussed later, that the apostles had predetermined to what part of the world each of the apostles would be sent. John's allotment was Asia Minor. Obviously Paul had already planted seeds there when John arrived. Because there was no rivalry among the apostles, they worked together. Whether John established all of those churches or simply served over them in Paul's absense, there is no doubt that John worked and served Asia Minor and all its churches out of his home base in Ephesus. Having said that, it is interesting that Paul had originally been "forbidden by the Holy Spirit to speak the word in Asia" (Acts 16:6). By Asia, it means the country named Asia, which is where Ephesus was located. Although Paul would later visit Ephesus, John may have already been there by that time. It is therefore possible that John did found the church in Ephesus. Coincidentally, the other country which Paul was forbidden from entering during his second journey was Bithynia (Acts 16:7) to which Andrew would minister.

Those who argue that John took over "orphaned" churches in Asia Minor argue that John had originally gone to Rome[114] and that it was then, under Nero, that John was exiled to Patmos, not years later under Domitian as stated by *every* ancient witness. Why? Is there any evidence of this? Frankly, the only ones who seem to hold to this untenable view are those with a certain theological agenda, as the reader will see.

Exile to Patmos

The book of Revelation was written by John and foretells the story of the anti-Christ and the second coming of Christ. The problem is that some people do not want to believe that this is a literal prophecy of End Times. Called "preterists", these interpreters want to make Revelation an allegory about Nero. The problems this view are too many and to great to discuss here,[115] save the most obvious. The Bible explicitly says that John "was on the island called Patmos because of the word of God and the testimony of Jesus" (Revelation 1:9). If John was exiled by Domitian, then there is no way that the book can be a prophecy about a man who had died almost thirty years before!

In an attempt to support their theologial agenda, some try desperately to shift the Patmos exile from Domitian to Nero. Bernard Ruffin implies that Tertullian and Jerome place John's exile under Nero,[116] but in fact they say nothing of the sort. They do not give the name of the emperor in question, but others do. Each and *every* church father who mentions the time or emperor places his exile under Domitian's reign in the mid 90s. *No* church father names Nero. Tertullian's quotation is simply that Rome is "where the Apostle John was first plunged, unhurt, into boiling oil, and thence remitted to his island exile."[117] He says nothing more. It is the other church fathers, including Clement of Alexandria, who identify the emperor as Domitian.[118] Moreover, the church fathers also state that he returned from exile under Nerva, or some say Trajan (for Nerva rule was very short). Can we really expect that he was in exile for over thirty years and multiple emperors?

Furthermore, based on the early church fathers' writings, John almost certainly never went to Rome until his arrest. None of the church fathers give any indication of John first traveling to Rome. Our two earliest sources say that he went to Ephesus and, as Irenaeus said, "remain[ed] among them [at Ephesus] permanently until the times of Trajan."[119] So say all others. How then did John come to exiled? If he never left Ephesus, how was he at Patmos?

Obviously, the quotations above refer to his home and mission only for they all concede that John was arrested and taken to Rome by Domitian, and thence to his exile on Patmos. How did this happen?

The *Acts of John*, our most sober apocryphal work on John, and among the most ancient, states that "it came to the ears of Domitian that there was a certain Hebrew in Ephesus, John by name, who spread a report about the seat of empire of the Romans, saying that it would quickly be rooted out, and that the kingdom of the Romans would be given over to another," which is the kingdom of God. Therefore, it says that Domitian sent soldiers to arrest John in Ephesus and bring him to Rome where he was tried for treason against Rome.[120] Why then was he not executed? This is the most intriguing part.

According to the most ancient of Roman customs, no prisoner who had survived a failed execution could be executed, for he was deemed to have been favored by the gods. In the *Acts of John* we are told that John was made to drink poison but that, as promised by our Lord Jesus (Mark 16:18), he did not die. Tertullian recounts a slightly different version, saying that, "the Apostle John was first plunged, unhurt, into boiling oil, and thence remitted to his island exile."[121] This account is the version that has been most often repeated, and considering Tertullian's close proximity to the events, his statement bears strong credibility.

So John left Israel, probably around 50 A.D. and traveled to Ephesus, probably with Jesus's mother, and remained there, as Irenaeus (as second generation disciple of John) said, until his arrest by Domitian. After having been boiled in oil and surviving, he was exiled to Patmos, Greece where he wrote the book of Revelation. Following Domitian's death John returned home to Ephesus. What then?

His Death

It is obvious that John lived to a ripe old age. So old that a "saying went out among the brethren that that disciple [John] would not die" (John 21:23). How then did he die?

The *Acts of John* offers up a strange tradition, saying that John was raptured like Elijah of old and never died.[122] This view was echoed by Hippolytus when he said that "his remains were sought for, but could not be found."[123]   Another curious legend, quoted by Augustine, relates the story that John, though buried, is but asleep awaiting the day that he would be awakened before the Second Coming in Last Days.[124] Thus John, it is said, is like a sort of ancient Rip Van Winkle who will awaken centuries later and will thus be alive when Jesus returns.

Now despite this theories, John 21:23 makes it clear that John did not believe the legends that he was not to die, and refuted this interpretation of Jesus's words. So most agree that John died peacefully at a ripe old age. Tertullian affirmed that John "underwent death."[125]   According to the fourth century Theodore of Mapsuestia John died under Trajan in 106 A.D.[126] Most place his death earlier, around 101 A.D. Estimates of his age at death also vary from eighty years of age to nearly a hundred. He was certainly the youngest of the apostles, and probably a teenager when he began to follow Jesus.   A conservative estimate is that he was over ninety years of age when he died, and at least eighteen or nineteen when called by Jesus. If we was born around 10 A.D., then he would have been ninety-one if he died in 101 A.D. and ninety-six if we take Theodore of Mapsuestia's estimation. In either case, John was the only apostle to die a natural death.

Summary

John, the beloved disciple, and the apostle of Jesus, left Israel and established his home in Ephesus, Turkey. It is there from which he set up a base and ministered to all the surrounding churches in Asia Minor.   He is credited with appointing overseers, elders, and others to care for the churches of Smyrna, Pergamos, Sardis, Philadelphia, Laodicea, and Thyratira,[127] all in modern day Turkey. He continued to live in Ephesus for many years until Domitian began to persecute Christians. The emperor had heard of the apostles, but only one remained alive, so he sent soldiers to arrest John in Ephesus and bring him back for trial.

In Rome John was subjected to torture and cast into a pot of boiling oil. Because John miraculously survived the boiling oil, he was deemed to have been favored by the gods, and not even the emperor could execute him, so John was instead exiled to the Greek island of Patmos, where he received a vision from the Lord and penned the book of Revelation.

After Domitian's death John was allowed to return to Ephesus where he continued to care for the churches. He died a natural death sometime between 101 and 106 A.D. His last words are alleged to have been, "Children, love one another."

5

Andrew

Andrew was the brother of Simon Peter (Matthew 4:18) and a follower of John the Baptist (John 1:40-41). It is he who first recognized Jesus as Christ, when he went to Peter and told him, "We have found the Messiah" (which translated means Christ)" (John 1:41). However, he is only mentioned thirteen times in the Bible, and only once in the book of Acts. Consequently, the Bible gives very little information about him, save that he was among the first called and the first to recognize Jesus as the Messiah. Despite this, there is probably less debate as to his missionary activities after the Biblical record than most of the other apostles. The greatest debate involves whether or not he went to the land of the "man-eaters" in the southern tip of modern day Ukraine and Russia. In all other respects the evidence for Andrew's mission field and martyrdom are united, as we shall see.

History and Traditions

The early church fathers say little about Andrew except that he ministered in Pontus, Galatia, Bithynia, Byzantium, Thracia, Macedonia, Thessalia, and Achaia,[128] as well as the possibility of mission work in Scythia (north of the Black Sea), as Eusebius declares.[129] Some even claim that he ministered in the Kingdom of Armenia.[130] They are also united in recording that he died in Achaia by crucifixion at the hands of its governor Ægeates as related in *Acts and Martyrdom of the Holy Apostle Andrew*.

The *Acts and Martyrdom of the Holy Apostle Andrew* is an apocryphal work which has been variously dated from as early as 80 A.D. to as late as the forth century.[131] It is another work of historical fiction which tells the story of Andrew's last days. According to the story, Andrew went to the city of Patrae (Patras), Achaia, in the southern part of modern day Greece. There he converted the wife of the governor Ægeates after miraculously healing her. He also converted her brother. On account of this "the proconsul Ægeates, being enraged, ordered the apostle of Christ to be afflicted by tortures. Being stretched out, therefore, by seven times three soldiers, and beaten with violence, he was lifted up and brought before the impious Ægeates" where he was ordered to renounce Christ or be crucified himself. He was then crucified with ropes in order to prolong his death and allow wild animals to feast upon him while he yet live.[132]   Of course the story also has many embellishments such as Andrew converting tens of thousands while hanging on the cross and even having Ægeates offer to release Andrew from the cross, but Andrew declining in favor of martyrdom.[133]   Allegedly Andrew survived for four days upon the cross, finally dying "the day before the kalends of December."[134]

Hippolytus believed that "Andrew preached to the Scythians and Thracians, and was crucified, suspended on an olive tree, at Patrae, a town of Achaia; and there too he was buried."[135]

The *Teaching of the Apostles* or *Didascalia Apostolorum* is, as aforementioned, an ancient Syrian document dating to around 230 A.D.[136] It says "Nicæa, and Nicomedia, and all the country of Bithynia, and of Inner Galatia, and of the regions round about it, received the apostles' ordination to the priesthood from Andrew, the brother of Simon Cephas."[137]   It also mentions specifically Andrew's work in Phrygia.[138]

The *Acts of Andrew and Matthias* is yet another apocryphal work which has been declared heretical, but carries some traditions which may be ancient or medieval, depending of its date, which is unknown for certain.[139] There is debate as to whether or not it is Matthew or Matthias, for the earliest manuscript contains Matthias, whereas later ones bear the name of Matthew (see Chapters 9 and 13 for more).[140] In the story Matthias was sent to Scythia, called the land "of the man-eaters," where he was blinded and imprisoned. Andrew then received a vision of the Lord, telling him of Matthias's plight, so he set out to rescue Matthias. Back in Scythia Matthias's eyes are miraculously restored and Andrew soon arrives to rescue him. Andrew then performs many miracles to show the frailty of their pagan gods and, in one part of the story,

50

he even resurrects a "great multitude" of men, women, and
children, and cattle who had been drowned. He then converted
many of the cannibals before leaving.[141]

Evaluation

After the Council of Jerusalem until the time of his
martyrdom there are but scant references by the church fathers
and historians. However, the references all seem to concur very
squarely with one another, save questions as to his excursions in
Scythia and Armenia.

Scythia is roughly equivalent to modern day Ukraine,
just south of Russia and north of the Black Sea. It was believed
to be occupied by cannibals or "man-eaters" as the *Acts of
Andrew and Matthias* says. Some have naturally questioned this
entire tale because of its wild exaggerations and the serious
questions as to whether or not either Matthew or Matthias had
ever been to Scythia. However, there is good reason to believe
that Andrew had visited Scythia and witnessed the gospel there.
First, cannibalism was known to have been practiced among the
barbarians of Scythia and eastern Gaul, beyond the boundaries
of Rome. The story may be absurdly exaggerated, but is based
on a historical reality. Second, to this day the Russian Orthodox
Church accepts St. Andrew as their patron saint.[142] It is natural
for the churches of certain countries to adopt patron saints, but
they naturally adopt those who had visited their country. It
would not make sense to adopt a patron saint that had never been
to Eurasia. Finally, Andrew's missions in the regions just south
of the Black Sea are well documented and disputed by very few.
It is logical that if Andrew's mission field encompassed the
region of Pontus, Bithynia, Phrygia, Byzantium, and even
Thracia (all of which border the Black Sea), then we might well
expect that Andrew continued up Thracia on the western coast of
the Black Sea and followed the northern coastline, entering into
Scythia.

Now if we accept that Andrew, if no one else, entered
Scythia, then it is again logical that he followed the Black Sea
coast around to the east and back down again into Turkey. This
would take him through the kingdom of Armenia, which lay

between the Black Sea and the Caspian Sea, northeast of modern day Turkey.

Later in life, he began to work in Greece, ministering in cities like Corinth, Philippi, Sparta, and Megara.[143] Presumeably Andrew was in Philippi when the Neronian persecutions began in Rome.[144] Despite what some revisionist historians claim, the persecutions were not restricted to Rome, although the majority of persecution was concentrated there. Nero was not popular with the regional governors, but most killed some Christians in order to appease the emperor, lest they be accused of neglecting their duty. Peter and Paul were not the only apostles to die under Nero, but they were the only ones to die in Rome. Andrew, however, appears to have escaped death under Nero, although just barely. History records that he died only a year (some say two years) after Nero's suicide.

Eventually Andrew made his way down to southern Greece in the city of Patrae (or Patras), in what was then the country of Achaia. There he converted the wife and brother-in-law of the regional governor Ægeates. This much seems certain as the story is repeated often by various different sources. When we discount the normal embellishments of the various stories, we are left with the same basic facts which no serious historians have rejected. Ægeates, in revenge for the conversion of his wife, ordered Andrew to recant his teachings or suffer upon the cross.[145] Refusing to do so, Andrew was fastened upon a cross with ropes, so that he would not bleed to death. This was done to prolong the agony and give wild animals a chance to feast upon him while he yet lived. Such barbaric tactics were not uncommon as there was no single method of crucifixion as often supposed. He would linger for days and hungry wild dogs would come and gnaw at his feet and legs while birds prey upon his head. The cross itself was of the "X" shape, thus it has become known as "St. Andrew's cross."[146]

Traditions vary as to how long it took Andrew to die. The *Acts and Martyrdom of the Holy Apostle Andrew* says that he was on the cross for four days before death,[147] but others say he was hung on the cross on November 28, which is but three days before his death,[148] which all traditions place on November 30, or more precisely, the eve of December 1.[149] Now this discrepancy is actually easily resolved, for the Jews began the new day at sundown, whereas the Romans began the new day at midnight, as in the modern age.[150] If he died on the eve of December 1, by Roman reckoning, then it was already four days by Jewish reckoning. This would explain the contradiction.

The year of his death is "uncertain." The traditional date is 69 A.D.[151] but martyrologists like Van Braght[152] and John Foxe place it in 70 A.D.[153] With no direct chronological markers with which to tie these dates to other calendar events, it is impossible to know which is correct. We can only say that he died on the night of November 30, in 69 or 70 A.D.

Bartolome Esteban Murillo – The Martyrdom of St. Andrew – 1675

One final anecdote is Andrew's final words. The various traditions expound his speech to long sermons, but most contain some variant of the fact that he said, "O cross, most welcome and long looked for,"[154] thus embracing his martyrdom.

Summary

Andrew's mission field began by the Black Sea. He apparently followed the sea around its coastline in a full circle. Beginning in modern day Turkey he ministered to Pontus,

Bithynia, Inner Galatia, and began a church in the famed city of Byzantium which would become the Roman capital under Constantine, under the new name of Constantinople. From there Andrew followed up along the western coast of the Black Sea to the country of Thracia in modern Bulgaria and the Romania. Continuing north he left the bounds of the Roman Empire and became one of the first to venture into Scythia, which is modern day Ukraine and southern Russia.

Scythia was a land then dominated by the pagan barbarians. They were considered savages and some tribes even practiced cannibalism. It is not know how much success Andrew had in Scythia, but the Russian Orthodox Church does consider him their patron saint, indicating that he may have left some small Christian communities behind. Nevertheless, whether he was successful or not, he began to move back down the eastern coast of the Black Sea, moving back toward the Roman Empire. He then passed through the small kingdom of Armenia in route, preaching the gospel there.

Once he returned to the Roman Empire, he moved his mission field to Greece, doubtless stopping by the churches he had worked with in Turkey along the way. In Greece he worked in Macedonia and Thessalia, staying in cities like Sparta and Philippi, where he is believed to have been when Nero's persecutions began. Finally, Andrew moved south into Achaia, Greece, visiting the churches of Corinth and Megara. In his last days, in either 69 or 70 A.D. he moved to the western portion of Achaia and the city of Patrae, or Patras. There he had success converting the wife and brother-in-law of the governor, who became enraged and ordered Andrew crucified without nails, and left to be exposed to animals. It took him three and a half days to die, having expired on November 30. His last words before being crucified are alleged to be, "O cross, most welcome and long looked for."[155]

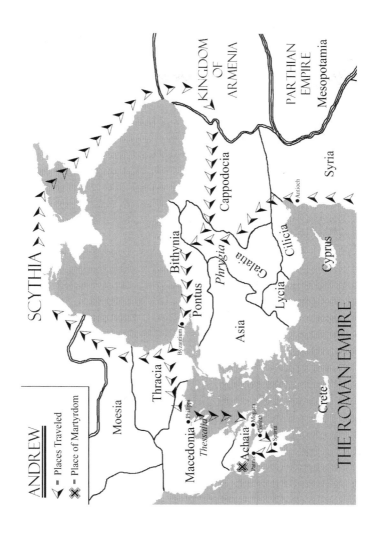

ANDREW
➤ = Places Traveled
✖ = Place of Martyrdom

SCYTHIA

KINGDOM OF ARMENIA

PARTHIAN EMPIRE
Mesopotamia

Cappodocia

Syria

Bithynia

Phrygia

Galatia

Cilicia

Antioch

Pontus

Lycia

Cyprus

Byzantium

Asia

Moesia

Thracia

Crete

Macedonia • Philippi
Thessalia

THE ROMAN EMPIRE

Achaia

55

6

Philip

Philip is famous for having witnessed to the Ethiopian eunuch (Acts 8:26-40) whom tradition ascribes as having founded the Ethiopian church.[156] However, many believe that this was actually Philip the Evangelist, whom they say was a different person from Philip the Apostle. For this very reason records of Philip and his deeds are arguably the most debated and even contradictory. Several different versions of his martyrdom have been written, and while some merge the stories, there is considerable debate as to which is true. This confusion may be explained if Philip the Apostle and Philip the Evangelist are indeed two different people, but are they? Is there another way to reconcile the problems with Philipine traditions?

History and Traditions

The Biblical Record

Philip is scarcely mentioned in the first three gospels, but has a relatively prominent role in John's gospel, as well as the book of Acts. He was from Bethsaida, which was also the city from which Andrew and Peter came (John 1:44). Many believe that he was also a fisherman and a follower of John the Baptist,[157] although the Bible is not specific on either point. What is specific is that it was Philip who told the apparently skeptical Nathaniel Bartholomew about Jesus. This flies in the face of those who make Philip out to be an indecisive and slow to understand apostle.[158]

In the book of Acts a man named Philip is seen converting many Samaritans, and yet some criticize the fact that Simon the Magician was among his converts (Acts 8:12-13) by suggesting that "he was being 'had' by a local cultist."[159] Once again, Philip (if this was the apostle) seems unfairly maligned by some, for neither Peter nor John said a word about Simon until after Simon showed the effrontery to attempt to bribe the apostles (Acts 8:18-24). It should also be noted that Simon offered an apology of sorts and asked the apostles to pray for him. Nothing else is then said of Simon in the Bible. However, this Philip is shown to continue his successful evangelism; most notably in the conversion of the Ethiopian Eunuch (Acts 8:26-40) whom tradition ascribes as having founded the Ethiopian church (see also Chapter 15).[160]

Is this the last we read of Philip in the Bible? Oddly enough, the controversy over Philip begins not with his life after the book of Acts, but within it, for there is a "Philip the Evangelist" who is described as one of the seven deacons (Acts 21:7) who were appointed to oversee the welfare of the Church (Acts 6:3-5). Some believe that this is the same Philip who was the apostle, whereas other deny this, and make Philip the Evangelist out to be a different person.

This is a debate reserved for the "Evaluation" section, but it should be noted that this confusion is doubtless one reason that there appear to be conflicting stories about Philip in the various traditions and histories. They were obviously confusing the two people, merging them into a single person, and thus resulting in contradictory accounts, which some then tried to resolve unsatisfactorily.

Extra-Biblical Records and Traditions

Papias is our earliest and best source in regard to Philip, although he says little except that Philip and his four daughters lived in Hierapolis.[161] Now Papias lived from 70 to 155 A.D. and was bishop of Hierapolis. It is believed he knew Philip, the father of the four prophetesses, personally. He was also a pupil of John the Apostle and was a friend of Polycarp.

Polycrates, who live from 130 to 196 A.D. served as the Bishop of Ephesus and was probably an associate of both Polycarp and Irenaeus. He mentioned "Philip, one of the twelve apostles, who sleeps at Hierapolis, with two of his aged, virgin daughters, while a third daughter lived in the Holy Spirit and rests in Ephesus."[162]

Clement of Alexandria affirmed that "Philip had children, and Philip gave his daughters in marriage."[163] Note that Clement says he gave more than one daughter in marriage.

Hippolytus said that "Philip preached in Phrygia, and was crucified in Hierapolis with his head downward in the time of Domitian, and was buried there."[164]

Gaius (Caius) of Rome said "the four daughters of Philip, who were prophetesses, were at Hierapolis in Asia. There grave is there, and so is their father's"[165]

Much later tradition by the sixth century Isidore of Seville claims Philip preached in Gaul (France), but Ruffin believes he mistook Galatia for Gallia.[166]

The apocryphal *Acts of Philip* says that he died in the time of Trajan.[167] It relates that "going through the cities and regions of Lydia and Asia"[168] he finally came "to the city of Ophioryma, which is called Hierapolis of Asia" with Bartholomew,[169] and there converted the wife of Nicanora the proconsul, which enraged him so he commanded "Philip and Bartholomew and Mariamme to be beaten; and after they had been scourged with the thongs, he ordered their feet to be tied, and them to be dragged through the streets of the city"[170] and "he ordered Philip to be hanged, and his ankles to be pierced, and to bring also iron hooks, and his heels also to be driven through, and to be hanged head downwards, opposite the temple on a certain tree; and stretch out Bartholomew opposite Philip, having nailed his hands on the wall of the gate of the temple."[171] In a strange piece of fiction Philip calls for a curse upon Nicanora which leads an angry Jesus to appear and chastise Philip because he sought to repay "evil with evil." Then Philip repented and accepted his martyrdom[172] whereas Bartholomew was rescued with the help of the Apostle John.[173]

Another later apocryphal work entitled the *Acts of Saint Philip the Apostle When He Went to Upper Hellas* recounts a story of Philip journeying to Athens where he debated the Greek philosophers who then wrote to Annas the high Priest complaining of his miracles and converts. Annas then came with hundreds of men but Philip prayed and Annas was cast alive into Hades and the hundred men were blinded until they repented.[174]

Lastly, is the Syriac apocryphal *Acts of the Apostles and The History of Philip* which records the story of Philip charting a ship to Carthage where he converted a Jewish man, and drew the ire of many Jews, but when the Roman prefect threatened the Jews for disturbing the peace, it was Philip who came to their aid and protected the Jews.[175]

Evaluation

The first question which must be addressed is whether or not Philip the Evangelist was the same as Philip the Apostle. Traditionally, they have been assumed to be the same person as accepted by Catholic tradition, but there is good reason to believe otherwise.

Acts 6:2-5 says:

> "The twelve summoned the congregation of the disciples and said, 'It is not desirable for us to neglect the word of God in order to serve tables. Therefore, brethren, select from among you seven men of good reputation, full of the Spirit and of wisdom, whom we may put in charge of this task.' But we will devote ourselves to prayer and to the ministry of the word. The statement found approval with the whole congregation ; and they chose Stephen, a man full of faith and of the Holy Spirit, and Philip, Prochorus, Nicanor, Timon, Parmenas and Nicolas, a proselyte from Antioch."

Now some argue that "the Twelve complained that administrative concerns were causing them to neglect the preaching of God's word, and thus they appointed the deacons to assist them ... since the college of deacons serve the Hellenistic wing of the Church, it was conceivable that the Twelve felt that one of their number should be a part of that body."[176] This seems logical, except when we read of this same Philip in Acts 21:8-9 wherein Paul entered "the house of Philip the evangelist, who was one of the seven" who had "four virgin daughters who were prophetesses." Why would one of the *twelve* be identified as "one of the seven"? Surely this must be a different Philip from the apostle or else he would not be designated as "one of the seven" (Acts 21:9), but one of "the Twelve" (Acts 6:2).

Interestingly enough, some, like Dave Hunt, even believe that Acts 8 is actually about Philip the Evangelist, not the apostle.[177] Whether this is true or not, there is other evidence that the apostle and the evangelist are different. Note that Acts

21:9 states plainly that Philip the Evangelist had "four virgin daughters." The various traditions say that all but one died a virgin,[178] but Clement of Alexandria said that "Philip gave his daughters [plural] in marriage."[179] This conflict could easily be resolved if we accept that they are different people, as Acts 21:8 implies.

More importantly, if Philip the Apostle and the Evangelist were different then this helps to explain the conflicting traditions which revolve around Philip. Consider, for example, that some have Philip dying in 54 A.D.,[180] others in 90 A.D.,[181] and some in the early second century under Trajan![182] Moreover, most make his missionary field in Asia Minor and Greece, while others place him in Scythia[183] or even in Carthage Africa![184] Now while Scythia is close to Asia Minor and consistent with that mission field, it makes no logical sense that Philip would travel to Carthage and then return to Asia Minor. If he went to Carthage we would expect him to establish a mission field in Africa. Finally, his martyrdom has been various described as being by stoned to death by Ebionites[185] or being hung upside down on a tree.[186] One again, if we assume *two* people named Philip, rather than one, then the conflicting traditions begin to make sense. The real question is "which is which"?

We know from Acts 21:9 that it was Philip the Evangelist who had the four virgin daughters who were prophetesses. We also know that Papias knew Philip the Evangelist and said that his four daughters lived in Hierapolis.[187] Consequently, we may safely assume that the traditions revolving around Hierapolis are about Philip the Evangelist rather than the apostle. This then leaves us with but scant references to Philip which we should examine.

Our first step is to establish where Philip's mission field resided. The *Acts of Saint Philip the Apostle When He Went to Upper Hellas* calls Philip "a Son of Thunder"[188] which was actually said of James and John (Mark 3:17). This is further indication of the author's confusion. In this story Philip is in Athens Greece, which we might expect would be a mission field close to Asia Minor. This apocrypha should then be rejected as conflated and probably referring to Philip the Evangelist.

This leaves only the traditions of Scythia and Africa. As discussed under the apostle Andrew, Scythia would be a mission field compatible with Asia Minor and Greece, so unless the two Philips both worked in the same mission field (certainly a possibility), we may assume then that only Carthage (in modern day Tunisia, Africa) does not fit.

By default we might assume then that Carthage was a separate mission field by a second Philip. If the Philip of Hierapolis was Philip the Evangelist, then Philip the Apostle would be the one who established a mission field in northern Africa and Carthage. Unfortunately, there is little information about Philip in Africa aside from the apocryphal Syrian *Acts of the Apostles*. This story, however, does not record the martyrdom of Philip. However, it does offer a possible clue.

The Syrian *Acts of the Apostles* tells the story of Philip's mission to Carthage and of a conflict with a sect of Jews in that country. Now Van Braght believed that Philip's head was fastened to a pillar and stoned to death by the Ebionite cult.[189] The Ebionites where a Jewish-Christian cult which was strictly legalistic and required gentiles to first convert to Judaism and be circumcised. Although the Syrian *Acts of the Apostles* clearly calls these Jews and does not record Philip having died there, it offers hints that the writer may have conflated the Jews and the Ebionites, for the Jews are depicted as saying that they would not "renounce Moses and believe in the Messiah."[190] Now the Jews were obviously not asked to renounce Moses, whom Jesus revered, but the Ebionites were so legalistic that they viewed the acceptance of gentiles without circumcision as a renunciation of Moses. Might these then have been Ebionites with whom Philip was in dispute? If so, then the tradition that Van Braght quotes fits well with Africa, and not the Hielapolis traditions which clearly make Philip's martyrdom a response by a pagan Roman to the conversion of his wife, and not in any way related to the Ebionite controversy.

Another piece of the puzzle lay in the vastly different dates offered for Philip's martyrdom. John Foxe,[191] like Van Braght, places Philip's death in 54 A.D. Although he does accept the Hierapolis tradition, that tradition actually places Philip's death under Trajan in the second century. However, this would make Philip over a hundred years old, and Hippolytus said that he died in the 90s under Domitian's reign.[192]

There is a simple answer to this complex problem which not only resolves the chronology, but also the silence of Philip the Apostle in relation to Philip the Evangelist. In short, if Philip died in 54 A.D. then he would have been the second apostle to die and his ministry would have been the second shortest. This would explain why so little was ever written about Philip.

One final piece of evidence that this may be the case is the fact that Roman's executed people by crucifixion, as in the Hierapolis tale (it was a form of being crucified upside down), but Jews traditionally executed people by stoning. Consequently, the story of Philip being tied to a pillar and stoned fits with the idea that he was killed by Ebionites, rather than a Roman prefect. The critic will answer, perhaps justly so, that those who claim Philip was stoned by Ebionites place his death in Hierapolis, and not in Africa. The answer is, of course, that this is on account of the conflated traditions.

Thus we are left with two choices. Either we have contradictory traditions or we have conflated traditions. I believe the latter is more logical, but makes it harder to separate the two. My tentative solution is that Philip the Apostle traveled to Carthage and established a mission field in north Africa. In circa 54 A.D. he was then stoned to death by Ebionites for sacrilege. It was Philip the Evangelist who traveled north and established his mission field in Asia Minor, Greece, and possibly Scythia (see Chapter 15). Because so little was written on Philip, whose career was cut short only twenty years after Christ, the Evangelist would eventually become conflated with the apostle by later traditions and historians who assumed them to be one and the same.

Summary

Although my solution is tentative, I believe that the traditions of Hierapolis and the Asia Minor mission field belong to Philip the Evangelist and not the apostle. I believe that the Apostle Philip, after witnessing the gospel in Judea, Samaria, and Syria, departed to establish a mission field in northern

Africa. There he found disciples but at some point he came into conflict with Ebionite Christians who tied him to a pillar and stoned him to death in the early to mid 50s, making him the second apostle to die a martyr.

7

Thomas

Although Bartholomew is listed before Thomas in many apostolic lists, Acts 1:13 list Thomas first. I have followed Acts here for the simple reason that the traditions of Bartholomew appear tied to those of Thomas. In order to discuss Bartholomew's history and reach a fair conclusion upon his life, it is necessary to discuss the history of Thomas first.

Thomas himself is often called the "Apostle to the Orient" or more specifically the "Apostle to India." His mission field was in the east, far beyond the Roman empire. This seems as well established as any post-Biblical fact regarding the apostles. We also have many more traditions and histories of Thomas than of most of the other apostles. Evidence supporting these traditions is also surprisingly strong given the relative historical obscurity of simple missionaries.

History and Traditions

The Biblical Record

It was Thomas who declared "unless I see in His hands the imprint of the nails, and put my finger into the place of the nails, and put my hand into His side I will not believe" (John 20:25). Because this is the primary anecdote about Thomas found in the gospels Thomas has unfairly been stigmatized as "Doubting Thomas," but this far from fair since the vast majority of those reading this book would never have believed it either. Thomas's doubt is natural, and Jesus did not chastise him, other than to say, "Because you have seen Me, have you believed? Blessed are they who did not see, and yet believed" (John 20:29).

What cast a better shadow upon Thomas's character is John 11:16. In that passage Lazarus has been declared dead, and while the other disciples thought there was no point going to the tomb, Thomas shows loyalty, love, and courage when he declared, "Let us also go, so that we may die with Him." Clearly he did not understand that Jesus was to resurrect Lazarus, but his comment shows a fierce love and loyalty, as well as proving that Thomas did not fear death. This character trait may be one reason he was chosen to go beyond the boundaries of the Roman empire, as we shall see.

The only other information we have about Thomas in the Bible is that he was called "the Twin" (John 11:16; 21:2). In fact, Thomas is the Anglicization of the Hebrew word for Twin, which is in Greek "didymus" (διδυμος). Thus "Thomas" is a nickname, like "Peter." The Bible does not record his true given name, but tradition ascribes to him the name Judah,[193] which is Judas in Greek. Since there were already two other apostles with this popular name, it is natural that Jesus would have given him a nickname to distinguish him from the other two.

Although we do not know the name of his twin brother, we must assume that Thomas's brother was not a believer, or at least not among the apostles. So it is that Thomas is one of the few apostles who has left a larger impression upon his post-Biblical life than what is recorded in the Bible.

Extra-Biblical Records and Traditions

There is a wealth of ancient historical records and traditions concerning Thomas. In fact, more has been said of Thomas that any apostle except Peter, and perhaps John. This is doubtless because he was a trailblazer who established mission fields outside of the Roman empire, and as far as India (some say China as well).

Perhaps the earliest confirmation of Thomas' travels to India is found in the second century by the missionary Pantaeus who arrived in India expecting to be the first to bring the gospel, only to find that there was already a Christian community there, and that the Indians had an Aramaic copy of Matthew's gospel.[194]

Hippolytus taught that "Thomas preached to the Parthians, Medes, Persians, Hyrcanians, Bactrians, and Magi, and was thrust through in the four members of his body with a pine spears at Calamene, the city of India, and was buried there."[195]

The *Teachings of the Apostles* (circa 230 A.D.[196]) says "India, and all the countries belonging to it and round about it, even to the farthest sea, received the apostles' ordination to the priesthood from Judas Thomas, who was guide and ruler in the church which he had built there, in which he also ministered there."[197]

Eusebius said that portions, or mission fields, were decided by casting lots and that India fell to Thomas.[198] He also claims to have seen authentic court records from the ancient Osroene (Mesopotamian) kingdom which record the following.

According to those records king Abgar of Edessa wrote a letter to Jesus shortly before His crucifixion, reading as follows:

> "I have heard of You, and of Your healing; that You do not use medicines or roots, but by Your word open the eyes of the blind, make the lame to walk, cleanse the lepers, make the deaf to hear; how by Your word You also heal the sick spirits and those who are tormented with lunatic demons, and how, again, You raise the dead to life. And, learning the wonders that You do, it was borne in upon me that (of two things, one): either You have come down from heaven, or else You are the Son of God, who bring all these things to pass. Wherefore I write to You, and pray that You will come to me, who adore You, and heal all the ill that I suffer, according to the faith I have in You. I also learn that the Jews murmur against You, and persecute You, that they seek to crucify You, and to destroy You. I possess but one small city, but it is beautiful, and large enough for us two to live in peace."[199]

According to these records which Eusebius had seen, Jesus answered saying that He could not come, but would sent a disciple to heal him. The final part of that record (which will be quoted under "Judas Thaddæus") says that Thomas sent Judas Thaddæus to Prince Abgar the Black who became a convert.[200]

The apocryphal *Acts of the Holy Apostle Thomas* is often considered to reflect false teachings, as Thomas pronounces curses upon enemies and similar deeds, but its antiquity makes it an important piece of tradition regarding

Thomas. It dates to at least the third century, and is another work of historical fiction. In it the Lord commanded Thomas to go to India, but Thomas acted like Jonah of old and refused to go, when "a certain merchant come from India, by name Abbanes, sent from the king Gundaphoros" seeking a carpenter for the king. Together they were kidnapped and brought back as slaves. "They began, therefore, to sail away. And they had a fair wind, and they sailed fast until they came to Andrapolis, a royal city." There he performed many miracles and converted the king.[201] Some of the legends found in *Acts of the Holy Apostle Thomas* are refreshing compared to other works of historical fiction at the time, although of little historical value. For example, in the story Thomas was commissioned to build a palace for the king, but he instead gave the money to the poor. When the king demanded to see the palace Thomas built, Thomas said that his palace was awaiting him in heaven. He then resurrected the king's brother who told Gundaphoros that he had seen the palace himself. It was then that Gundaphoros converted to Christianity.[202]

The *Consummation of Thomas the Apostle* is yet another apocryphal work, sometimes considered heretical. It purports to tell the story of Thomas' martyrdom. In it King Misdeus of India imprisons Thomas on the charge of sorcery because of his miracles. He is then executed with spears by four soldiers.[203] The legendary parts of the story also claim that the King's son had become demon possessed and, having remembered the miracles of Thomas, the king went to the tomb to seek Thomas' bones which he believed had mystic healing powers. There Thomas appeared to him saying, "You did not believe in me when alive; how will you believe in me when I am dead? Fear not. Jesus Christ is kindly disposed to you, through His great clemency." His son was then healed.[204]

A different account is found in the "Martyrology of Jerome" in which Thomas was praying in a cave when radical Hindus discovered him and speared him to death on July 3, 72 A.D.[205]

Still other traditions say that he was thrown into a furnace[206] in Calamia, India[207] but like Shadrach, Meshach, and Abegeno he survived and was thus finally slain with a spear.[208]

Although the origin of the story is unknown, Marco Polo recorded a tradition wherein the last words of Thomas were, "Lord, I thank Thee for all Thy mercies. Into Thy hands I commend my spirit."[209]

Still other traditions say Thomas first went to Ethiopia,[210] and others that he traveled to Carmania, Hyrcania, Bactria, and Magia[211] (all in Iran and Afghanistan). The kingdom of Armenia is also sometimes considered one of his mission fields.[212]

One final tradition, is the late oral tradition found in the Rabban song, which was sung by Indians for centuries. In it, Thomas is alleged to have gone to China in 49 A.D.[213]

Evaluation

Like the Apostle Peter, the records and traditions of Thomas are too plentiful to address singly. Consequently, it is best to address each tradition separately and then merge our conclusions together.

The Abgar Records

The tiny kingdom of Osroene was absorbed by Mesopotamia which was a part of the Parthian empire. Its capital, Edessa, is northeast of Syria and lay just outside the borders of the Roman empire. At the time of Christ its ruler was Abgar V, called the Black. This much is historically accurate. Whether or not Judas Thaddæus truly visited and converted the king is not as certain, because some scholars, perhaps cynically, argue that the documents Eusebius read were forgeries designed to support the eastern Orthodox church's traditions. In fact, the church of Assyria traces its bishops back to Thomas, much as the Catholic church traces its bishops back to Peter.[214] Furthermore, the date given for the crucifixion is the year 340 by the Edessene calendar which is believed to correspond to 30 A.D. and would be an incorrect date of the crucifixion.[215]

Now since the records actually say more about Judas Thaddæus than Thomas I shall reserve judgment for that section. Here it is sufficient to say that this argument seems more of a contrived debate between the Catholic church and the Eastern Orthodox church. If the documents are real then Thomas ministered to Osroene, and its neighboring kingdom of Armenia, before the Council of Jerusalem. Its close proximity to Syria makes this a possibility. However, if the documents were forgeries then Thomas would not have gone to either kingdom until after the Council of Jerusalem and then only if he took the land route to Parthia and India, rather than the sea fairing route (see discussion below).

The Parthian Traditions

That Thomas ministered in Parthia seems beyond reasonable doubt. Virtually all historians and traditions from at least Hippolytus record Thomas visiting some part of what was then Parthia.[216] These include Carmania, Hyrcania, Bactria, Media, Persia, and "the land of the Magi,"[217] all of which lay in modern day Iran and Afghanistan. Furthermore, unless Thomas took the route by sea, he would naturally have had to pass through most of these countries in order to reach India, giving a further indication that Thomas had at least visited them en route to his mission field.

Parthia was an empire that originated in ancient Persia and sought to reclaim much of the glory of the old Persian empire. After Alexander the Great conquered Persia, the land had become a part of his empire, but when he died the Greek empire was divided among his generals. The eastern Greek empire was called the Seleucid Empire. As early as 200 B.C. the tiny Parthian empire, then made up of what is Turkmenistan and the furtherest tip of northern Iran, began to war with the Seleucids. By the time of the Romans the Seleucid Empire was threatened on both the east and west. Eventually Parthia took in what is today Iran, Iraq, Turkmenistan, and a part of what is now Syria and Turkey. The Indo-Parthian empire was a semi-autonomous state, southeast of Parthia, which encompassed modern day Afghanistan, Pakistan, and the northern part of India including the Punjab.

As the reader can see, Thomas would almost certainly have had to pass through many of these regions to reach India, assuming he traveled by land. However, if he traveled by sea, as depicted in the Gundaphorus tradition, he would still have visited Indo-Parthia, for that was his kingdom. Let us examine that tradition more closely.

70

The Gundaphorus Traditions

The apocryphal *Acts of the Holy Apostle Thomas* is quickly rejected by many on account of its alleged gnosticism. In fact, it does reflect a cultic view of Christianity, which does not emphasize grace, but these ideas merely reflect its author and not the underlying historical basis to which archaeology has lent support. As with all historical fiction, we cannot take the story at face value, but, given historical support, we may assume the underlying characters and historical backdrop are real. Until the nineteenth century, however, even this was suspect.

The historicity of king Gundaphorus was verified in the nineteenth century when ancient first century coins bearing his name were discovered.[218] Many now believe that Gundaphorus was actually a title rather than a name, but the historical setting and dates fit very well with the Gundaphorus tradition. According to the histories and traditions, Thomas was taken captive as a slave and shipped to Gundaphorus's kingdom in 49 A.D. He then arrived sometime in 50 A.D.[219] We know that in the early 50s Kushan empire overran Indo-Parthia, and conquered much of northern India.[220] There is no doubt that by 52 A.D. Thomas had arrived in southern India (see below), meaning that he had left northern India no later than that same year. These facts fit. Thomas would have left Gundaphorus's kingdom when it came under siege. More important is that this invasion could explain a tradition which I reject; namely the legend that Thomas had gone to Peking, China in 49 A.D.[221]

There seems little doubt that Thomas never went to China. Our chronology does not even give Thomas enough time to make such a long trip, nor are there any ancient traditions or histories to support it. Nevertheless, there is a late tradition, or legend, that Thomas founded the church in Peking. How could such a legend have originated? There is only one logical explanation. Had Christianity existed in Gundaphorus's kingdom, or been a Christian himself, then the Kushanites would have heard the gospel from their prisoners. As the conquerors returned home to Peking some may have been converts or perhaps merely related news of the new religion. They would have reported second hand accounts of St. Thomas, which by legend would eventually become associated with any Christian sects in China. In other words, Chinese Christians would say that they received the gospel through Thomas, even though Thomas had never visited China. Although by no means proof, this theory can explain the origin of the legend, assuming Thomas truly did visit Gundaphorus's kingdom.

It is believed that Thomas disembarked at Pattala[222] and sailed up the Indus river to Taxila, the "Athens of India"[223] in what is today Kashmir, Pakistan of the Punjab region. Once again, if Thomas traveled to India by the overland route, he would have passed through modern day Pakistan. If he traveled by sea, then the tradition bears another historical accuracy. In either case it is highly likely that Thomas did at least pass through this kingdom and witness the gospel to Gundaphorus, whom he presumably converted.[224]

The Kerala Traditions

The best supported stories all revolve around Thomas's arrival in India on Malabar coast in circa 52 A.D.[225] There was already a Jewish community and a trade port in Malabar, Kerala in the first century, which would make it the most logical place for Thomas to go if he was establishing a mission.[226]

Aside from the vast, and overwhelming, traditions and histories of Thomas's journey to southern India, there is strong secondary evidence from India itself. Firstly it is now known Pallivaanavar, a mid-second century king of Kerala, was a Christian.[227] Second, we know that at the end of the second century the missionary Pantaeus arrived in India, expecting to be the first to bring the gospel. Instead, he was shocked to find a large Christian community there. The Indians also had a copy of Matthew's gospel. This makes sense for at the time the apostles left Israel only the gospel of Matthew had been written,[228] and there is no other way they could have received the gospel of Matthew, if not from an apostle! Now while this second story is generally attributed to Bartholomew, rather than Thomas, the appearance of a Christian king in Kerala certainly indicates that Thomas had served in Kerala, for Bartholomew is never said to have visited south India.

The Malabar coast of India is located in one of three small kingdoms found in southern India in those days. The Chera Kingdom on the west coast was the smallest of kingdoms and it is there where Thomas landed in the modern day state of Kerala, India. Evidence strongly supports the fact that Thomas remained there in Kerala promulgating the gospel for nearly seven years, until 59 A.D. when he decided to move further east to the then kingdom of Chola in what is today the Tamil Nadu state in India.

The Mylapore Traditions

It was in 59 A.D. that Thomas moved across from the west coast of southern India to its east coast. There he came to the capital of the kingdom of Chola, which was called Calamia.[229] Today it is Mylapore, Madras which is a part of the grand city of Chennai, in the state of Tamil Nadu, India. Traditions say that Thomas traveled throughout many other areas of southern India, but becoming aged and weak, he settled in Mylapore around 69 A.D.[230] This much is certain.

The rest of the Mylapore traditions actually revolve around Thomas's martyrdom. As with other apostles the works of historical fiction have sometimes created some contradictory accounts, but all seem in agreement that he died from a spear in or near the caves of what is today called "St. Thomas Mound" in Chennai, India.[231] The specifics of this are discussed below under "The Martyrdom Traditions."

Miscellaneous Traditions

Along with the histories of Thomas's travels to India many often forget that Thomas is sometimes connected with Ethiopia and even China! Oddly enough some say that Ethiopia, Parthia, and India were all assigned to Thomas.[232] Logically, unless Thomas took the sea route, Ethiopia would in no way be in the direction of Parthia and India. Now it is true that the apocryphal *Acts of the Holy Apostle Thomas* said that Thomas sailed down the Nile river when we was taken to Gundaphorus, so this may have been the origin of the story, but this seems to have little historical support, for even if he took the sea route, they would have sailed down the Red Sea, not the Nile. It is possible that Thomas could have stopped at Ethiopia before entering the Gulf of Aden, but the most logical explanation actually provides further indirect proof that Thomas went to India. This is because Ethiopia is called in Hebrew "Cush."

However, India also a "Kush," the "Hindu-Kush," not to mention that the Kushan empire ruled India for many years. Consequently, the most logical answer is that later translators and copyists mistook the African Cush for the Hindu Kush. This makes the most sense, especially since most westerners were unfamiliar with Indian geography. Consequently, the false assumption that Thomas went to Ethiopia is actually indirect evidence of his excursion into the Indies.

We, therefore, have no reason to accept either the sea route or the Ethiopian visit. Had Thomas traveled by sea, it would have been impractical for him to have moved northward to the region of Carmania and Hyrcania in Parthia which lay just south and southwest of the Caspian Sea. This is especially true since he would have to return to India afterwards, thus retracing his steps unnecessarily. This is compounded by the fact that his arrival in southern India in 52 A.D. is all but certain. If he left Israel shortly after the Council of Jerusalem he would have three to four years at the most to reach south India. I am, therefore, of the firm belief that Thomas traveled overland. Nonetheless, the overland route is not without problems.

One problem with the overland route is again in the timetable. We know that Thomas did not leave Israel until after the Council of Jerusalem. That council has variously been dated, with the most credible dates being between 48 and 50 A.D. If the council was in 48 A.D. and Thomas left soon after that, then the overland route is not only likely but probable as four years would be enough time for Thomas to establish missions in the countries to which he is credited. If he left with the company of Thaddæus and Bartholomew (see chapters 8 and 11) then he would have parted ways with them after staying in certain cities where they would reside. This would mean that Thomas did not need to have a prolonged stay in those areas. Counting the difficulty of travel in those days, we can calculate that it might take a minimum of nine months to travel to northern India assuming he didn't stop anywhere on the way. Of course, we assume he stopped at no fewer than five countries; Hyrcania, Bactria, Carmania, Media, and Persia. If he arrived in Indo-Parthia at Taxila in 50 A.D. then he would have spent no more than two to three months in each of those countries. This is entirely possible, and even probable, but only if the council of

Jerusalem was in 48 or 49 A.D. at the latest. If it was much later than that, then the sea route becomes more likely, but would eliminate the probability that Thomas ever visited Carmania, Hyrcania, Bactria, Media, and Persia. For this reason, I prefer the land route. I believe that the council of Jerusalem was probably in 49 A.D. based on Galatians 1:18; 2:1.[233]

This still leaves a few other questions. One, which I have alluded to previously, is the oral tradition that Thomas visited Peking China in 49 A.D.[234] As I stated earlier, this legend likely arose when the Kushans invaded Indo-Parthia and discovered Christian communities there that had been established by Thomas. The 49 A.D. date alone is reason enough to reject the tradition at face value, for Thomas may not have even left Judea until that year. Furthermore, no corroborating evidence for this tradition exist, even in the form of a late written tradition.

A final question is in regard to the date of Thomas's death. Van Braght believed that it was in 70 A.D.[235] but most traditions place it two years later in 72 A.D. According to Jerome, it was July 3, 72 A.D.[236] but many eastern Churches commemorate Thomas's death on December 21. The Syrian and Syro-Malabar churches favor July 3, whereas the Indian Orthodox Church favors December 21. How came such a difference? The answer could be in the fact that Thomas's bones are believed to have been transferred to Edessa on July 3 by the Kushan emperor Vasudeva I. Hence the enshrining of Thomas's bones in Edessa could have become confused in the west with his original entombment. I therefore tentatively then favor December 21.

One final note, is the interesting fact in regard to the Thomas traditions that the earliest Christian communities in India were found to be using symbols of the cross hundreds of years before it became prominent in the west. It was not until after the time of Constantine that the cross became a symbol of Christianity. Various different symbols, such as the fish, were predominantly in use before that time. However, in India the cross was already being used![237] Why?

This question could take a chapter all by itself, and is not particularly relevant, so I will merely abbreviate my answer. In Rome crucifixion was the standard mode of execution for criminals. The cross was largely a symbol of death and criminal punishment. This is why even Christians were reluctant to use the symbol until Constantine outlawed crucifixion. From that time onward Christians were no longer reluctant to see that Christ had transformed death into life on a cross, an instrument of death. The cross was thus a symbol of how Jesus turned death into life! In India crucifixion was not as common or popular, although by no means unheard of. It is, therefore, logical that without the stigma of Roman execution, the Indians took the symbol of the cross more readily than the west.

The Martyrdom Traditions

There are at three different accounts of St. Thomas's death. All in some way depict him as dying by a spear wound, but each differ in the circumstances surrounding it.

According to some famous medieval martyrologies Thomas was tortured with red hot plates and then cast into an idol (or oven) where he was supposed to be cooked alive. However, like Shadrach, Meshach, and Abednego (Daniel 3), Thomas was not consumed by the flames, so soldiers pierced him with a javelin or spear.

Thomas Thrown into an Oven – 1742

The apocryphal *Consummation of Thomas the Apostle* depicts Thomas's martyrdom as an execution by order of Misdeus the king. He was charged with sorcery on account of his miracles and four soldiers speared him to death.[238]

The last tradition is local, and held by most Indian Christians. In that story Thomas was somewhat of an ascetic, like John the Baptist. He often went to pray in secret, and had been praying in a cave when radical Hindus discovered him and slew him with a spear. Some accounts claim that he managed to crawl back to a local church before uttering his famous last words; "Lord, I thank Thee for all Thy mercies. Into Thy hands I commend my spirit."[239]

Now one thing seems certain. The existence of a king Misdeus of India has been confirmed in the writings of the Kushan emperor Vasudeva I. It is said that "Vasudeva may have been the Indian king who returned the relics of the Apostle St. Thomas from Mylapore, India in 232 CE, on which occasion his Syriac Acts (the 3rd century *Acts of Thomas*) were written. The relics were transferred triumphally to the town of Edessa, Mesopotamia. The Indian king is named as 'Mazdai' in Syriac sources, 'Misdeos' and 'Misdeus' in Greek and Latin sources."[240]

This fits with the record of Gregory of Tours (538 to 594 A.D.) who said "Thomas the Apostle, according to the narrative of his martyrdom is stated to have suffered in India. His holy remains (*corpus*), after a long interval of time, were removed to the city of Edessa in Syria and there interred. In that part of India where they first rested, stand a monastery and a church of striking dimensions, elaborately adorned and designed."

Further, to this very day in Mylapore, Madras (near Chennai) there lies "St. Thomas Mount" which is believed to be where Thomas was slain. The tradition and maintenance of the cave supports the latter story.[241]

Now this does leave one question. Was Thomas executed or killed while praying in a cave? It may be that both stories bear part of the truth. It is probable that Misdeus ordered the arrest of Thomas who sought refuge in the cave and was praying for guidance and wisdom when soldiers discovered him and slew him on the spot.

Summary

Thomas may have visited Edessa shortly after the resurrection and ascension, or he may have passed through it, and neighboring Armenia, en route to India after the Council of Jerusalem. In either case, he most likely took the overland route, passing through the Parthia kingdoms of Hyrcania, Bactria, Carmania, Media, and Persia, thereby entering into the Indo-Parthian kingdom of northern India. There he went to their capital city of Taxila and witnessed to king Gundaphorus whom tradition says became a Christian.

By 52 A.D. Thomas had left northern India and sailed down to Kerala, on the Malabar coast of southern India. There he established a lasting mission and probably gave the locals a copy of Matthew's gospel in Aramaic. There was a local Jewish community there as it was a trade city, and Thomas doubtless witnessed to the Jewish community there. He stayed there in the Chera (hence, Cherala or Kerala) kingdom for seven years, before moving to the east coast in the Chola kingdom of what is today Chennai, Tamil Nadu.

For almost ten years Thomas served in missionary work in the region, spreading the gospel. Becoming aged and weak, he finally settled down in Mylapore region in circa 69 A.D. Finally, in 72 A.D. he drew the wrath of king Misdeus who ordered the arrest of Thomas for sorcery. Apparently he never got his trial as he was discovered praying in a cave and slain with spears, presumably on the 21st of December. His body was buried by faithful followers on that spot, now called "St. Thomas Mound" until the Kushan emperor Vasudeva transferred his remains to Edessa in the early third century.

Thomas is often called the "Apostle to the Orient" because his work extended further east than any other apostle. He is credited founding the church in India and to this very day the church of *Mar Thoma* is named after him. Surely "Apostle to India" is a more fitting title than "Doubting Thomas" for the man who ventured further than any apostle.

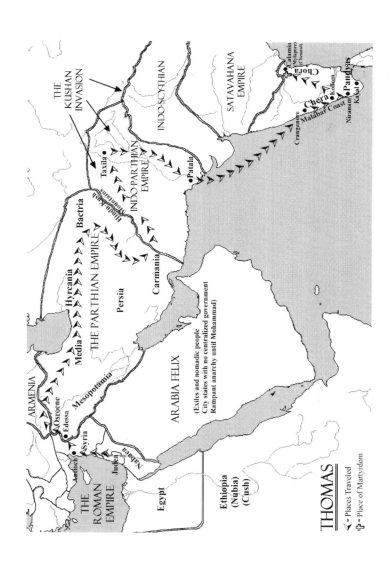

THOMAS

◄ - Places Traveled
✝ - Place of Martyrdom

8

Nathanael Bartholomew

With the possible exception of Philip there is no apostle whose post-Biblical history is so confusing and conflated as that of Bartholomew. He has been associated with Philip in Turkey, with a mission in Armenia, and even with India. Additionally, his martyrdom has been variously ascribed to crucifixion, flaying (skinning), and decapitation. Even the country of his death is variously attributed to Armenia or India.

History and Traditions

The Biblical Record

Bartholomew (בַּר-תַּלְמַי) is Aramaic for the Son of Tal'may. *Bar* (בַּר) means "son" in Aramaic (in Hebrew it is *ben* [בֵּן]). Bartholomew is, therefore, not his given name. John calls him Nathanael, which is another common name among the Jews, so it is natural that they might prefer to call him Bartholomew. Some have speculated that he was a descendant of "Maacah, the daughter of Talmai, king of Geshur" (2 Samuel 3:3), and therefore of the lineage of king David.[242] This may be entirely possible, although we cannot confirm it.

As to Bartholomew himself, the Bible says almost nothing about him. It was he who asked "can anything good come out of Nazareth" (John 1:46), but Jesus said of him, that he was "an Israelite in whom there is no deceit" (John 1:47). Unlike some of the other apostles Bartholomew does not appear to have known Jesus before his calling (based on John 1:45-51). Nevertheless, Jesus knew the hearts and minds of men and saw in him an apostle, but what happened to Bartholomew after Jesus's ascension?

Extra-Biblical Records and Traditions

The Bartholomew portion of the *Acts of Abdias* and the *Martyrdom of the Holy and Glorious Apostle Bartholomew* are virtually identical works which necessarily predate Julius Africanus (160 to 240 A.D.) who some believe translated the *Acts of Abdias* into Greek. My quotations are from *Martyrdom of the Holy and Glorious Apostle Bartholomew* in which it is said, "To this India, then, the holy Bartholomew the apostle of Christ went, and took up his quarters in the temple of Astaruth."[243] Having achieved the notice of the king, he was called before him and :

> "Polymius, the king of that country, happened to be standing opposite the apostle; and he had a daughter a demoniac, that is to say, a lunatic. And he heard about the demoniac that had been healed, and sent messengers to the apostle, saying: My daughter is grievously torn; I implore you, therefore, as you have delivered him who suffered for many years, so also to order my daughter to be set free. And the apostle rose up, and went with them. And he sees the king's daughter bound with chains, for she used to tear in pieces all her limbs; and if any one came near her, she used to bite, and no one dared to come near her. The servants say to him: And who is it that dares to touch her? The apostle answered them: Loose her, and let her go. They say to him again: We have her in our power when she is bound with all our force, and do you bid us loose her? The apostle says to them: Behold, I keep her enemy bound, and are you even now afraid of her? Go and loose her; and when she has partaken of food, let her rest, and early tomorrow bring her to me. And they went and did as the apostle had commanded them; and thereafter the demon was not able to come near her."[244]

Polymius then, although not converting to the faith himself, looked upon Bartholomew favorably and allowed him to preach the gospel freely. Soon, however, this attracted the ear of king Astreges[245] who "ordered the holy apostle Bartholomew to be beaten with rods; and after having been thus scourged, to be beheaded."[246]

Hippolytus said that "Bartholomew, again, preached to the Indians, to whom he also gave the Gospel according to Matthew, and was crucified with his head downward, and was buried in Allanum, a town of the great Armenia."[247]

Euesbius also records that Bartholomew preached to India and even translated the gospel of Matthew into their language.[248]

Chrysostom (347 to 407 A.D.) said that he preached in Lycaonia,[249] which is in modern day Turkey, as does the "martyrology of Jerome."[250]

Sophronius, the bishop of Jerusalem, (560 to 638 A.D.) said that Bartholomew preached "to the Indians who are called 'the Happy.'"[251]

Also of importance is the appearance of Bartholomew in the apocryphal *Acts of Philip*.[252] As aforementioned, it relates that "going through the cities and regions of Lydia and Asia"[253] Philip and Bartholomew came to Hierapolis where the proconsul Nicanora ordered "Philip and Bartholomew and Mariamme to be beaten; and after they had been scourged with the thongs, he ordered their feet to be tied, and them to be dragged through the streets of the city"[254] and also that they "stretch out Bartholomew opposite Philip, having nailed his hands on the wall of the gate of the temple."[255] However, while Philip is martyred Bartholomew is said to be rescued with the help of the Apostle John.[256]

Still other traditions and histories record that Bartholomew died in Armenia at the hands of king Astyage who had Bartholomew flayed (skinned) alive on a cross.[257] This is alleged to have taken place in 70 A.D.[258] Some records place his death specifically in Albanopolis in modern Azerbaijan.[259]

Evaluation

As with Peter and Thomas, it is best to divide our evaluation into smaller sections because of the difficulty of piecing the stories together. By examining the different aspects of the story we can more easily decipher fact from fiction.

Connection to Philip

We know that the gospels often pair Bartholomew's name with that of Philip (Matthew 10:3; Mark 3:18; Luke 6:14), although in Acts he is paired with Matthew (Acts 1:13). Consequently, it is not surprising that he may have been Philip's traveling companion at one time or another. It is certainly possible that they witnessed the gospel together, but that time

83

had to end not too long after the Council in Jerusalem, for they had different mission fields and could not remain together. This fact alone contradicts the *Acts of Philip* stories. However, there are many other reasons to reject the *Acts of Philip*.

First, according to the *Acts of Philip* Bartholomew witnessed the martyrdom of Philip which allegedly took place in the reign of Trajan.[260] Other traditions apparently "corrected" this date to the reign of Domitian because of the implausibility of having so many apostles living well into the second century.[261] In either case, the evidence that Bartholomew was already dead by this time is overwhelming. The latest date for Bartholomew's death is 70 A.D.[262] and most traditions place his martyrdom even earlier in 62 A.D.[263] Thus Bartholomew was long dead before this Philip's martyrdom.

Second, I have already demonstrated that the stories of the Apostle Philip and Philip the Evangelist have become hopelessly conflated. The fact that Bartholomew and Philip may have been traveling companions at one time is doubtless the source for the conflated stories, but cannot be true.

In short, Bartholomew may have traveled with Philip early on, and some of their work may have been in Asia Minor, but after the dispersion of the apostles following the Council of Jerusalem they went their separate ways. I believe Philip departed for Africa (see chapter 6), and Bartholomew appears to have headed for the kingdom of Armenia.

Bartholomew in Armenia

Armenia was an independent kingdom which lay between the Roman empire and the Parthian empire and encompassed the four corners of modern day Turkey, Syria, Iraq, and Iran,[264] between the Black Sea and the Caspian Sea. Today the country of Azerbaijan occupies much of the territory it once held.

That Bartholomew preached in Armenia is acknowledged by virtually all scholars, but there is a question as to how long he preached there, and more importantly whether or not he died there. The evidence is strong that sometime after the Council of Jerusalem Bartholomew worked in Armenia, and he may have even established himself before then, as Armenia was not far from Antioch.

Later Armenian tradition claims that "the mission of St. Bartholomew in Armenia lasted sixteen years,"[265] but this seems an exaggeration. 70 A.D. is the latest date we have for Bartholomew's death,[266] and 62 A.D. is more likely (see below).[267] Since we know that Bartholomew at least visited India (see below) in 60 A.D.,[268] then we would be hard pressed to give Bartholomew more than ten years, unless he ministered there before the Council of Jerusalem. Another option is that sixteen years combined the ten years before Bartholomew left for India with six years after his alleged return, assuming he did return. This option might be the best, but its acceptance obviously hinges upon whether Bartholomew died in India or returned to Armenia as we shall see.

The truth is that because of Bartholomew's influence and reverence in Armenia, where he became a patron saint, the people had a natural tendency to want to export his martyrdom to their native country. This seems to be unconsciously admitted by a lecture at an Armenia church wherein it was said, "By commonly accepted tradition, the honor of sowing the first seeds of Christianity in Armenia, and of watering them with their blood, rests with St. Thaddeus and St. Bartholomew, who are consequently revered as the First Illuminators of Armenia."[269] In other words, where the seeds are sown must also be where the watering with blood takes place, but this is simply not always so. As I will discuss in detail under "Bartholomew's Martyrdom," the traditions of Bartholomew's death in Armenia may have been transferred from elsewhere to accommodate this desire concerning their beloved saint.

In any case, if we leave room for Bartholomew's missions in Syria, Lycaonia (and other Asia Minor countries), Arabia, Persia, and India, then it would be hard to imagine Bartholomew spending more than ten years in the country before leaving for India. Nevertheless, ten years is a considerable time and it is obvious that Bartholomew spent the vast majority of his ministry working in Armenia and thus becoming their patron saint.

Bartholomew in India

Like Armenia, the evidence that Bartholomew visited India is ancient and strong. In addition to the *Martyrdom of the*

Holy and Glorious Apostle Bartholomew, which dates to at least the second century, Eusebius recounted the story of a second century missionary named Pantaeus who arrived in India and found that they already had an Aramaic copy of Matthew's gospel which they said had been left to them by Bartholomew.[270]

Additionally, although there are problems with the chronology and specifics, it seems apparent that the names of kings and governors of which are spoken in the apocryphal writings do correspond to India rulers of that time.[271] Obviously such traditions could only have arisen from people acquainted with India, and not from the western writers who recorded these events. More specifics are discussed below as this debate involves the question of Bartholomew's martyrdom. It is sufficient to say here that Bartholomew certainly visited India, in what was the Satavahan empire,[272] on the west coast of central India, north of Thomas's main mission field, but south of Gundaphorus's kingdom, which was by the time of Bartholomew's arrival already conquered by the Kushan empire. He arrived around 60 A.D.[273] but his mission was relatively short lived, as he either died in 62 A.D. or returned to Armenia no later than 64 A.D. and thence dying there in 70 A.D.

Miscellaneous Traditions

Now very little information seems to exist as to the countries he visited en route to India. Interestingly enough, the *Martyrdom of the Holy and Glorious Apostle Bartholomew* says that "historians declare that India is divided into three parts; and the first is said to end at Ethiopia, and the second at Media, and the third completes the country."[274] As I mentioned before, the reference to Ethiopia apparently arose by confusion of the African Cush with that of the Hindu-Kush. Obviously Bartholomew never visited Ethiopia. Some argue that he visited south Persia, and even Arabia. Both are possible, and even probable if he took a sea route from Persia, or an Arabian port, near the Persian Gulf. However, it is uncertain how much work he did in either country.

One final issue of interests is in regard to the tradition in the *Acts of Abdias* that Bartholomew's ascetic lifestyle was so extreme that he did not bathe or change clothes for years![275] This is clearly a piece of fiction designed to make the humble lifestyle of the apostles compatible with the eastern ascetic idea which rose to prominence in the Middle Ages. The *Acts of Abdias* was itself written by a man of suspect theology. It may contain some traditions which offer a glimpse of history, but the story is embellished to fit the theology of its author. The fact is that Jewish law required cleanliness! Ritual cleanliness was not for the Temple alone, but for daily life. This is the reason that Jews did not catch the Black Plague when it raced across Europe! Jews were clean, changed clothes, took baths, and had no rats. No Jew, Christian or not, would go without a bath for years. Such a habit is not spiritual at all. Indeed, it was the Jews themselves who originated the saying, "cleanliness is next to godliness."

Bartholomew's Martyrdom

Some of the accounts of Bartholomew's martyrdom in Armenia are virtually identical to those which place the martyrdom in India. Still other accounts differ on the specifics of his execution. The *Martyrdom of the Holy and Glorious Apostle Bartholomew* says that Bartholomew was beaten, scourged, and then beheaded in India. The *Acts of Abdias* says that Bartholomew was beaten and crucified in Armenia. Hippolytus said that he "was crucified with his head downward." Many others say that he was flayed alive and then beheaded, or even crucified (although one would assume they were crucifying a corpse if he had been skinned)!

Despite this confusion there is actually much more common ground than might at first be imagined, and historical research in India has also revealed a surprising answer. Let us, therefore, begin with the place of his death.

In most of the ancient traditions Bartholomew wins the favor of a king Polymius whose people worshipped a god named Astaruth or Ashtaroth. Finally, Bartholomew invokes the wrath of a king Astreges or Astyages.[276] The location is variously identified as either India or Armenia. Now history has recorded no kings by any of these names in Armenia in the first century, and it is unknown to what extent the ancient god Ashtaroth was still revered, if at all, in Armenia. This make the tradition more legendary, until we look at India.

A.C. Perumalil noted that Sophronius, the bishop of Jerusalem, had described Bartholomew as preaching "to the Indians who are called 'the Happy.'"[277] He believes that city-state in the first century called Kalyana was called India Felix or India Happy by Rome.[278] It was located near Mumbai/Bombay,[279] in what was the Satavahan empire of central India. More interesting is that he identified the governor of Kalyana as a certain Pulumayi, who reigned until 62 A.D.[280] He believes that Polymius is an westernization of Pulumayi. Moreover, he argues that Ashtoreth is a westernization of the Hindu god Astamurti who was worshipped in Kalyana.[281] Finally, he argues that the king of Satavahan was Aristakarman whom he identified with the Astriagis of the legend.[282] Now this later identification is suspect, especially since at least one kings list appears to place his reign thirty years earlier.[283] Likewise, Pulumayi I reigned too early and Pulumayi II ruled too late. However, the king of Kalyana at this time is not known, as the tablet has been damaged.[284] It is possible that the ruler known as Pulumayi II was actually Pulumayi III, for they had no numbers attached to their names. Since it was a hereditary dynasty, it is possible that there was a Pulumayi between these two rulers.

Now a cynic might say that Perumalil is merely trying to lend credibility to his native India's traditions, but there is no doubt that Armenia also sought to elevate their own patron saint as well. One thing which Perumalil's thesis does offer is evidence that kings and rulers of a similar names did at least exist in a relative time frame to the travels of Bartholomew. Moreover, if Perumalil is correct, then Pulumayi died in 62 A.D.[285] which just happens to be the best probable date for Bartholomew's death. If this is so, then it follows logically that king Aristakarman ordered the death of both Pulumayi and Bartholomew. Let us then consider the date of death.

The traditional date for Bartholomew's death is August 24, 62 A.D.[286] This is not without some controversy, of course, for the exact day has been suggested as August 29, because this is the day said to correspond to the Coptic calendar's September 11, in which the Egyptians commemorate his death. To make matters worse, the eastern church celebrates his feast day on June 11, but the west retains August 24. In any case, 62 A.D. is the best attested date. Those who offer a later date of 70 A.D.

usually do so on the assumption that Bartholomew returned to Armenia before his death.[287]   Since Bartholomew allegedly arrived in India in 60 A.D., it is clear that a great deal of time could not have elapsed before either his martyrdom or his return journey.   Now if Pulumayi granted religious freedom for Bartholomew then his death in 62 A.D. either meant that Bartholomew would have had to leave India, returning to Armenia, or more likely that he would have been executed along with Pulumayi. This, combined with the fact that the names of the governors and kings described in martydom accounts appear to correspond to Indian rulers of the day, but not with any Armenia rulers known to exist, suggest that 62 A.D. should be the preferred date.

This leaves the question of how he died. It is obvious from each and every story that Bartholomew was tortured before his death. Virtually all record some form of beating before his execution. Many traditions say that Bartholomew was skinned alive, but the *Martyrdom of the Holy and Glorious Apostle Bartholomew* only says that he was "scourged," which is very similar. In fact, "scourge" actually comes from the Latin word for "flaying" or "skinning." This is because the whips used in scourging had tiny bits of metal and bone tied to them, thereby tearing the flesh from the person's body.[288]

Now scourging was a cruel form of punishment (and sometimes execution) used in the Roman empire but neither India nor Armenia were a part of Rome. Flaying, on the other hand, had been used in China and the east, so we may assume that India preferred flaying to scourging, whereas Armenia, generally considered "western," would have preferred scourging.

The mere fact that most traditions record that Bartholomew was either beheaded or crucified after being flayed also indicate that he was still alive, and no one can survive being flayed. Consequently, we might be tempted to assume that he was beaten and scourged to the point to where his flesh was falling off of his body, but he was not actually flayed or skinned. However, beheading the dead was not uncommon, particularly in the east. Often the head would be displayed for a time as a warning to lawbreakers. So we are left with a choice. If he died in Armenia, he was most likely scourged beyond recognition and then crucified, but this could have been an attempt to make the patron saint's life emulate that of our Lord. If he died in India then he may well have been flayed and decapitated after death.

Giovanni Tiepolo – Martyrdom of St. Bartholomew – 1722

Obviously, neither choice is pleasant, but the Indian thesis fits best for three reasons. First, though not without problems there does appear to be Indian rulers with names similar to those of the traditions, but not in Armenia. Second, if the story had been transferred and assimilated into Armenian tradition than the attempt to westernize the history of Bartholomew's death would fit naturally. Finally, the best dates for Bartholomew's death fit perfectly with the events of India, but create problems with Armenia.

So I believe that the tales of Bartholomew's martyrdom have been assimilated into Armenia, and the people and places in India were thence westernized to fit with an Armenian martyrdom. Although the problem has not been completely solved, the facts best fit his martyrdom in India.

Summary

Nathanael Bartholomew spent the majority of his missionary career in the kingdom of Armenia, northeast of Syria and the beyond the limits of the Roman empire. After perhaps a decade of work there, feeling that he had left behind a solid foundation, he then embarked for the east around 59 or 60 A.D. Perhaps he had heard news of Thomas's missions in the country of India and was intrigued. For whatever reasons he took the most direct route, which would be sea. He, therefore, moved directly south to the sea port in the Persian gulf. There he may have spent some brief time witnessing in the southern Persian port. His ship would most likely have made at least one stop before entering the Arabian sea. That stop would probably be on the tip of Arabia in what is today Adu Dhabi.

From there he traveled to the trading port of the Satavahan empire in central India, in what is today Mumbai (Bombay). He arrived in circa 60 A.D. and there encountered the regional governor of the city whose daughter was alleged to have been demon possessed and kept in a cage. Bartholomew ordered her release and to their surprise she did not attack him, but lived thereafter a normal life. Although not a convert, the governor accepted Bartholomew and allowed him to freely witness the gospel in India.

While there he gave the Indians a copy of Matthew's gospel in Hebrew/Aramaic, but some claim he translated the gospel into their own language. Because of the short duration of his stay, it is more likely that he merely oversaw a translation made by a convert. In either case, news soon reached the king of the Satavahan empire who was angered by the news that this stranger was preaching against the local god. He appears to have ordered not only Bartholomew's execution, but also that of the governor, who, if tradition be our guide, repented and trusted in Christ before his execution.

Bartholomew himself was beaten and flayed. His head was then removed and displayed as a warning. Despite this, and even because of it, the Christian community in India grew and flourished until it was discovered almost a hundred years later by missionaries who had thought to arrive in a country untouched by the gospel![289]

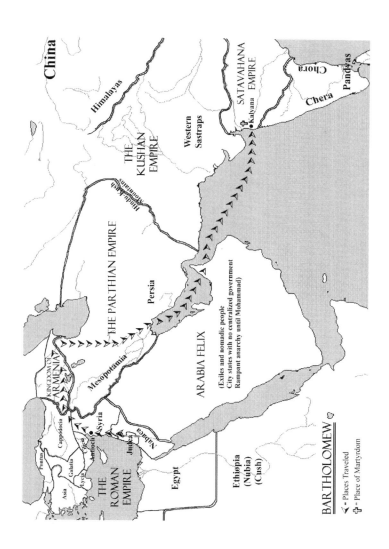

China

Himalayas

THE KUSHAN EMPIRE

Hindu-Kush Mountains

THE PARTHIAN EMPIRE

Western Sastraps

SATAVAHANA EMPIRE

✞ Kalyana

Chora

Pandyas

Chera

Persia

Mesopotamia

KINGDOM OF ARMENIA

Cappadocia

Pontus

Asia

Galatia

Lycia

Syria

Antioch

Edessa

Judea

Nabtea

ARABIA FELIX

(Exiles and nomadic people
City states with no centralized government
Rampant anarchy until Mohammad)

THE ROMAN EMPIRE

Egypt

Ethiopia
(Nubia)
(Cush)

BARTHOLOMEW

↗ = Places Traveled
✞ = Place of Martyrdom

93

9

Matthew Levi

Matthew Levi is one of only two apostles to write a gospel. His was the first written in the language of Hebrew while they were yet in Israel before the Council of Jerusalem.[290] This fact alone makes Matthew one of the best known apostles, and yet his post-Biblical history is one of the most obscure. Very little has been passed down to us through the ages, and most of what has been passed down is of late origin. To make matters worse, the traditions handed down to us are conflated with those of Matthias, making them often contradictory. Despite this, we do have some strong evidence of his post-Biblical history, even if the specifics remain a mystery.

History and Traditions

The Biblical Record

Matthew wrote the first gospel, and yet nowhere does he state this fact. Indeed, he only mentions himself by name twice. Once is in Matthew 9:9 where it is revealed that he was a hated tax-collector, and the other time is simply in the apostlic list (10:3). How then do we know that Matthew was the author at all?

Aside from the "undisputed"[291] unity of tradition and ancient history, the Bible gives ample clues. Consider, for example, that the gospel of Matthew makes numerous references to specific coins of the realm (17:24, 27; 18:24 etc.)?[292] Why? Surely no fisherman would be interested in such trivialities. Only a tax-collector, it is argued, who was used to working with money would have been so specific as to the denominations and types of money used.

The fact that he does not mention himself is also in accordance with the humility of the apostles, for John also fails to mention himself, although he is central figure in many passages. Instead he simply refers to "the disciple whom Jesus loved" (John 19:26).

When the gospel was written is disputed, save that, as Tertullian records, "Matthew wrote the Gospel in the Hebrew tongue, and published it at Jerusalem,"[293] which means it must have been written sometime before the Council of Jerusalem. C.I. Scofield believed that tradition points to a date as early as 37 A.D., just a few years after the Crucifixion and resurrection.[294] Merrill Unger places it between 40 and 45 A.D.[295] In any case, it was certainly before 48 or 49 A.D., for it was taken by some of the other apostles with them to far away lands, including India (see chapter 8). What then of Matthew's life after he wrote the gospel?

Extra-Biblical Records and Traditions

Unlike many of the other apostles, most of our extra-Biblical records and traditions are nearly worthless. The earliest manuscripts record nothing of significance and later traditions are conflated and contradictory, as will be discussed under "evaluation."

Hippolytus said, "Matthew wrote the Gospel in the Hebrew tongue, and published it at Jerusalem, and fell asleep at Hierees, a town of Parthia."[296]

Clement of Alexandria has often erroneously been quoted as saying that Matthew died a natural death in old age,[297] but in fact the reference, never quoted, appears to be a quotation from Heracleon who is talking about confessing our faith in Jesus when faced with martyrdom. He then said, "all the saved have confessed with the confession made by the voice, and departed. Of whom are Matthew, Philip, Thomas, Levi, and many others."[298] Problems with this and its interpretation are discussed below. Clement of Alexandria also said that Matthew worked in Judea for fifteen years.

The apocryphal *Acts of Abdias* may contain one of the older preserved traditions of Matthew. In it Matthew goes down to Ethiopia at the invitation of the eunuch for the queen called Candace (mentioned in Acts 8). There he enters a city called Naddaver and encounters a king Aeglippus who is dominated by two court magicians. In various stories, apparently inspired by Moses and Pharaoh's court magicians, Matthew performs miracles the magicians cannot duplicate. Eventually when Matthew resurrects the king's son, the magicians flee to Parthia.

However, when Hyrtaeus succeeded his brother to the throne of Ethiopia he orders Matthew assassinated, and he is stabbed in the back, thus meeting his martyrdom in Ethiopia.[299]

The *Acts and Martyrdom of St. Matthew the Apostle* is a late tradition which dates to the early middle ages, about the sixth century. The earliest manuscripts read "Matthew," but later medieval manuscripts actually read Matthias (see chapter 13). One online critic calls it "a sequel to the Acts of Andrew and Matthias."[300] In the story Matthew is called a "king" in the land of the "man-eaters." There he is slain by another king named Phulbanus by nailing him to the ground, and setting him on fire.[301]

Similar traditions, such as the one recorded by Venantius Fortunatus around the fifth or sixth century, said that Matthew was nailed to the ground and decapitated in Naddaver, Ethiopia.[302]

Matthew Executed in Ethiopia – 1742

It is useful to note that later medieval manuscripts of the *Acts of Andrew and Matthias*, discussed under the chapter on Andrew, contain the name of Matthew rather than Matthias.

This is important to keep in mind when reading the later traditions of Matthew.

Evaluation

Various traditions place Matthew in Egypt, Ethiopia,[303] Parthia,[304] Syria, Macedonia,[305] and even Scythia.[306] However, the majority of these traditions date late, even to the middle ages. The earliest sources say almost nothing about Matthew. Hippolytus, for example, only said that he wrote the book of Matthew in Jerusalem in Hebrew and that he allegedly died in Parthia, presumably of natural causes.[307] Although others have cited Clement of Alexandria as supporting a natural death, this may not be true at all. The citations, unless they be from some lost writings of Clement, are absent from all known text. This may be from confusion about a second hand quotation by Clement which not only says nothing about how Matthew dies, but also showed that Matthias and Matthew were conflated even as early as the second century, for he says, "Matthew, Philip, Thomas, Levi, and many others."[308] Now Matthew and Levi are one and the same. Moreover, notice that Thomas certainly died a martyr, and all the ancient traditions also say Philip died a martyr (see chapter 6 for more on this debate).

What is most interesting about Clement's quote is not the assumption that Matthew died peacefully (which it does not say) but that the conflation of Matthew and Matthias appears to have existed already. This becomes readily apparent in the later traditions of both Matthew and Matthias. To an extent it is understandable.

In Hebrew Matthew is *Matthay* (מַתַּי) which is transliterated into the Greek as *Matthaios* (ματθαιος). Matthias has the same Hebrew root and is *Matthiyah* (מַתִּיָה) which is transliterated into Greek as *Matthias* (ματθιας). Obviously it is easy to see how the names can be conflated, for they are two different versions of the same root name. Moreover, if pronounced out loud, *Matthaios* (ματθαιος) actually sounds more like Matthias (pronounced "Matt-eye-os") than does the *Matthias* (ματθιας), pronounced "Matt-eeas." The problem first appears explicit in the apocryphal *Acts of Andrew and Matthias*. The earliest manuscripts all read Matthias, but later medieval manuscripts read Matthew, as does the *Acts of Abdias* in its replication of the story.[309] Conversely the *Acts and Martyrdom of St. Matthew the Apostle* contains the name Matthias in later medieval manuscripts, but the earliest manuscripts contain Matthew! Add to this the fact that they *Acts of Andrew and Matthias* and the *Acts and Martyrdom of St. Matthew the Apostle* both take place in the "land of the man-eaters" and we can easily see beyond a shadow of a doubt that Matthew and Matthias are conflated in the traditions.

Having established that this conflation took place early in the tradition, we can safely reject the stories that Matthew went to Scythia and even Macedonia, for there is ample evidence from the earliest of times that Matthew went Africa. Ancient tradition even holds that Egypt is where Matthew translated his own gospel into Greek for the benefit of his gentile followers in Egypt and neighboring Ethiopia.[310]

According to Clement of Alexandria in Egypt, Matthew spent fifteen years in Israel and its regions before departing for foreign missions. There was a large Jewish community in Egypt, and it is most likely to those communities that Matthew traveled. This places Matthew in Egypt around 49 A.D. shortly after the Council in Jerusalem. It is logical that if he established his mission in Egypt, he would also have visited neighboring Ethiopia to the south. He may have even met with the Ethiopian eunuch of Acts 8, and it is logical to assume that he may have been a contact, inasmuch as he would have been the first Christian to enter Ethiopia after his conversion by Philip.

It is of interest to note that there were many Jewish Ethiopians owing to the legends (probably false) that the Queen of Sheba (whose kingdom in the southern tip of the Arabian peninsula ruled over Ethiopia) had children by King Solomon.[311] As Matthew usually ministered to Jews and Jewish communities, it would be natural for him to go to the Jewish communities in Ethiopia as well.

Thus we can establish that Matthew served in Egypt and Ethiopia. The question then is "how did he die?"

With the possible exception of what is recorded in the *Acts of Abdias* all the traditions involving martyrdom are late post-Nicene, and even medieval traditions. Although many of those may trace back earlier to non-extant writings, we cannot know this for sure. It is best, therefore, to compare the traditions and see if there are any common threads. Starting with the *Acts of Abdias* we are told that Hyrtaeus, the brother of Aeglippus, had Matthew assassinated and so Matthew was stabbed in the back in Ethiopia.[312] The *Acts of Matthew*, erroneously places Matthew's death in Scythia where it is said a king Phulbanus ordered him nailed to the ground and set on fire.[313] Venantius Fortunatus tells a similar story in Ethiopia where Matthew was nailed to the ground and decapitated by order of Hytacus.[314] Finally, John Foxe preferred a tradition wherein Matthew was speared to death by a Hircanus in Ethiopia.[315]

Now note that of these four accounts, three take place in Ethiopia, two involve Matthew being pinned to the ground, and two involve Matthew having been pierced (either by a spear or knife). However, none of the names correspond to one another, except for the similarities in Hyrtaeus, Hytacus, and Hircanus. Let us, therefore, first examine the names of the people involved.

Ethiopian kings list record that the Queen of Ethiopia from 40 to 50 A.D. was a Queen Garsemot Kandake. This would have been at the time that Philip converted the Ethiopian eunuch (Acts 8). Now the *Acts of Abdias* calls the Queen's name Candace which is clearly a Greek form of her name. In this regard the *Acts of Abdias*, which borrowed from ancient sources, is correct. However, the king who replaced her was Hatosza Bahr Asaged and he ruled from 50 to 78 A.D. It is debatable whether or not Hyrtaeus and even Fortunatus's Hytacus could be Latin or Greek forms of Hatosza (although the latter is possible). Could they have merely been mayors or governors under Hatosza? This is possible. Given the favorability of evidence supporting Matthew's ministering in Ethiopia and the connection to Queen Candace, we may assume that Hyrtaeus is at least based on a historical personage.

The next question is whether or not Matthew truly died in Ethiopia, or in Hierees of Parthia as Hippolytus believed. Because Hippolytus is a much more credible source than the *Acts of Abdias* many have been tempted to accept him at his word, but Hippolytus shows almost no knowledge of Matthew beyond his writing of the gospel in Hebrew and having published it in Jerusalem. His statement could well be based on the assumption that Clement of Alexandria called Matthew's death natural (as suspect interpretation). In short, Hippolytus does not show much knowledge of Matthew's history as his record of Matthew's life is reserved to but a single sentence! Moreover, I have not been able to find any historical or archaeological references to such a city in ancient Parthia. Also note the wide variant of names connected with Matthew's death : Hyrtaeus, Hircanus, and Hytacus. Could Hierees be yet another confusion of names which Hippolytus mistook for a city, rather than a governor? All of this is speculation, but so is the assumption that Matthew left twenty three years worth of mission work in Africa to go to a small town in Parthia of no historical note for unknown reasons.

If we accept that Hippolytus may have been mistaken, then we again fall back to the most ancient source being that of the *Acts of Abdias* whose original source may, in fact, predate Hippolytus. It shows some knowledge of history in recording the name of Queen Candace as the queen under whom the eunuch served. In its account of Matthew's martyrdom he is assassinated. John Foxe accepts a similar version of the story. Also owing to the similarities between the martyrdom account of the *Acts of Matthew* and Fortunatus's, we should agree that Matthew died in Ethiopia. The best evidence seems to favor assassination, although this is a tentative assessment.

The final question is then when he died. Although John Foxe places his death around 60 A.D.[316] Matthew would still have been in Egypt at this time where he is credited with translating Matthew in Greek.[317] The *Acts of Abdias* claims that he spent twenty three years in Ethiopia,[318] but this is probably a conflation of his time in both Egypt and Ethiopia. If so, then we arrive at about 71 A.D by combining this with Clement's statement about his serving fifteen years in Israel. Fifteen years after the resurrection takes us to 48 A.D. and twenty three years later takes us to 71 A.D. Van Braght believed that he died in 70 A.D.[319] Conceding a rounding off of partial years, this seems best.

Summary

With little information at our disposal we can only safely conclude that after completing his gospel in Hebrew while still in Jerusalem Matthew departed for the Jewish communities in Egypt where he spent many years. Eventually, he moved south into Ethiopia where he did mission work, perhaps meeting with and coordinating with the Ethiopian eunuch of the former Queen Candace. After serving there for many years, around 70 or 71 A.D., Matthew was most likely assassinated by the command of a local governor or politician.

Claude Vignon – The Martyrdom of St. Matthew – 1617

10

James Alphæus

James is called the "son of Alphæus" and an apostle. He is one of two apostles named James, but ironically many believe that there are *three* Jameses in the Bible. There is James "the Greater" of whom we have already spoken. There is this James "the son of Aphaeus," who most believe is also called James "the Less." Finally there is a James "the Just," or so history calls him. Now the question is whether of not James "the Just" is the same as James "the Less." Which is James "the son of Aphaeus"? The answer is not as easy as some might think. The Bible says almost nothing about James "the son of Alphæus" unless he be either "the Less" or "the Just," or both. Even then, the Bible speaks of him only briefly. Our first task is, therefore, to determine exactly who were each of these individuals.

Was the Apostle James also "the Just"?

Tradition is overwhelmingly of the opinion that the Apostle James "the Less" is one and the same as James "the Just." However, many modern day scholars, mostly Protestants, believe that they were different persons. Usually the difference boils down to whether or not James "the Just" was Jesus's brother by Joseph and or a more distant step-brother. However, the answer is not as simple as this, as the reader will see.

When I study the Bible I do not concern myself with what Catholics, Protestants, or others may say. I am not worried about what Jerome or Aquinas or Calvin or Luther said. I am only concerned with what the Bible says. For that reason I will take the reader through all the critical passages step by step, and the reader can reach their own conclusions, as I did.

Logically the first step we must take is to identify each of the individuals identified by the three different titles. Then we must seek to see whether or not they can be tied to one another. This must be done *before* we can assume anything.

Merrill Unger, for example, assumes that James "the son of Alphæus" is the same as James "the Less," but then denies that he is the same as James "the Just."[320] As we shall see, however, if James "the son of Alphæus" is not James "the Just" then he cannot be James "the Less." Why?

Mark 15:40 refers to "Mary the mother of James the Less and Joses" (Mark 15:40 : cf. 16:1). This is the only passage in the entire Bible where the nickname "the Less" is to be found. This James "the Less" is then said to be the brother of a Joses (the Greek rendition of Joseph) and the son of a Mary. In Mark 6:3 Jesus's critics explicitly said, "Is not this the carpenter, the son of Mary, and brother of James and Joses and Judas and Simon? Are not His sisters here with us?" It is then clear that this James "the Less" is one and the same as the James listed here.

Lest there be any doubt, let us examine all the parallel passages. First are the passages which discuss the women who were at the cross when Jesus was crucified.

Matthew	Mark	Luke	John
"Among them was Mary Magdalene, and Mary the mother of James and Joseph, and the mother of the sons of Zebedee." (Matthew 27:56)	"Among whom were Mary Magdalene, and Mary the mother of James the Less and Joses, and Salome." (Mark 15:40)	"Now they were Mary Magdalene and Joanna and Mary the *mother* of James; also the other women with them" (Luke 24:10)	"Standing by the cross of Jesus were His mother, and His mother's sister, Mary the *wife* of Clopas, and Mary Magdalene." (John 19:25)

Now Matthew makes it clear that these were not the only women at the cross. He says that "many women were there" (Matthew 27:55), but we can affirm that Mary, the mother of Jesus, was there along with Mary Magdalene, Salome, the mother of James (the Greater) and John, and this Mary, wife of Clopas (or Cleophas). We can also ascertain that either Mary, the mother of Jesus, or Mary, the wife of Cleophas, had sons named James and Joseph (Joses). At this point I will not discuss Mary, the wife of Cleophas, but reserve that debate for later, because we must now look at the passages related to Mark 6:3 which seem to confirm that James "the Less" is the same as that in Mark 6:3.

Matthew	Mark
"Is not this the carpenter's son? Is not His mother called Mary, and His brothers, James and Joseph and Simon and Judas? And His sisters, are they not all with us? Where then *did* this man *get* all these things?" (Matthew 13:55-56)	"Is not this the carpenter, the son of Mary, and brother of James and Joses and Judas and Simon? Are not His sisters here with us?" (Mark 6:3)

So this James "the Less" also has brothers named Joseph (Joses), Judas, and Simon (or Simeon in the Hebrew). The controversy, however, is in that he is also called a brother of Jesus. Catholics believe that the Virgin Mary remained a virgin her entire life. Protestants believe that Mary was a virgin when Jesus was born but that she afterwards consummated her marriage to Joseph and had other children. Consequently, and ironically, Catholics and Protestants have taken these passages and shaped them to fit their own theology. Catholics see this as Jesus's step-brothers by a different marriage, while Protestants say that it was his immediate step-brothers and step-sisters, the sons and daughters of Joseph and Mary. Note that I said ironically. There is a reason that this is ironic.

If James "the Less" is the son of Joseph and Mary then it would seem that he cannot be James "the son of Alphæus." The reasons are apparent not only from the fact that he is called Alphæus's son, but also by the fact that Jesus's brothers were said to be unbelievers, apparently jealous of his fame (John 7:5). So we have here a contradiction among both Catholics and Protestants! Protestants accept James "the Less" as the son of Joseph and Mary but forget that Jesus's step-brothers were not believers (John 7:5), thus he could not be James "the son of Alphæus." Catholics, on the other hand, often take the passage to mean that he was the son of Mary's sister but forget that no one names both of their daughters by the same name, for he was also a son of Mary! How then can this be resolved?

Four solutions have been offered. Let us look at each of them carefully.

1. Jesus's Half-Brothers by Another Wife

Many Catholics argue that Joseph was married previously and had children by a previous marriage. While theoretically possible, there are three major problems with this view.

105

First, they present no evidence other than the assumption that Mary had no other children; an assumption not supported in the Bible. On the contrary, the Bible says that Joseph "kept her a virgin *until* she gave birth to a Son" (Matthew 1:25). Nothing is said of what happened afterwards, but seeing as how he is rightfully called her husband the marriage must have been consummated, for a marriage that is not consummated is annulled. And so we may agree with the Catholic father Saint Jerome who said, "she was known [sexually] after she gave birth."[321]

Second, if Joseph's first wife had died, then we might ask how old Joseph was. While it was not uncommon for older men to marry teenage girls, it seems slanderous to assume that the teenage Mary married a man with sons as old as, or older than, she was, for the Catholic scholar Bernard Ruffin notes that ancient tradition made James "the Just" over eighty years old when he died in 62 A.D.[322] Some say he was ninety-four.[323] If true, this would mean that he was born no later than 17 B.C., and as early as 31 B.C., thus at least twelve to twenty six years Jesus's senior. This is not a problem unless we assume that Joseph was his father, for Mary would then be marrying someone whose children may have been as old as, or even older, than her, and this seems a rather slanderous attack on the man whom God chose to be Jesus's earthly father.

Finally, James is not called the "son of Joseph" but the "son of Alphæus," which would eliminate Joseph who had no ancestor by that name.[324] Any legitimate view must explain the origin of the "son of Alphæus," by which Matthew is also called (Mark 2:14).

2. Cousins, as Sons of Mary of Cleopas; Mary's Natural Sister

Another argument is that James "the Less" is the son of "Mary, the wife of Cleopas" (John 19:25) and that she was Mary's natural sister. In favor of this view is the natural translation of the Greek in John 19:25 which says, "Standing by the cross of Jesus were His mother, and His mother's sister, Mary the *wife* of Clopas." Later "Syriac, Persic, and Ethiopic versions distinguish Mary the wife of Cleophas from his mother's sister, by placing the copulative and between them, and so make two persons."[325] However, John's gospel was not written in Syriac, Persic, or Ethiopic, and so it is best to accept it as it is written. Nevertheless, this does create several seemingly insurmountable problems. First, if Mary is Mary's natural sister then we would be faced with the fact that a father named both of his daughters Mary! This seems highly absurd. Second is again the problem with the title "son of Alphæus" rather than "son of Cleophas," which will be discussed in more detail below.

3. Cousins, as Sons of Mary Alphœus; Later Remarried to Cleophas

A slightly better option is sort of a merger between the first and second views. It holds that Mary, the wife of Cleophas, had children by a previous marriage to an Alphæus. This is a theoretically possibility but rest entirely on assumption. Moreover, James is not called a cousin, but a brother. The Hebrew word for cousin is *dodan* (דּוֹדָן) and the Hebrew word for aunt is *dodah* (דּוֹדָה), found in Exodus 6:20, Leviticus 18:14, and 20:20. Nevertheless, if we accept the possibility that "brothers" and "sisters" is used in a more generic sense, then we still have a better option; the fourth option.

4. Cousins, as Sons of Mary of Cleopas; Mary's Step-Sister

This final view suggests that Mary was the Virgin Mary's step-sister, and that Cleophas was Joseph's brother. Certainly it would not be uncommon to see the word "sister" used of step-sisters or half-sisters, and this obviously eliminates the problem of having two daughters named Mary. However, it is not without problems. The most obvious is one which each and every one of these views has; who is Alphæus?

John Gill, the eighteenth century Calvinist, provided what may be the best answer. Although it is somewhat tentative, it would answer the seeming problem and leave us with the inevitable conclusion that the Apostle James was James "the Less" and hence James "the Just."

According to John Gill, Cleophas and Alphæus are different Hellenizations of the same Hebrew names. Consider that Joshua and Jesus are both different Hellenizations of the Hebrew name *yeshua* (יֵשׁוּעַ), which is short for *yehoshua* (יְהוֹשֻׁעַ). In this case the argument is similar. Gill said that Cleophas was "a name frequently to be met with in Talmudic and Rabbinic writings; and so a Jewish writer observes, that הילפא והוא אילפא, 'Chilpha is the same as Ilpha'; and in Greek may be pronounced either Cleophas, or Alphæus."[326] For the English reader not acquainted with Hebrew, I will try to make the argument more simple. Greek and Hebrew have different alphabets and some of the letters found in Semitic languages like Hebrew do not exist in Greek, or even English. Therefore substitutions are made to a letter similar. In this case the only difference in "Chilpha" and "Ilpha" is the omission of the Hebrew *chet*, "ch" (as in Hanukah or Chanukah), which does not exist in Greek. The Greek letter kappa (κ) could substitute for it, leaving us with either Cilphas or Ilphas, if it is omitted altogether. If the "l" and "i" somehow became inverted, then we would have "Cliphas" and "Ilphas." Further Hellenization then renders more appropriately as Cleophas or Alphæus.

Now this suggested remedy is tentative to be sure. Were the "l" and "i" not inverted, it would be a better argument, but the only alternative seems to be that *neither* James "the Less" nor James "Just" (assuming they are not the same) can be the apostle. This would quite literally leave us with an apostle of whom absolutely *nothing* is said! Let us, therefore, examine that possibility.

Galatians 1:19 seems to indicate quite strongly that "James, the Lord's brother" *was* the apostle. It says, "I did not see any other of the apostles except James, the Lord's brother." Thus "the Lord's brother" was an apostle. Now the argument against this is that Paul uses the term "apostle" loosely, as if synonymous with missionary or evangelist, but Paul uses the word "evangelist" in 1 Timothy 4:5. Nonetheless, they base their argument on Paul's use in 1 Corinthians 15:5, 7. There Paul is briefly recounting the Lord's appearances after His resurrection. He says:

> "He appeared to Cephas, then to the twelve. After that He appeared to more than five hundred brethren at one time, most of whom remain until now, but some have fallen asleep; then He appeared to James, then to all the apostles; and last of all, as to one untimely born, He appeared to me also. For I am the least of the apostles, and not fit to be called an apostle, because I persecuted the church of God."

They thus argue that "James, then to all the apostles" must be *in addition* to the "twelve" of verse five. This, however, is suspect for two reasons. First, if we take "then" to imply that it could not have been a second time, then we must reject Peter as an apostle, for verse five say "He appeared to Cephas [Peter], *then* to the twelve." Obviously Peter was one of the twelve, so He had seen Peter twice. Could He not have seen James twice? Could He not have seen "all the apostles" twice? In fact, we know that He appeared to them more than twice. Consequently, this argument is not strong enough to prove that James was not the apostle, as Galatians 1:19 states.

The final argument is that "the Lord's brother" could not have been the apostle because Jesus's natural brothers were unbelievers (John 7:5). However, we have already concluded that James "the Less" is not the natural brother of Jesus, but is the same as that found in Mark 6:3. We must, therefore, accept that the term "brother" is being used in a loose filial sense of Jesus's cousin. It is true that Jesus had brothers and sisters, who may well have been there along with his cousins, but there is simply no way to get around the fact that James "the Less" is the "Lord's brother" and that the "Lord's brother" apparently is an apostle, but *not* the "son of Joseph"!

Let it be noted that this simple fact eliminates the "coincidences" found in varying traditions. Ruffin, for example, is one of the few Catholics who believes that James Alphæus is not James the Just, but he believes that they both died in Jerusalem by stoning "in the same persecution"![327] Perhaps the reason is that they are one and the same.

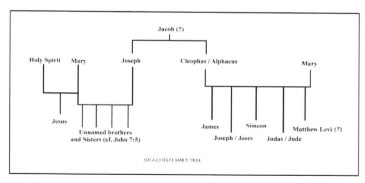

SUGGESTED FAMILY TREE

109

Let the reader also be aware that I am an evangelical Protestant who has even been accused of "anti-Catholicism" for my strict stand against certain Catholic teachings and dogma. However, when I study the Bible I do not seek to support any dogma, bias, or teaching; but to understand the word of God. Based on Matthew 13:55-56, 27:56; Mark 6:3, 15:40; Luke 24:10; John 7:5, 19:25; and Galatians 1:19, I have reached the tentative conclusion that James "the son of Alphæus" is James the Less and the "Lord's brother" to whom history has attached the name "James the Just."

History and Traditions

The Biblical Record
Assuming that James Alphæus is James the Less and James the Just, the Bible has more to say that most of the apostles. If they are not the same, as I believe, then it says absolutely *nothing* about James.

According to Peter, James the Greater, and John were a part of Jesus' inner circle (cf. Matthew 17:1; Mark 5:37, 14:13; Luke 8:51, 9:28). However, after James the Greater's execution (Acts 12:2) it seems that James the Less rose very quickly to prominence among the twelve, and seems to have already been among the more prominent of the disciples, for following Peter's escape from prison (after James's execution) he told his followers to "Report these things to James and the brethren" (Acts 12:17). Thus we might assume that James the Less was considered more esteemed.

It is also apparent from the Bible that James had become a spokesperson for the "party of circumcision" (Galatians 2:12) when the dispute between Jewish and gentile converts arose. However, James's prominence and importance at the Council of Jerusalem was arguably the deciding factor in convincing the "party of circumcision" to accept gentiles with but minor reservations, such as abstinence from sexual sin (Acts 15:13-29).

James is again encountered upon Paul's return to Jerusalem in Acts 21:18. There he immediately goes to visit James "and all the elders." It is clear from this that James was among the few apostles who remained in Jerusalem, and that

James was either the head of the elders, or in some other prominent position which was held in great esteem by the elders. Traditions may give us the precise answer, but here we shall restrict ourselves to the Bible alone.

So it is clear that while Peter, James, and John were the inner circle of Jesus, it was "James and Cephas [Peter] and John who were reputed to be pillars" (Galatians 2:9) after the death of James the Greater. James the Less then became one of the most prominent of all the apostles. It is interesting to note that Peter seemed to have look up to James as inferred by Galatians 2:12. However little is said of James the Less in the gospels, he quickly became a man of importance in the church following the death of James the Greater. He was apparently an overseer for the church elders of Jerusalem, and a spokesman for the Jewish Christian party at the Council of Jerusalem. His decision is what determined the favorable outcome of that council.

Extra-Biblical Records and Traditions

Although I usually refer to "traditions" as opposed to "history," there is more history of James the Just than there is "tradition." He seems to have been one of the most important of the early church leaders and is the only apostle to be mentioned by the first century Jewish historian Josephus.

Josephus's account is short, but said that "Ananus assembled the Sanhedrim of judges, and brought before them the brother of Jesus, who was called Christ, whose name was James, and some others; and when he had formed an accusation against them as breakers of the law, he delivered them to be stoned."[328]

Hegesippus was the earliest Christian "chronologer" who lived in the first part of the second century, called the "sub-apostolic age." His account is the longest and most detailed, saying:

> "James, the Lord's brother, succeeds to the government of the Church, in conjunction with the apostles. He has been universally called the Just, from the days of the Lord down to the present time ... he used to be found kneeling on his knees, begging forgiveness for the people – so that the skin of his knees became horny like that of a camel's, by reason of his constantly bending the knee in adoration to

111

God, and begging forgiveness for the people. Therefore, in consequence of his pre-eminent justice, he was called the Just ... Now some persons belonging to the seven sects existing among the people, which have been before described by me in the Notes, asked him: 'What is the door of Jesus?' And he replied that He was the Saviour. In Consequence of this answer, some believed that Jesus is the Christ. But the sects before mentioned did not believe, either in a resurrection or in the coming of One to requite every man according to his works; but those who did believe, believed because of James. So, when many even of the ruling class believed, there was a commotion among the Jews, and scribes, and Pharisees, who said: 'A little more, and we shall have all the people looking for Jesus as the Christ.' They came, therefore, in a body to James, and said: 'We entreat thee, restrain the people: for they are gone astray in their opinions about Jesus, as if he were the Christ. We entreat thee to persuade all who have come hither for the day of the passover, concerning Jesus. For we all listen to thy persuasion; since we, as well as all the people, bear thee testimony that thou art just, and showest partiality to none. Do thou, therefore, persuade the people not to entertain erroneous opinions concerning Jesus: for all the people, and we also, listen to thy persuasion. Take thy stand, then, upon the summit of the temple, that from that elevated spot thou mayest be clearly seen, and thy words may be plainly audible to all the people. For, in order to attend the passover, all the tribes have congregated hither, and some of the Gentiles also.' The aforesaid scribes and Pharisees accordingly set James on the summit of the temple, and cried aloud to him, and said: 'O just one, whom we are all bound to obey, forasmuch as the people is in error, and follows Jesus the crucified, do thou tell us what is the door of Jesus, the crucified.' And he answered with a loud voice: 'Why ask ye me concerning Jesus the Son of man? He Himself sitteth in heaven, at the right hand of the Great Power, and shall come on the clouds of heaven.' And, when many were fully convinced by these words, and offered praise for the testimony of James, and said, 'Hosanna to the son of David,' then again the said Pharisees and scribes said to one another, 'We

112

have not done well in procuring this testimony to Jesus. But let us go up and throw him down, that they may be afraid, and not believe him.' And they cried aloud, and said: 'Oh! oh! the just man himself is in error.' Thus they fulfilled the Scripture written in Isaiah: 'Let us away with the just man, because he is troublesome to us: therefore shall they eat the fruit of their doings.' So they went up and threw down the just man, and said to one another: 'Let us stone James the Just.' And they began to stone him: for he was not killed by the fall; but he turned, and kneeled down, and said: 'I beseech Thee, Lord God our Father, forgive them; for they know not what they do.' And, while they were thus stoning him to death, one of the priests, the sons of Rechab, the son of Rechabim, to whom testimony is borne by Jeremiah the prophet, began to cry aloud, saying: 'Cease, what do ye? The just man is praying for us.' But one among them, one of the fullers, took the staff with which he was accustomed to wring out the garments he dyed, and hurled it at the head of the just man. And so he suffered martyrdom; and they buried him on the spot, and the pillar erected to his memory still remains, close by the temple. This man was a true witness to both Jews and Greeks that Jesus is the Christ."[329]

Hippolytus was one of the few who did not count James the Just as the apostle, but declared that James the Just was the bishop of Jerusalem.[330] He said of the apostle, whom he believed to be different, "James the son of Alphæus, when preaching in Jerusalem, was stoned to death by the Jews, and was buried there beside the temple."[331]

Clement of Alexandia, also writing in the first century, said, "For he says that Peter and James and John, after the Saviour's ascension, though pre-eminently honoured by the Lord, did not contend for glory, but made James the Just, bishop of Jerusalem."[332] He also said, "James the Just ... was thrown down from the parapet and beaten to death with a fuller's club."[333]

The so-called *Teaching of the Apostles* said, "Jerusalem received the ordination to the priesthood, as did all the country of Palestine, and the parts occupied by the Samaritans, and the parts occupied by the Philistines, and the country of the

Arabians, and of Phœnicia, and the people of Cæsarea, from James, who was ruler and guide in the church of the apostles which was built in Zion."[334] It also said that "James had written from Jerusalem."[335]

Likewise, the "*Apostolic Constitutions*" also called him "James the bishop" and said only that he was martyred.[336]

Note that all of these sources are first and second century accounts. I will, therefore, not quote the later sources, for these are sufficient and strong enough in themselves, combined with the citation by Josephus.

Evaluation

There is very little here to evaluate as all ancient sources seem to agree with one another. The only debate seems to be whether or not James "the son of Alphæus" was also James the Just. That issue I have already debated, and reached the conclusion that they are one and the same. This eliminates the problems with having two separate Jameses dying by stoning in 62 or 63 A.D. on Passover near the Temple. The confusion is merely one over Jesus's family tree, which is never easy to decipher when the Bible offers little in the way of the apostles' genealogies. Still, this solution seems the best, in light of Galatians 1:19 and Mark 6:3, 15:40.

Summary

James "the son of Alphæus" was cousin of Jesus, who is called in the affectionate sense, "the Lord's brother," for His true filial brothers were not believers (John 7:5). After the death of James the Great, he seems to have risen to prominence among the apostles and become one of the "pillars" of the apostles (Galatians 2:9). He was appointed overseer of the elders of the church in Jerusalem[337] and was the leader of the Jewish Christian party. Even after the majority of the other apostles left Judea for the mission field, James the Just remained in Jerusalem ministering the gospels to the Jews there.

It was a few short years before the Jewish revolt in Judea that James the Just was mercifully spared the Jewish war to come, for following the death of governor-procurator Festus, the Sanhedrim saw an opportunity. They confronted James the Just, who had the respect and admiration of the people, and they ordered him to stand upon the parapet of the Temple and renounce the Lord Jesus before everyone on Passover. James may have remained silent and refused to answer them, for they clearly were taken by surprise when he instead proclaimed the gospel before everyone. Immediately they rushed up on the temple parapet and cast him down. Because he did not die from the fall the enemies of the Christians began to stone James while others tried fruitlessly to protect him. The death blow came when a man struck him on the head with a club. This took place on Passover of either 62, or possibly 63 A.D.

11

Judas Thaddæus

Judas Lebbæus was surnamed Thaddæus to distinguish him from the other Judas. Speculation has attempted to make him variously the brother of James the Less or Simon the Zealot, or both. He has often been associated with the epistle Jude. His post-Biblical history is largely restricted to Mesopotamia, and his death remains largely a mystery with a few varying late traditions. What then do we know about this apostle?

History and Traditions

The Biblical Record

The only record we have of Judas Thaddæus in the Bible is when he asked to the Lord, "what then has happened that You are going to disclose Yourself to us and not to the world?" (John 14:22). The question is actually a good one, although some have tried to find fault with it. It shows a curious nature in Thaddæus which is good. Beyond this, however, the Bible says nothing. Some critics even question whether or not this Thaddæus was one and the same as the Lebbæus found in some gospels.

As with all names in antiquity it is sometimes hard to distinguish between individuals, because they did not have firsts, middle, and last names as today. Sometimes they would be called the "son of" their fathers, such as Judas son of Alphæus, but this was too clumsy for ordinary use, so surnames became popular. This is the case with many of the apostles, such as Peter and presumably Thomas, as well as Matthew and others who had common names. Here is another example.

It has been argued that Thaddæus and Lebbæus are the same name transliterated into Greek differently,[338] but more than likely Thaddæus is a surname as Merrill Unger believes.[339] Which view we take depends on the underlying root word for Thaddæus which is debated. D.A. Carson believes Thaddæus comes from a root "roughly" meaning "beloved."[340]   Joseph Thayer believes that it come from תַּדַי (thadday) meaning courageous.[341]   Merrill Unger believes it is from תּוֹדָה (thodah), meaning to praise or to give thanks.[342]   Obviously, names change form, particularly when transliterated into a different language which has a different alphabet.   Consequently, it is hard to say which of these views is correct, except to say that Thaddæus and Lebbæus are clearly the same person occupying the same space in the apostles list.   He is best known as Judas Thaddæus, and probably the Addæus of Syriac writings.

Extra-Biblical Records and Traditions

Syrian traditions revere a man named Addæus.   Some Syrian writings contain the name Thaddæus.   These were the same man, but whether or not he was the apostle is to be debated.   For the purposes of this section, I will list the traditions of Addæus as well as Judas, and reserve debate for later.

The *"Teachings of the Apostles"* relates that "Edessa, and all the countries round about it which were on all sides of it, and Zoba, and Arabia, and all the north, and the regions round about it, and the south, and all the regions on the borders of Mesopotamia, received the apostles' ordination to the priesthood from Addæus the apostle, one of the seventy-two apostles, who himself made disciples there, and built a church there, and was priest and ministered there in his office of Guide which he held there."[343]

Hippolytus believed that Judas Thaddæus and the Thaddæus of the Edessa traditions were not the same person, but he also said that "Jude, who is also called Lebbæus, preached to the people of Edessa, and to all Mesopotamia, and fell asleep at Berytus, and was buried there."[344]   In regard to the Thaddæus of Edessa, he said, "Thaddeus ... conveyed the epistle to Augarus" and was one of the seventy-two disciples.[345]

The most controversial record of Thaddæus is quoted by Eusebius who copied what he said he found in the official government archives of Edessa.   If true this would be the earliest account of Thaddæus and a first hand account.   As will debated later, some are highly suspicious of this.   Nevertheless, the records say that king Abgar of Edessa wrote a letter to Jesus shortly before His crucifixion, saying:

actual Bible, but is the translators opinion. "Son of" is preferred by the NAS, NIV, NLV, NKJB, RSV, Tyndale's, and the ASV. "Brother of James" is preferred by the King James Bible, Webster's, Darby's, the Douay-Rheims Bible, and the Geneva Bible. Note that the New King James reads "son of" whereas the older King James versions read "brother of." Which is correct?

There are three dominant reasons that I believe "son of" is the proper translation. First, if the Greek use of the *genitive*, translated "of James," could be used of either brothers or fathers, sisters or mothers, then it would be ambiguous. Obviously Greek, like all other languages, does not cater to ambiguities. The *genitive* use of a name should properly be used of one or the other, but not both. Since the *genitive of relationship*[356] is used throughout the Bible in relation to "the son of" or "daughter of" it is logical to assume that is the case here as well.

Second, is the fact that Luke uses the specific word "brother" (αδελφος) in regard to Andrew (Luke 6:14). If Luke uses "brother" (αδελφος) for Andrew why would he not use it for Judas? The likely answer is that this Judas Thaddæus is the "son of" a man named James, and not the brother of James the Less.

The final argument is perhaps the strongest, at least in regard to whether or not Jude was the apostle. Jude 17 says, "you, beloved, ought to remember the words that were spoken beforehand by the apostles of our Lord Jesus Christ." This implies that Jude was not one of "the apostles of our Lord Jesus Christ," and therefore not Judas Thaddæus.

Was the Thaddæus of Abgar Legend the Apostle?

The alleged archive of which Eusebius quotes states that Thaddæus, or Addæus, was one of the seventy (some say seventy-two) disciples (cf. Luke 10:1, 17), and not the apostle, yet the "Teachings of the Apostles" calls him both the apostle *and* one of the seventy.[357] Hippolytus believed that this is an entirely different Thaddæus from the apostle, but then conflated Thaddæus and Jude.[358] This cannot be the case.

Most other traditions make it clear that this was indeed Judas Thaddæus. For one thing, Thaddæus was most likely Judas's surname, and not a proper name. It is therefore highly unlikely that two followers of Jesus would both be called Thaddæus. Furthermore, every extant tradition claims that Judas Thaddæus ministered to Edessa and Mesopotamia. If he did not evangelize Edessa, what did he evangelize? If he went to Mesopotamia, then he would naturally have gone to Edessa, the bridge, so to speak, into Mesopotamia. It is thus clear that the association of Thaddæus with the seventy disciples is a mistake, as will become evident. The next question is then whether or not the legend is true.

The Legend of Thaddæus and Abgar

The majority of traditions regarding Thaddæus, or Addæus in Syriac, revolve around the ancient kingdom of Osroene, a nominal part of the Parthian empire, in a country called Mesopotamia. It's capital, Edessa, is not far from Syria and Antioch where the apostles set up camp for a time. On the modern day map it lay close to the Syria-Turkey border near the Euphrates river.

For the time being I will not debate whether or not Thaddæus ministered in Edessa, for its seems he did, but whether or not the "archives" which Eusebius had seen were real or forged, as many scholars now believe.

At first glimpse it seems highly absurd to declare a court document from a government archive a "forgery" without even looking at the document, let alone being removed from that document by two thousand years. Add to this the fact that Eusebius was no fool and we might be inclined to reject the critics as simply more revisionist historians seeking tenure. However, there are three reasons to believe that Eusebius's "archives" had indeed been forged by someone in the Osroene kingdom before Eusebius's day.

First, the archives which Euebius quoted state that "these things were done in the year 340" of the Osroene calendar.[359] According to Cleveland Coxe that date corresponds "with the fifteenth year of Tiberius."[360] If that is so then the document is inaccurate for Luke 3:1 makes it very clear that the baptism of Jesus took place "in the fifteenth year of the reign of Tiberius Caesar."[361] Thus the crucifixion did not take place until 343 or 344 according to the Osroene calendar!

Second, the document confuses the apostle Thaddæus with one of the seventy (Luke 10:1). Surely if the document was written at the time of Thaddæus's visit they would have known that he was an apostle, and not one of the seventy.

Finally, the document cast strong suspicion upon itself when the king tells Jesus, "the Jews murmur against You, and ... they seek to crucify You." This statement seems extremely unrealistic for two reasons. 1. Crucifixion was a Roman punishment, not a Jewish one. The original plan was to try Jesus for heresy and have him stoned to death. It was only when Jesus was acquitted by Jewish law that Caiaphas contrived to bring Jesus before Pilate. Consequently, the mention of crucifixion implies this was written after Jesus's death, and not before. 2. The conspiracy was a secret not even known the apostles! How could the king of another country know this? Had the conspiracy been so well known as to be reported to a foreign king, surely the multitude of Jesus's followers would have appeared at the trial instead of Caiaphas's thugs who showed up before anyone else was even awake in the morning!

Eusebius himself seems to have believed the archival records because he said Edessa was a Christian city "to this day."[362] However, we know that whether or not Abgar was a Christian, there were several rulers hostile to Christianity, including Abgar VI whom at least one tradition holds martyred Thaddæus. Therefore, it seems that a later Christian king may have altered or added to the old archives in hopes of "restoring" Edessa's Christian heritage or affirming one of their patron saints' visit.

So while the archives of Edessa, which Eusebius quoted, are not reliable or accurate enough to be true history, they nevertheless record a very ancient tradition which is echoed almost uniformly for centuries. Let us look at that tradition.

Thaddæus in Edessa
Even though we can dismiss Eusebius's archival report, it does provide strong evidence for the antiquity of the all but universal traditions of Thaddæus in Edessa. It seems almost certain that the traditions and legends revolving around an apostle barely mentioned in the Scripture is no accident. The very fact that some traditions confuse him with one of the

seventy (Luke 10:1) as opposed to an apostle, serves as further proof that the stories were not simply an attempt to make some great apostle their patron saint, but instead grew out of the truth.

Now while we cannot confirm that Abgar the Black did convert to Christianity, the antagonism of Abgar VI (see below) may reflect this fact. Osroene was not under Roman jurisdiction and so the edicts of Nero were of no interest to them at all. Edessa did indeed have a long history of Christianity in their country, and its proximity to Antioch makes it very likely that more than one apostle visited during the reign of Abgar the Black.

Given the overwhelming support for Thaddæus ministering in Edessa and the surrounding areas, there can be little doubt that he served in Mesopotamia and the surrounding regions, as the traditions state. It is also fairly apparent that his entire ministry career focused on the western Parthian empire. It is also probable that Abgar the Black was a convert, explaining not only the uniform traditions but also the relative freedom which Thaddæus must have had to witness the gospel in Mesopotamia.

Thaddæus and Simon?

The *Acts of Abdias* is a collection of ancient traditions of varying dates. They are then compiled together. It is in the *Acts of Abdias* that we first have an extant tradition of Simon the Zealot returning to meet "his brother" Judas Thaddæus. Now I will discuss the alleged fraternal relationship of Judas Thaddæus and Simon the Zealot under Chapter 12 : Simon the Zealot. However, it is important to note here that they are almost certainly not brothers. I believe that this confusion arose from a conflation of Simon the Zealot with Simeon the brother of James the Less and the belief that Judas Thaddæus was the Jude of the epistle. Consequently, the traditions seem tied to conflated stories of Simon. Moreover, the tradition which has Simon returning to do missionary work with his brother also conveniently ties their martyrdom together with two pagan priests who plagued the Apostle Matthew. In other words, "poetic license" seems to have been taken. A more full discussion follows in the next chapter, but here I merely conclude that Simon probably never did return to the Middle

East, and the traditions of Thaddæus and Simon dying together are probably of late origin, and not reliable

Thaddæus's Death

The traditions of Thaddæus's death are diverse and contradictory. They can be broken down into four different views, shown below.

Place of Death	Manner of Death	Earliest known Tradition
Lebannon	Natural causes	Third century
Edessa	Illness	Third century
Edessa	Crucified	Late third century
Persia	Beaten to death	Uncertain (*Abdias*)

Notice that in two he dies a natural death and in two he dies in Edessa, both of which claim a king Abgar was ruling the kingdom. I have already rejected the idea that Thaddæus and Simon traveled or died together (but see Chapter 12 for a defense of this), and so we are left with three views. Let us now break these down and examine these facts more closely.

Hippolytus said that he died in Berytus (Beruit), Lebanon of a natural death.[363] Given the assertion of the *Teaching of Addæus the Apostle* that he died of an illness we might be inclined at first to believe that this Syriac tradition merely transferred his death from Berytus to Edessa because he was a patron saint there.[364] However, upon closer examination, these two traditions actually cancel each other out. Here is why.

Many of the old Syriac traditions consider Thaddæus of Edessa to be different from Thaddæus the apostle. Those traditions have Thaddæus dying in 45 A.D.![365] Hippolytus actually concurs that Thaddæus the apostle is not Thaddæus of Edessa and yet his record of Thaddæus dying of natural causes in Lebanon is borrowed from that tradition. Remember that these early traditions are conflated because of confusion between Thaddæus the apostle, Thaddæus of Edessa, and Jude, the brother of James. I believe the first and second are the same, whereas Hippolytus believed that the first and third were the same. A closer examination of the apocryphal *Teaching of Addæus the Apostle* may help the reader understand the confusion.

125

According to Edessan tradition king Abgar V mourned the death of Thaddæus while Dorotheus believed that Abgar VI crucified him.[366] Interestingly enough, the *Teaching of Addæus the Apostle* further says that "some years after the death of Abgar the king, there arose one of his contumacious sons, who was not favorable to peace" and began to persecute the church.[367] Now Abgar (V) the Black died around 50 A.D. and Abgar VI arose to power around 71 A.D.[368] John Foxe records Thaddæus's martyrdom as 72 A.D. Since Abgar VI reigned until 91 A.D. it is clear that Agbar VI was apparently the "contumacious son" who persecuted the church, as Dorotheus believed. It is also equally clear that Thaddæus did not die before 50 A.D. since he was at the council of Jerusalem, along with all the other apostles. Consequently, we must believe that the apocryphal *Teaching of Addæus the Apostle* conflated the histories of the two Abgars, and Thaddæus did not die during the reign of Abgar (V) the Black, but in the reign of Agbar VI.

This leaves us the tradition recorded by Dorotheus. Both he and the *Teaching of Addæus the Apostle* record a persecution of Christians following the death of Abgar (V) the Black. Since Thaddæus probably died around 72 A.D., it would seem that Abgar VI was the "contumacious son" who persecuted those his forebear had once loved. According to Dorotheus, Judas Thaddæus was crucified. The Syriac tradition says that he died on "the fourteenth of the month Iyar"[369] which would be early May, but his feast has been variously held on June 19 and October 28.

Summary

Because of his conflation with Jude and confusion of his relationship to one of the seventy (Luke 10:1) there is little reliable information on Thaddæus except that he spent at least five years in Edessa preaching the gospel,[370] apparently with the blessings of Abgar (V) the Black. It may also be that Abgar (V) the Black was a convert, whose son became bitter over the intrusion of a "foreign" religion.

Thaddæus spent the next fifteen years or more ministering in Mesopotamia, Syria, Edessa, Persia, and possibly even northern Arabia.[371] In 71 A.D. king Abgar VI became king of Edessa. He wrote to the king of Parthia to warn him of the intrusion of a "foreign" religion in his land.[372]   Whether Thaddæus returned to Edessa or was captured and brought back in chains, he was apparently crucified in 72 A.D.[373]

12

Simon the Zealot

The reader has doubtless noticed that some traditions make James the Less and Judas Thaddæus brothers. These same traditions go a step further in assuming, with no evidence, that Simon the Zealot was the same Simon found in Mark 6:3, and hence a brother to James and Judas. Thus Simon the Zealot is conflated with Simeon (or Simon), the brother of James the Less. Consequently we are again left with the difficult task of separating fact from fiction. Can this be done?

The Bible mentions Simon only in the apostolic list. Nowhere is anything else said of him. There is not the slightest evidence that he is the brother of James the Less, let alone the brother of Judas Thaddæus. If these *assumptions* are removed, then it becomes easier to distinguish between the traditions, for it will become apparent that conflation of the various Simon's has created much of the confusion and contradictions involving his ministry and death. By looking at each tradition individually, it will become more clear which are reliable, and which have erred.

History and Traditions

Hippolytus, who confuses Simon the Zealot with Simon, the brother of James Alphæus, said, "Simon the Zealot, the son of Clopas, who is also called Jude, became bishop of Jerusalem after James the Just, and fell asleep and was buried there at the age of 120 years."[374]

Dorotheus, the bishop of Tyre, in the late third century, said that after preaching in North Africa he sailed up to Britain where he was crucified, circa 74 A.D.[375]

Eusebius, Dorotheus's disciple, follows a different tradition. Like Hippolytus he believes that Simon the Zealot was the same as Simon the brother of James the Less and later bishop of Jerusalem. Like Hippolytus he believes that Simon died at age 120, but unlike Hippolytus he said that Simon was tortured and crucified in Syria under Domitian's reign. However, his proof is the citation of Hegesippus:

> "Simon, son of Clopas ... was tortured for many days in giving his witness, so that all, even the governor, were astounded at how he endured it all at 120 years of age; and he was sentenced to crucifixion."[376]

So Eusebius's belief is based on the assumption that Simon, son of Clopas, is the same as Simon the Zealot.

The *Acts of Abdias* follows Dorotheus's tradition except that Simon the Zealot returned from Britain and joined Thaddæus who then ventured into Persia. There they allegedly encountered the same two pagan magicians that Matthew had driven out of Ethiopia. Finally in the city of Suanir, Persia (somewhere east of Baghdad, Iraq) the magicians stirred up a mob who speared Judas to death, and sawed Simon in half.[377]

As there are few ante-Nicene records, I will cite later traditions such as Basil the Great, of the fourth century, who said that Simon died of natural causes in Edessa.[378]

Isidore of Seville said that Simon moved across Egypt, Cyrene, Africa, Mauritania, and Libya[379] and then became first to venture north to Britain,[380] but later visited his "brother" Judas in Persia[381] and was ultimately crucified in Syria under Nero's edict in 68 A.D.[382] This is also the opinion of Nicephorus of Constantinople.[383] Likewise, this is supported in Coptic tradition, with the exception that Coptic tradition has Simon's dying in Persia.[384] Still other traditions have him dying as early as 65 A.D.

An interesting, but late, legend says that Simon was one of the shepherds at Jesus's birth, but few place stock in this late legend.[385]

Evaluation

Simon's Relationship to the Other Apostles

As we have seen with the last few apostles, there is confusion among the ancients, and moderns, as to the exact familial relationship of some of the apostles to one another. Judas (from the Hebrew Judah), James, and Simon were all very common names. The appearance of three brothers by these names in the Bible (Mark 6:3) is scarcely proof that James Alphæus the Less, Judas Lebbæus Thaddæus, and Simon the Zealot were all brothers. Jude, the brother of James (mentioned in Mark 6:3), is not one of the apostles by his own admission (Jude 17), and neither is the Simon of Mark 6:3. That Simon and Jude are brothers of James the Less, and believed to be members of the seventy (Luke 10:1), but were not apostles. If we bear this in mind, then it is much easier task to distinguish between the fact and fiction of the Simon traditions.

Simon in Africa

With the exception of Hippolytus who confuses Simon the Zealot with Simon the brother of James the Less, all traditions and histories record that Simon at least went to Egypt in north Africa. The majority also say that he traveled across north Africa to Cyrene (Libya), the country called Africa, and Mauritania. This makes perfect sense. When the apostles went out to establish churches and mission fields, they were given certain regions to evangelize. If Simon ventured to Egypt it is logical to assume that he continued across northern Africa to establish the church in all of Roman Africa, even as Matthew evangelized Egypt and then moved down into Ethiopia and the north eastern region of Africa.

Simon in Britain

Now we come to the first truly controversial aspect of the traditions of Simon. Some might even call it a rubicon of sorts, for once we have decided whether this story is true or not, it will effect our decision upon whether Simon ever returned to the middle east.

Nearly every ancient source still in existence (although that is relatively few) records that after he had reached the western shores of northern Africa, he sailed up to the new Roman colony in Britain. Some have questioned this because of the lack of evidence of any Christian communities in Britain until centuries later, but given the wars that ravaged Britain under Roman occupation, this is not particularly surprising. What is surprising is the discovery of a second century stone engraving of the Lord's Prayer.[386] This is proof enough that

Christianity had at least been introduced to the island within the first hundred years after Jesus Christ. It is not beyond reason to believe that it was one of Jesus's disciples who brought it there.

Dorotheus believed that Simon remained in Britain where he was crucified, circa 74 A.D.[387] Later traditions, however, follow the belief that he returned from Britain to the middle east where he died under Nero's reign. Those who favor these stories point out that Queen Boadicea of Britain revolted against Rome circa 60 A.D.[388] and argue that Simon would have been expelled. Certainly the country was to be engulfed in war for the next twenty years, but the revolt actually began in central western Britain and would not have had an immediate impact upon Simon. Nevertheless, the revolt of Queen Boadicea is a rubicon for our study of Simon. As a missionary he could certainly have been in sympathy for the British and stayed, but he would almost certainly not have been able to leave if he chose the British as his allies. This would fit with the theory that he was crucified by Romans in 74 A.D. He would have been seen as aiding and abetting the enemy and subject to crucifixion.

Conversely, some hold the view that he was forced to leave Britain not too long after his arrival in order to escape the war that would ravage Britain for the next few decades. According to this view, it is around this time that he would have returned to the middle east. If this view is correct then his return actually shortened his life, for all the traditions of Simon in the middle east place his death in either 65 or 68 A.D. under the reign of the emperor Nero. Our decision may hinge upon whether the evidence truly favors Simon as returning to the middle east at all. If he did, then he left Britain around 60 A.D. If he did not, then he must have remained there until his death in 74 A.D.

Did Simon Return to the Middle East?

It is not easy to know if Simon truly returned to the middle east. Most of the traditions that involve Simon's return to the middle east are filled with factual errors, such as the idea that he and Thaddæus were brothers who traveled together, but the greater problem is not whether or not they traveled together (for they were certainly friends), but the time table. If Simon returned from Britain and met with Thaddæus then it would probably be sometime in 61 A.D. at the earliest. In these traditions, however, they travel to Lebanon, Armenia, Persia, and possibly even part of Arabia. Now consider that they were not sight-seeing but establishing churches and missions. Today the average missionary is expected to spend a minimum of six month in each country, unless he is just an assistant or aid. If Simon and Thaddæus traveled to all these countries and established churches then they would have had to do it in less than four years according to one strain of the tradition, and seven in the other.

Now the seven year curtain is obviously enough time, but, as will discussed below, the 68 A.D. martyrdom date is not acceptable since it hinges upon false historical assumptions. This leaves us with two possibilities, which become more clear after debating the method and time of Simon's martyrdom.

Simon's Death

There are six major traditions involving the death of Simon the Zealot, as listed below.

Place of Death	Manner of Death	Earliest known Tradition
Jerusalem	Natural causes	Second century
England	Crucifixion	Third century
Syria	Crucifixion in the 90s	Fourth century
Edessa	Natural causes	Fourth century
Syria	Crucifixion in 65 A.D.	Sixth century
Persia	Sawed in half	Uncertain (*Abdias*)

We can safely reject the first, despite its early source, because Hippolytus is clearly conflating Simon the Zealot with Simeon the brother of James the Less, and later overseer of Jerusalem. This is, therefore, a mistake on Hippolytus's part. It may also explain the late tradition that he died of natural causes in Edessa, for many Jews were expelled and persecuted by Rome after the fall of Jerusalem in 70 A.D. Basil the Great may have, therefore, taken Hippolytus's word for his death, but transferred it to Edessa where Simon might have been expected to relocate following the fall of Jerusalem. Certainly there is no way that Simon could have been in Jerusalem in 70 A.D. when the city fell, for all those Jews who survived were either put to the sword or enslaved, and a Christian bishop would have been slain by the rebels even before Rome took the city.

This leaves us with four choices, two of which differ only in the date of his death. Note that in three of the traditions Simon is said to have been crucified, and in two he is alleged to visit "his brother" Judas Thaddæus. Since we have already ruled out that this Simon was related to James the Less, we may also doubt any relation to Judas Thaddæus without evidence. However, it is possibly that they visited each other, as they were obviously friends and apostles. Let us examine then the two strains of this tradition to see which, if either, is viable.

In one of the two traditions where Simon and Thaddæus travel together, they die in Persia. As discussed in the previous chapter, this particular story lacks credibility for two reasons. First, it is probably of a late date, and second, the appearance of two magicians whom Matthew allegedly drove out of Ethiopia has all the earmarks of dramatic license. It also contradicts the weight of evidence that Thaddæus died under Abgar VI. If this is so then he obviously could not have died with Simon in Persia.

The second strain is more plausible until we examine it closely. In this view Simon and Thaddæus return to their homes after finishing several years of mission work together. Simon is said to return to Syria where he is crucified in 65 A.D. under Nero's edict. This theory almost makes sense, until we compare it that of Eusebius which is almost identical save the date of death. Eusebius quoted the second century author Hegesippus as proof that Simon was crucified at 120 years of age under the emperor Domitian. The later tradition then shifts his martyrdom from the 90s to 65 A.D. under Nero, but here is where both fall apart, for Hegesippus was actually describing the crucifixion of Simon, son of Clopas![389] As a result neither of these views is acceptable unless we *assume* that Simon the Zealot was Simon, the brother of James and son of Clopas. Of course if we assume that, then we must reject *all* the other traditions, for this Simon, son of Clopas, was the overseer of Jerusalem and lived in Judea and Syria his whole life (see Chapter 15)!

This then nullifies both traditions that Simon died in Syria. Simon the Zealot was not Simon the overseer of Jerusalem. Both traditions conflate the two, and must therefore be rejected. This leaves us with only one alternative. Simon never returned from Britain. He remained in Britain when war engulfed the country. He chose to ally himself with the British and was therefore considered a traitor to Rome. This explains a great many things, including why we know so little of Simon's work in Britain. When the Romans finally squashed the rebellion, they also destroyed the churches and missions which he had established. He was executed around 74 A.D. as a traitor to Rome. Christianity had come to Britain, but the stamp of Roman oppression crushed much of his work. Nevertheless, he had planted the seeds that would one day grow into one of the most historically Christian countries in the world.

Summary

Simon's mission field was to preach the gospel to Roman Africa. One of three sent into Africa, Simon moved across northern Africa from Egypt to Cyrenaica (Libya), the country then called Africa (Tunisia and northeastern Algeria), and finally to the western end of northern Africa in Mauritania (which is actually north of modern day Mauritania in Morocco and northwestern Algeria). By this time he had probably spent at least ten years establishing churches and mission fields with his followers. It is at this time that he decided to travel far north to the relatively new Roman colony of Britain.

No sooner did Simon arrive in Britain and establish his missionary field than a British revolt threatened his work. After Nero seized Queen Boadicea's land and had her daughters raped and tortured,[390] the Queen led a revolt which was to begin a war which would last for more than two decades, even after her death (which was shortly after the revolt began). I believe the mass of evidence favors the belief that Simon chose to stay with his new converts and continue his mission works. Because of the coming war, however, he had to make up him mind to stay there most likely for the rest of his life. This is exactly what I believe happened.

As the Romans reconquered much of Britain and crushed opposition, they almost certainly destroyed the churches which Simon had established. Finally, in 74 A.D. Simon was captured by Romans and crucified as a traitor to Rome.

Although his churches were destroyed and forgotten, he had planted the seeds which would one day blossom and bear great fruit.

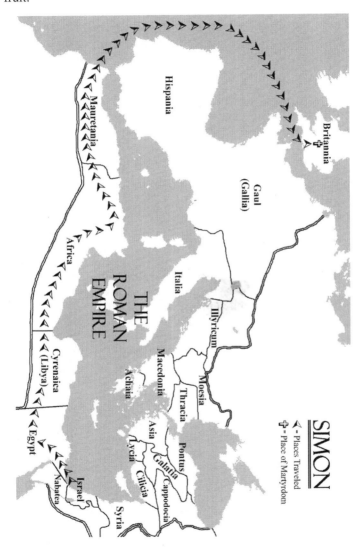

13

—

Matthias

As has been the case with the last few apostles we have examined, the traditions concerning Matthias are conflated and few. In fact, there is less information on Matthias than any other apostle. There is a reason for this, as the reader will learn.

Perhaps it should not be a surprise that there is relatively so little known about Matthias, for the Bible says little about him as well. We only know that he was one of the seventy disciples (cf. Luke 10:1), and that he was elected to replace Judas by the eleven (Acts 1:23-26). Beyond this nothing is said of him in the Bible.

How then can we know anything about him? Because there is actually more written on Matthias after the Bible than in the Bible. The problem is that Matthias is conflated with Matthew due to the virtual identical names (as discussed more fully in chapter 9). In Greek Matthew is *Matthaios* (ματθαιος) and Matthias is *Matthias* (ματθιας). Obviously it is easy to confuse the two. This is one way in which the conflation of traditions start, but when we are able to recognize the conflations, it becomes easier to decipher fact from fiction. This is the case with Matthias as well.

History and Traditions

Hippolytus said, "Matthias, who was one of the seventy, was numbered along with the eleven apostles, and preached in Jerusalem, and fell asleep and was buried there."[391]

Eusebius claimed that Matthias was the eighth bishop of Jerusalem,[392] sometime between 34 and 132 A.D.[393]

St. Jerome believed that he was the first to go to Ethiopia but later returned to Judea.[394]

The *Acts of Andrew and Matthias*, mentioned under Andrew, may or may not even refer to Matthias. The earliest manuscript contains Matthias's name, but later manuscripts read Matthew.[395] In the story Matthias was sent to Scythia, called the land "of the man-eaters," where he was blinded and imprisoned. Andrew then received a vision of the Lord, telling him of Matthias's plight, so he set out to rescue Matthias. Back in Scythia Matthias's eyes are miraculously restored and Andrew soon arrives to rescue him.[396]

The *Acts and Martyrdom of St. Matthew the Apostle* is yet another late tradition dating to around the sixth century. The earliest manuscripts read "Matthew," but later medieval manuscripts actually read Matthias. One critic calls it "a sequel to the Acts of Andrew and Matthias."[397] In the story Matthew (or Matthias) is called a "king" in the land of the "man-eaters." There he is slain by another king named Phulbanus by nailing him to the ground, and setting him on fire.[398]

Traditions concerning his martyrdom are once again late and confused. Most agree that he died in Judea, but the specifics vary. Some claim it was Rome who executed him for refusal to sacrifice to Jupiter, but most believe that he was killed by Jewish priests on charges of blasphemy because of Jesus. He is variously said to have either been hung on a cross (Romans) or tied to a large rock and then stoned (Jews), and sometimes beheaded afterwards.[399] Most say that he was stoned by the Jews[400] but the dates vary from 51 A.D.[401] to as late as 69 to 70 A.D.[402]

Evaluation

All the traditions place Matthias predominantly in Judea for an extended period of time. Only three traditions have him venturing outside of the Holy Land. The *Acts of Andrew and Matthias* and possibly the *Acts and Martyrdom of St. Matthew the Apostle* claim he traveled to Scythia, but these can be rejected as both late and conflated traditions (see chapters 5 and 9). This leaves us with only Jerome who believed that Matthias ventured into Ethiopia before returning to Judea.

Now concerning Jerome's assertion that Matthias went to Ethiopia, it is again apparent that Jerome has mistaken Matthias for Matthew. He is the only one that records Matthias going to Ethiopia, but many have recorded Matthew there. The problem is not uncommon as we have seen with the *Acts of Andrew and Matthias* and the *Acts and Martyrdom of St. Matthew the Apostle*. The Greek names are virtually identical, save a single letter. Therefore, we can safely reject the Ethiopian tradition as well.

So there can be no doubt that Matthias was one of three apostles who was assigned to remain in Judea, Samaria, and Galilee. James the Greater and James the Less were the other two. According to Eusebius Matthias was the eighth, of fifteen, bishops of Jerusalem before Hadrian expelled Jews from Israel.[403] This would be a span of about a hundred years, and many of those names listed as bishops did not die until their old age. This either means that the office of bishop (or more properly, overseer) was not a lifetime appointment or, more likely, that he was including some of the seven deacons (or more accurately, elders) who were appointed by the apostles (Acts 6:3; 15:2, 4, 6, 22-23; 16:4).

If, however, Eusebius recorded the names of the elders, he did not record them all. In fact, none of the seven mentioned in Acts 6:5 are listed. It may be that these seven were not the same as the elders, but a special group of disciples. In either case, it seems that James the Just and Matthias both served as overseer for the church in Jerusalem, or perhaps Matthias was an elder. What is certain is that Matthias served in Jerusalem, assisting the church there.

As to his death we must again eliminate the fiction, and arrive at the facts. If the Roman's executed Matthias for refusal to sacrifice to the gods, then this would have to have been during one of the persecutions, for before Nero Jews were allowed to pay a tax to escape the requirement for sacrificial offerings. After Nero, there was a peace which followed. Although Christians did continue to come under persecution, it was not the state who persecuted them until the time of Domitian. Now Nero reigned from 54 to 68 A.D. and Domitian from 81 to 96 A.D. However, the possible dates that we have for Matthias's death are 51 A.D. or 69 to 70 A.D. If he died in 51 A.D. then he would, as a Jew, be exempt from the requirement to sacrifice to Jupiter. If he died in 69 to 70 A.D. then Jerusalem would have been under siege by Rome, and Matthias would either have fled

Jerusalem, or been within the city walls under siege. In either case, we can eliminate the theory that he was martyred by Rome.

Most accounts say he was killed by Jewish radicals on account of Jesus. Given the probable dates for his death, and the circumstances which existed in Israel at this time, this seems to be the best, and most attested, view.

As to manner of this death, we must again use deductive logic. If he was not executed by Rome, then the use of a cross would not come into play as Jews had no such instrument of execution. All other accounts say that Matthias was stoned, which was the most common form of execution and/or mob killing in Judea at that time. It is doubtful that he would have been decapitated afterwards.

This leaves us only with the question of when he died. The first date offered has been 51 A.D. However, if Eusebius's "bishop" list has any credibility at all this cannot be, for James the Just is universally credited with being the first overseer of Jerusalem, and he did not die until 62 A.D. How then could Matthias be the eighth overseer of Jerusalem? Perhaps he was just one of the elders. This is plausible and would explain why so little was written of Matthias. If he did die in 51 A.D. then he would have been the second apostle to die.

Alternately, if he died in 69 or 70 A.D. then the city of Jerusalem was already under siege by the Romans. Within the city walls the Sicarii and other revolutionary groups held a tight grip on the city and enforced martial law. Josephus's account of what went on within the city is terrifying, but by no means exhaustive. It makes perfect sense that Matthias would have been killed at this time, for Christians were seen as sympathizers with Rome for our love of gentiles and our alleged rejection of Moses.

Both theories have strengths. If he died in 51 A.D. then we would understand why traditions about Matthias are so few in number, but we would wonder how he could ever have been considered the eighth "bishop" in line after men who did not die until many years later. If he died in 69 or 70 A.D. then his death would fit the dire circumstances of Jerusalem, and even be a blessing, for not only would he receive the martyrs crown (cf. James 1:12; Revelation 2:10), but he would be spared the barbarity and atrocities that were to take place when Rome breached the walls of the city. I, therefore, tentatively prefer the 69 or 70 A.D. date.

Summary

Matthias was one of three apostles who remained in Judea, Samaria, Galilee, and the nearby regions. He served in the church at Jerusalem most likely as an elder, and possibly as its overseer for a time. Although it is possible he died early in 51 A.D., it is more likely that he was stoned to death by Siccarri and other radical Jews when Rome besieged the city of Jerusalem, sometime between 69 and 70 A.D.

Rembrandt – Paul at His Writing Desk – 1627

14

—

Paul

Paul was the most influential of all the apostles, and yet he was not an apostle in the beginning. In fact, he persecuted Christians and condoned their executions. With all the zeal and fervor of a fanatic he hunted down Christians until he himself became a convert. From that day forward Paul used all the zeal he once used to hunt Christians and diverted it to spreading the gospel.

Paul has wrongly been called "the second founder of Christianity."[404] This rather blasphemous saying nevertheless reflects Paul's influence. Of the twenty-seven books of the New Testament Paul wrote thirteen (some say fourteen) of those books, and featured prominently in the book of Acts, written by one of Paul's companions, who also wrote one of the four gospels. One could argue that half of the New Testament is related to Paul in some way. This is, of course, an exagerration for the epistles of Paul are relatively short compared to the gospels, but they are doctrinal and instructional.

Contrary to those who called Paul Hellenistic because of his emphasis upon gentiles, Paul was virulently opposed to Hellenism (cf. 1 Corinthians 1:20, 27; 3:18; Colossians 2:8; Acts 9:29) and a student of Gamaliel, the Pharisee leader (Acts 22:3), of the Hillel descent.[405] He openly criticized Peter for "living like the gentiles" and then telling gentiles to live like Jews (Galatians 2:14). So those who try to argue that Paul was a Hellenistic Jew who opposed the "Jewish Christianity" of Peter and John[406] show themselves to be ignorant of both Judaism and Christianity, for there was no apostle more "Jewish" than Paul.

One can obviously see why Paul was so controversial. He was one of the most influential, if not the most influential, of apostles who is responsible for half of the New Testament books. He was the founder of the majority of churches in Turkey, Greece, and Rome; many of which were started before the other apostles ever left Israel. Some say that he even went as far as Spain.

History and Traditions

The Biblical Record

Paul first appears in the Bible as Saul. It was he to whom the murderers of Steven cast his robe (Acts 7:58). Of him it is said, "Saul was in hearty agreement with putting him to death" (Acts 8:1). It is said that he then "*began* ravaging the church, entering house after house, and dragging off men and women, he would put them in prison" (Acts 8:3). Fearing persecutions Christians fled Judea, and many went to Syria. Not content to drive them out of Jerusalem, Saul set out for Damascus to find and arrest the Christians when he experienced a life changing event. Saul was struck blind after having a vision of the Lord Jesus Christ who asked him, "Saul, Saul, why are you persecuting Me?"

The tramatic event shook Saul's convictions and changed his life. He took the new name, Paul, to show that he was no longer the same man, but he did not go to the apostles at that time. Instead he retreated to Arabia where he spent close to three years studying the Scriptures and re-evaluating his understanding of the Messiah promised therein (Galatians 1:17-18). After three years (on or during the third year by Hebrew reconning), he then went to meet Peter and James the Just, but did not initially speak to any of the other apostles, for they did not trust him. Nevertheless, Barnabas took Paul to meet the apostles and convince them of his sincerity (Acts 9:26-27).

Paul then went out together with Barnabas and others, and began to evangelize Asia minor (modern day Turkey). For over a dozen years (Galatians 1:18) Paul and his companions traveled throughout the countries that now make up Turkey creating and establishing churches. They passed through Cyprus, Lycia, and Galatia, when they returned to Jerusalem around 48 or 49 A.D. to attend the council of Jerusalem and persuade the other apostles that God was no respecter of persons and that they should put no obstacle in the way of gentile converts that was not Christ Himself. Having won over the apostles, the church of Jerusalem began to open the doors to gentile missions and the Great Commission began to be fully realized.

144

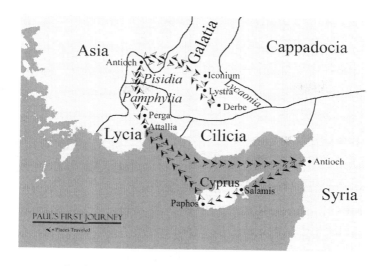

Paul returned to Asia minor to continue his work, but because of a dispute over John Mark he left without Barnabas who ventured to Cyprus with Mark. Paul eventually moved further out into Greece, expanding his original mission field. Returning to Antioch Paul spent some time there before setting out on his third mission trip.

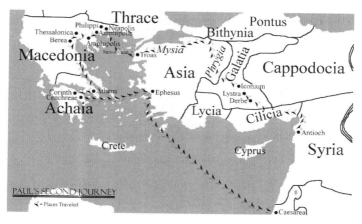

Setting out again to strengthen all the churches he had previously established (Acts 18:23), he passed through Turkey and Greece when he began to feel conflicted. He wanted to go to Rome, but he also felt the urge to return to Jerusalem. He resolved to go to Jerusalem first, and then head to Rome to meet with the church which had probably been established by Aquila and Priscilla (see notes in Chapter 2; cf. Romans 16:3).

Upon arrival in Jerusalem Ananaias, the High Priest, had brought up false charges against Paul (Acts 24:1). He was imprisoned for two years as the governor Felix had hoped he would be offered bribe money to release Paul (Acts 24:26), but instead Paul preached the gospel with his limited freedom and appealed to Caesar (Acts 25:11-12). Finally Festus replaced Felix as governor. Then Festus and king Aggripa brought Paul before them to hear his defense. Paul then preached the gospel to king and governor. Ironically, Agrippa said that he not requested an appeal to Caesar they would have released him (Acts 26:32). Instead Paul was sent a prisoner to Rome to be heard by none other than the emperor Nero.

Nikolai Bodarevsky – The Apostle Paul On Trial – 1875

On the long sea voyage the prisoner ship was wrecked by a storm off the coast Malta (Acts 27). Eventually they were rescued and brought to Rome in 60 A.D. where Paul was kept under house arrest with limited freedom for two years. This was permitted because Nero was not yet concerned with the affairs of state and had allowed the great Seneca, his advisor at the time, to manage most of the the country's affairs in his name.

It is as this point that the book of Acts abruptly ends. Different theories have been presented for this, but the most obvious and logical reason is that the book ends with Paul awaiting trial because that is when Luke finished writing his book and sent the transcript to Theophilus, who had commissioned the history (Acts 1:1). This seems too simple an explanation for some, but if I write a history of America, will I not end it today, even if unfolding events have not yet come to fruition? Should it not be the same with Luke? The real question is what happened afterwards? Was Paul released? Did Paul remain in prison until his execution three years later? If released, where did he go and why did he return?

Extra-Biblical Records and Traditions

There is more said of Paul than perhaps even Peter. Considering that Paul's post-Biblical history is so much shorter than the others, this should be somewhat surprising, but given his influence upon the Bible and the fact that he founded most of the ancient churches in Roman lands, we should not be surprised.

Clement, one of the earliest overseers (bishops) of Rome who lived in the first century, said, "Paul also obtained the reward of patient endurance, after being seven times thrown into captivity, compelled to flee, and stoned. After preaching both in the east and west, he gained the illustrious reputation due to his faith, having taught righteousness to the whole world, and come to the extreme limit of the west, and suffered martyrdom under the prefects. Thus was he removed from the world, and went into the holy place."[407]

Irenaeus declared that the "church in Ephesus [was] founded by Paul"[408] and calls Paul a co-founder of the church in Rome.[409]

Dionysius, an overseer (or bishop) of the church at Corinth, wrote in 170 A.D. that Paul was the planter of the Roman church, along with Peter and that "they suffered martyrdom at the same time."[410]

Tertullian stated that Paul was beheaded[411] in Rome.[412]

Hippolytus said, "Paul entered into the apostleship a year after the assumption of Christ; and beginning at Jerusalem, he advanced as far as Illyricum, and Italy, and Spain, preaching the Gospel for five-and-thirty years. And in the time of Nero he was beheaded at Rome, and was buried there."[413]

Eusebius believed that Paul was aquitted following the end of Acts based on 2 Timothy 4:16-17,[414] and that he did not suffer martyrdom until arrested later in Nero's reign when he was beheaded.[415]

The apocryphal *Acts of Peter* mentions Paul, saying that he traveled to Spain between his first imprisonment and his return.[416]

The *Acts of the Holy Apostles Peter and Paul* relates the story that after the fire in Rome, Paul sought an audience with the emperor, but he refused, fearing he would stir up more trouble. So Paul was banned from all of Italy. Paul then landed in Sicily and entered Italy with the help of Peter's disciples. Reaching Rome he found Simon Magus conspiring with the Jewish enemies of Peter and Paul. Having preached the gospel there it is claimed that Nero's wife Libia became a convert and fled the palace. Thus Peter, Paul, and Simon Magus were called to meet Nero. After hearing each of their accounts "both Peter and Paul were led away from the presence of Nero. And Paul was beheaded on the Ostesian road."[417]

A very late tradition, found only in the *Acts of Abdias*, says that after his head was chopped off, milk flowed from the body in place of blood.[418] It also claims Paul died two years after Peter, but John Foxe believed that he contradicted himself in regard to chronology, and thus rejected the chronology of *Abdias*.[419] Many late traditions say that he died in the last year of Nero.[420]

Evaluation

His First Roman Imprisonment

Acts ends with Paul still imprison and awaiting trial. It is the all but universal opinion that Paul was released after his first trial. It is true that some say that Paul was executed and that Luke didn't record this because he did not want a downbeat story to the triumph of Christianity,[421] but this argument is frivolous. However, some might wonder why the demonic Nero did release Paul, and this is a fair question. If we are to understand, then we must understand the politics of Rome in Nero's time.

When Nero first became emperor he was still a boy of sixteen years.[422] His chief advisor was a famed stoic philosopher named Seneca who had been appointed the young emperor's tutor. The advisor was chosen very wisely, but the pupil was not interested in stoic virtures. Nero allowed Seneca to handle most of the affair of state up until 62 A.D. when Seneca was forced to retire.[423] Before then it seemed as if all was well with the empire.

Now most all church historians place Paul's trial in 62 A.D. A few place it a year or two earlier,[424] but in either case, it is clear that Seneca was still the dominating factor. Interestingly enough, there are apocryphal writings purporting to be letters exchanged between Seneca and Paul. This is because Seneca's stoic philosophy was seen by some of the more Hellenistic elements in the Christian church to be similar to that of Jesus. Their desire to make Seneca a pseudo-convert is doubtless behind these letters.[425] Certainly stoic philosophy extolled the virtues of morality, and hence there is no doubt that Seneca would have sided with Paul against the charge of *superstitio illicita* (illegal superstition).[426]

The importance here is that Christianity not only came to the forefront of Rome and the empire, but to the ears of the young emperor himself. After Paul's release, it is apparent that Nero, who hated stoic philosophy and the ideals of virtue, also hated Christianity. The emperor was so debased he said to have castrated one of his lovers, a young boy, so as to make him "a girl" and enjoyed all manner of debauchery, violence, rape, and cruelty.[427] His hatred for Seneca's love of virtue became more acute with time, and eventually he would order Seneca to commit suicide or face something far worse. At the same time Nero had begun to persecute Christians, he also arrested and tried some prominent stoics.[428]

So it seems clear that Paul's first trial ended in an acquittal, but that Nero gained personal knowledge about this new religion that denied the emperor's deity and extolled the virtues of morality which he despised so much in the stoics. It is also probable that some prominent senatorial families may have been Christians at this time, such as the Marcellus and Pudens found in the *Acts of Peter*.[429] This would give Nero even more reason to hate Christians, for the word of Jesus was rapidly expanding across the empire.

Paul in Spain?

In Romans 15:24 Paul states his desire to go to Spain. At this time he had not even been to Rome, but hoped to stop by Rome en route to Spain. Circumstances would change his plans, but following his release from prison Paul visited many of his churches in Macedonia and Achaia. Tradition, however, says that he also fulfilled his desire to take the gospel to Hispania.

In the first century Clement spoke of Paul journeying to "the farthest bounds of the West."[430] "The farthest bounds" could only be Hispania. If this Clement was truly the Clement of Philippians 4:3 as some believe, then he would have known Paul, lending credibility this statement.

If Clement's statement is not clear enough, Hippolytus is more lucid, saying, "he advanced as far as Illyricum, and Italy, and Spain."[431] Some doubt this because he does not mention Spain in any of his pastoral letters, written during his final days in his second imprisonment. Nonetheless, Paul does not give details of his fourth journey in these letters, and only mentions a few places relevant to his discussions. This is, therefore, not sufficient grounds to reject the tradition which dates back to the first century, and possibly one of Paul's colleagues.

Owing to the fact that we know Paul, a trailblazer, wanted to go to Spain, and seeing the antiquity of the traditions, with no evidence to the contrary, I believe it is safe to believe that Paul did indeed reach Spain. He may have even been in Spain when news of Peter's arrest reached him.

His Return to Rome

Why Paul returned to Rome and when he died are tied to one another. Some hold that he was arrested and brought back to Rome,[432] while other traditions say that Paul returned of his own accord.[433] Both have problems, and both have benefits.

Merrill Unger believed that Paul was arrested and brought to Rome around 67 A.D.[434] The problem is that under

Nero's edict there could be no appeals even for Roman citizens. Confessing to be a Christian was sufficient grounds of execution without trial.[435] Moreover, although revisionist historians are wrong to claim that persecutions were restricted to Rome,[436] it is true that persecutions were concentrated there. Persecutions outside Italy were sporatic, as Nero was increasingly unpopular and most governors had no desire to destabalize their communities. Some would kill a token number of Christians to satisfy any query from Rome, but then stop. If Paul was arrested it would have been because he was recognized as the leader of the Christians, but Peter was already a captive (and by Unger's chronology dead). Why was Paul alone targeted? Why were the other apostles not targeted? Could it be because Nero remembered Paul and sought him out? This is possible, but it is not likely that Paul ever met Nero again face to face, as Christians were now facing summary execution. There is another alternative as expressed in the apocryphal writings.

The *Acts of the Holy Apostles Peter and Paul* says that Paul returned to Rome in hopes of assisting the church. The *Acts of Peter* also implies that Paul returned of his own accord. Why? Surely he would not have been so naive as to willingly walk into the "lion's mouth" (cf. 2 Timothy 4:17). The answer to this lays in two factors. One; what his intentions were. Two; when he returned.

If Paul had heard of the fire in Rome and of Peter's subsequent arrest, might Paul's fatherly instincts for his church have kicked in? Could it be that he thought Seneca was still Nero's advisor and believed he could reason with emperor? Since Seneca's retirement was kept secret from the public this is possible. Or perhaps he simply wanted to enter Rome surreptitiously to help his flock in times of distress. All of these are possibilities if he returned to Rome in 65 A.D. If it was later then this becomes less and less of a possibility. Why? Consider this famous quote by the pagan historian Tacitus:

> "Nero fastened the guilt and inflicted the most exquisite tortures on a class hated for their abominations, called Christians by the populace. Christus, from whom the name had its origin, suffered the extreme penalty during the reign of Tiberius at the hands of one of our procurators, Pontius Pilatus, and a

most mischievous superstition, thus checked for the moment, again broke out not only in Judaea, the first source of the evil, but even in Rome, where all things hideous and shameful from every part of the world find their centre and become popular. Accordingly, an arrest was first made of all who pleaded guilty; then, upon their information, an immense multitude was convicted, not so much of the crime of firing the city, as of hatred against mankind. Mockery of every sort was added to their deaths. Covered with the skins of beasts, they were torn by dogs and perished, or were nailed to crosses, or were doomed to the flames and burnt, to serve as a nightly illumination, when daylight had expired."[437]

The atrocities to which Christians were subject goes far beyond even what Tacitus records in this passage, for he offers only a brief glimpse here. Had Paul heard of these incidents he would surely have known that there was no hope of reasoning with Nero. Seneca himself was ordered to commit suicide in 65 A.D. While it is possible that Paul wanted to be with his suffering children, the possibility of Paul's returning to Rome on his own is only probable if he was in Rome shortly before or after the fire in Rome. If more than a year had passed, it is more likely that Paul was somehow recognized and arrested. Given Clement's strange statement that Paul "had been seven times in bonds"[438] this possible (but see notes on Andronicus in chapter 15), but once again hinges upon the year of his death, so let us examine that.

Date of His Martyrdom
Four dates have been variously given for Paul's execution. The first is that he died with Peter in 65 A.D.,[439] the second is that of Aurelius Prudentius Clemens (a fourth century poet) who claimed that Paul died on the same date as Peter, but a year after,[440] the third view is that he died "two years later" in 67 A.D.,[441] and the last view is that he died in the "last year of Nero" which was 68 A.D.[442]

The last view seems to be taken from Hippolytus's remark that Paul had been "preaching the Gospel for five-and-thirty years."[443] Since Hippolytus places Paul's conversion a year after the resurrection in 34 A.D., this would place Paul's execution in 69 A.D. Of course, Nero was already dead by that time, so it is assumed that this is a rounded off number and his death is pushed back to 68 A.D.[444] Later writers, taking this at face value, have since argued that Paul died in the fourteenth year of Nero, which was his last.[445] Given Hippolytus's antiquity we might be inclined to accept this, but the first view is actually older than Hippolytus, dating back to at least the mid-second century, so we must examine the other views first before reaching a conclusion.

The *Acts of Abdias* says that Paul died two years after Peter.[446] Since most (but by no means all) place Peter's death early in the persecutions, this would mean Paul died around 67 A.D. Now there are multiple problems with this chronology. First, *Abdias*'s source is probably much later than Hippolytus or Dionysius. Second, John Foxe noted that *Abdias* appears to contradict himself in his own chronology, for he seems to place Peter's crucifixion before the end of Paul's first trial (which he apparently believed to be his only trial). Said John Foxe, "if it be true which Abdias also saith ... then must it be ten years betwixt the martyrdom of Peter and of Paul ... so Abdias seemeth neither to agree with other authors, nor with himself."[447] A final curiosity among advocates of this view is the decision of the famed chronologer Archbishop Ussher, who advocates the 67 A.D. date, and yet inexplicably had Paul acquitted by Nero *a second time* after the fire in Rome and after the writing of 1 and 2 Timothy when Paul clearly states his belief that he would die![448]

What then of Aurelius Prudentius Clemens's claim that Paul died on the same date as Peter, but a year after?[449] This argument seems sound at first, for it explains why Dionysius believed that Peter and Paul died "at the same time"[450] while other authors have them dying in different years. However, for this very same reason we may reject the view. Prudentius was a fourth century poet who may have assumed this in order to reconcile the seemingly contradictory views of the historians of his day. This view is also the least supported in history. Therefore, let us examine the earliest tradition.

The earliest extant record that we have regarding the time of Paul's execution is that of the second century bishop Dionysius of Corinth. His statement was made in a matter of fact manner to the church in Rome, where Paul had died. In it he said simply that Peter and Paul "suffered martyrdom at the same time."[451] Not only is this the earliest tradition, but because of the manner in which it is given, we may assume that the church of Rome did not contest this view. Dionysius is simply speaking of the great martyrs of the church and of those who died in Rome and of whom the Roman church of that time honored.

Moreover, if Archbishop Ussher believed that Paul had been acquitted *a second time* by Nero even while slaughtering Christians in the Circus Maximus, then this would mean that Ussher agreed that there was a second imprisonment in 65 A.D.[452] On this Ussher is completely correct. However, the only reason that Ussher could possibily see Paul's being released while Christians were being used as human torches seems to be belief that Paul died two years after Peter. Nevertheless, he agreed that Paul had returned to Rome early during the start of the persecutions. In this respect Ussher lends ironic support to the theory that Peter and Paul both died on the same day.

Logically, there is no reason to doubt this most ancient tradition. Peter, we know, was held a prisoner for at least nine months (see chapter 2). If Paul returned to help the church he too would have been captured. Nero was not interested in trials or appeals (for there would have been thousands of Roman citizens demanding appeals). When Nero decided to execute the church leaders, he would have had them both executed at the same time. Peter, who was not a citizen of Rome, suffered the torment of crucifixion after seeing his wife led away to execution. Paul, being a Roman citizen of high standing, was given the more merciful execution of beheading (of which all historians agree). This took place approximately June 29, 65 A.D.

Summary

Who better to replace the traitor of Christ, Judas Iscariot, than one who became a traitor to the enemies of Christ. Paul, whether he be reconned as the twelfth or thirteenth apostle, once persecuted the church, only to become one of its most fiercest supporters and missionaries.

A trailblazer, Paul ventured out into the gentile world long before the other apostles began to fully embrace the Great Commission. After studying the Scriptures in Arabia for a number of years Paul moved into Syria and from there to Cyprus and Asia Minor in the countries then called Lycia and Galatia, as well as the surrounding regions in what is the southwestern tip of Turkey. He returned to Jerusalem for the famous council of Jerusalem around 48 or 49 A.D. but soon returned to the mission field, entering into the ancient countries of Cilicia, Galatia, and skirting around the edge of the country called Asia until coming to the seaport city of Troas. From there he crossed over into Macedonia and Achaia (modern day Greece). His third journey revisted many of the same cities, but also further expanded the churches in Asia Minor and Greece.

It was then that Paul was arrested upon his return to Judea. He was to be brought in chains before the emperor Nero, and Christianity was to be cast into the forefront of world history; from a small Judean religious sect of Judaism to a religion that caught the eye, and wrath, of Nero.

While still under the influence of the great senator Seneca, Paul was granted his freedom in 62 A.D., but Nero now knew about this religious sect and his hatred for all things good and pure, which had led him to rape vestal virgins,[453] plunged Christianity into his crosshairs.

In the meantime Paul returned to his missionary work, strengthing the church of Greece and Asia, and probably venturing as far as Spain. This took place over two years when news arrived of a travesty in Rome which threatened the church there. On July 19, 64 A.D. a massive fire erupted, just "coincidentally" in the rich housing community where Nero had wanted to build his "Golden House."[454] After the fire Nero almost immediately set about building that Golden House in commemoration to himself. The people of Rome suspected Nero was behind the fire, and so Nero set out to deflect blame to the Christians he hated so much. Did they not prophesy that the world would end in fire?

Peter was arrested in Rome and thrown in prison, doubtless while they tried to "extract" a confession. Other Christians were executed, but upon seeing that they would not fight in the arena Nero soon devised more devious manners of execution. Early in 65 A.D. Paul arrived in Rome. Whether he had been arrested or returned on his own in hopes helping the church, he was taken immediately to prison. This time Paul had no doubt that there would be no acquital, and he probably was not even given a trial. In the month or two he spent in prison awaiting execution he composed his last few epistles, comforting himself knowing that "I have fought the good fight, I have finished the course, I have kept the faith" (2Timothy 4:7). His reward was coming soon. Somewhere around June 29, 65 A.D. both he and Peter were put to death. Paul was beheaded, and then buried in the catacombs.[455]

Tintoretto – Execution of St. Paul – 1552

15

The Apostle's Companions

It has been demonstrated from history that all the apostles, save John, died a martyr's death. Unique among history is the fact that their blood, surrendered peacefully, wrought more change and won more victories than all the blood surrendered by force throughout human history.

What of the apostles' companions? Did they too die a martyr's death? Some of the apostles' companions are better known to readers today than some of the apostles. Mark and Luke, for example, who wrote part of the New Testament, or even Barnabas who journeyed with Paul. Did these men also die martyrs?

Of all the names mentioned in the Bible, some merely in passing, we do not know about most. Many are listed by Hippolytus as members of the seventy (Luke 10:1), but his list is suspect in some respects. For example, he list Luke as a member of the seventy and yet Luke was a gentile who almost certainly was not a convert at the time Jesus selected the seventy. Some others who appear on his list may not have been converts until later and thus were not among the seventy. Nevertheless, we do know about some of these men; usually, the martyrs.

Not all of the apostles' companions died a martyr's death, but many did, and those are the ones whom faithful followers recorded for honor among the saints. I have listed, therefore, only those companions of which we have reliable (or reasonable) information; most of whom were martyrs. They are listed alphabetically for easy reference.

Andronicus

Andronicus is mentioned only in the book of Romans where Paul refers to him, and a Junias, as "my kinsmen and my fellow prisoners, who are outstanding among the apostles, who also were in Christ before me" (16:7). Since Andronicus and Junias are called "fellow prisoners" with Paul, it is clear that this would have to have been before Paul was taken to Rome, for when he wrote the epistle to Rome he had not yet been to Rome (cf. Romans 1:11; 15:24). It is probable that this took place during one of Paul's journeys for he was called before proconsuls on more than one occasion (cf. Acts 13:8-12; 18:12). This would also explain Clement's statement that Paul "had been seven times in bonds."[456]

Hippolytus calls Andronicus, but not Junias, one of the seventy,[457] which is quite possible given Paul's testimony that he was "in Christ before me" (16:7). Further, according to Hippolytus he was a bishop of Pannonia.[458] Now Pannonia is not a city, but a region which would correspond today to the region where Hungary, Croatia, Bosnia, and Serbia meet.

According to the early martyrologists they died under Nero's persecution.[459] Whether they died in Pannonia under Nero's edict or had come to Rome at some point, the testimony of the early martyrologists, little as it may be, is clear that they died under Nero's brutal persecution. What manner of death we do not know. They may have been fed to lions, or used as human torches, or perhaps one of Nero's other devious tortures. We can only say that they died for Christ under Nero's reign.

Henry Siemiradzki – Nero's Torches – 1877

Antipas

Antipas is mentioned by the apostle John, wherein the Lord Himself calls him "My witness, My faithful one, who was killed among you" (Revelation 2:13). This testimony alone is strong enough. From this we know that Antipas served in the chuch of Pergamum, which is modern day Aeolis, Turkey. We also know that he died a martyr's death worthy of the Lord's mention in Revelation. According to the early martyrologists his manner of death was particularly cruel. It is said that he was sealed in a bronze idol and cooked to death. This took place approximately 95 A.D. during the early phase of Domitian's persecution,[460] probably about the same time John was arrested and brought to Rome.

Aquila and Priscilla (Prisca)

Aquila and Priscilla (or Prisca) were husband and wife. They are mentioned three times in the book of Acts, and three times in the epistles of Paul. Although a Jewish native of Pontus (northern Turkey) Aquila had been living in Rome until Claudius expelled the Jews (Acts 18:2). They met Paul in Corinth, Achaia (Greece) and soon became close friends and associates. They worked building tents together (Acts 18:3) and were with Paul as traveling companions for at least the latter part of his second journey (Acts 18:18). Aquila and Priscilla also appear to have shown good knowledge of the faith, for it was they who first enlightened Apollos to a deeper understanding of the Lord Jesus (Acts 18:26).

Paul's love for them is obvious, for he states in Romans that they risked their own lives for him (16:3). We also know that they were at Rome when Paul wrote his epistle to Rome (16:3) and appear to have been of some prominence there since they were the first to whom Paul addressed his postscript after commending Phoebe (16:1). Since they had originally come from Rome before the expulsion by Claudius, it is reasonable that they returned to Rome and helped to found the church there. This seems to be what the early church fathers believed as well.

The *Apostolic Constitutions* says that Aquila was the "brethren of Clement, bishop and citizen of Rome, who was the disciple of Paul."[461] In apocryphal stories attributed to Clement, Aquila is seen assisting Peter in Rome against the heresies of Simon Magus.[462] He is also portayed as a fellow traveler with Peter by some church fathers.[463] Now I have rejected the Simon Magus apocrypha as mere personification of the theological war with gnosticism, but even as a work of historical fiction the appearance of Aquila as a man of prominence in the church of Rome, and a colleague of Clement (who would later become overseer, or bishop, of Rome), would make no sense unless he was well known to the church of Rome as one of their founding members. If tradition is to be believed then they became traveling companions of Luke after the death of Paul and evangelized Greece and Macedonia,[464] although the accounts of their martydom cast doubt upon this.

As to how they died, we only know that they both appear as martyrs under Nero's terrible reign.[465] Given that they were leaders in Rome, this is entirely probable. The exact manner of their death we can only guess. They might have been fed to wild animals or used as human tortures, or worse. One crime which Nero was known to have used was to cut open the belly of Christian prisoners and pour grain in the open wounds. Pigs would then be released to feed upon the victim.[466] Whatever the manner, they died martyrs and deserve to be remembered as among the best of Paul's companions who laid down their lives for Christ.

Aristarchus

Aristarchus is found five times in the Bible. He is called one of "Paul's traveling companions from Macedonia" (Acts 19:29). He was also imprisoned with Paul during his first imprisonment (Colossians 4:10). Tradition ascibes to him the title of overseer at Thessalonica for some time after this,[467] and he is also called one of the seventy by Hippolytus.[468] Later he is said to have been found in Rome, captured by Nero's men and fed to the lions in the arena.[469]

Barnabas (Joseph Barnabas)

"Joseph [was] a Levite of Cyprian birth, who was also called Barnabas by the apostles (which translated means Son of Encouragement)" (Acts 4:36). It was Barnabas who was to become one of the apostle Paul's closest friends and colleagues. When most of the apostles were in fear of the new convert Paul, it was Barnabas who trusted Paul and defended him before the apostles (Acts 9:27).

Despite what was to be a close association, they did have a fall out of sorts when Paul became angry at John Mark, Barnabas's cousin (Colossians 4:10), because of perceived abandonment (Acts 15:38). Barnabas refused to leave Mark, and so they parted ways. Barnabas then set out with John Mark for Cyprus (Acts 15:39). This is the last we read of Barnabas in Acts, although he mentioned in several of Paul's epistles and they remained friends. What happened to Barnabas after this?

Some apocrypha claims that Barnabas preached the gospel in Rome during the reign of Tiberius Caesar,[470] but this seems to be pure fiction, for Tiberius died in 37 A.D. and Barnabas was already with Paul in Jerusalem about that time (cf. Acts 9:27, Galatians 1:18). Moreover, it was Paul who first ventured out to gentiles, so he would never have ventured to Rome so early by himself. This tradition can be rejected.

Hippolytus called Barnabas a bishop of Heraclea in the Aegean sea, but this is almost certainly conflated with Barsabas, because Hippolytus believes they are one and the same (see below).[471] Once again, we can reject this tradition as it has no support from any other source.

The best source we have for Barnabas comes from the *Acts of Barnabas* which is one of the earliest aporyphal writings and one with the fewest embellishments. It claims to have been written by John Mark, although most doubt this with good reason.[472] Nevertheless, most accept it as a predominantly historical work with only mild additions. It is also of interest for its introduction of the gospel of Matthew. In one passage it is said that Barnabas had just received copies of a gospel from Matthew which he began to distribute. It also says, "Barnabas, having unrolled the Gospel which he had received from Matthew his fellow-labourer, began to teach the Jews."[473] This agrees with the fact that Matthew was the first gospel written and distributed before the council of Jerusalem. Most of the apostles apparently took it with them, but did not have any of the other gospels as of yet.

As to the story itself, Barnabas and John Mark are said to have traveled to Cyprus and neighboring islands. It was on Cyprus, however, where most of their work was done. How many years were spent in these missions is not said but the end of Barnabas is described as taking place when a man named Barjesus "was enraged, and brought together all the multitude of the Jews; and they having laid hold of Barnabas ... took Barnabas by night, and bound him with a rope by the neck; and having dragged him to the hippodrome from the synagogue, and having gone out of the city, standing round him, they burned him with fire, so that even his bones became dust."[474] John Mark is said to have escaped along with Timon (cf. Acts 6:5) and fled to Egypt.

Most accept this as historical, but the chronology is difficult. Some place it in 64 A.D. shortly before the death of Paul,[475] but others place it late in 73 A.D.[476] Neither view seems acceptable.

Paul mentions Barnabas in 1 Corinthians 9:6, but no where does Paul send greetings to or from his close associate as he normally did. We cannot attribute this to the falling out for Paul explicitly sends greetings from "Barnabas's cousin Mark" (Colossians 4:10). Since he was reconciled with Mark by this time, we can only assume that Barnabas died sometime between the writing of 1 Corinthians and Colossians. Moreover, if the *Acts of Barnabas* is to be taken as largely historical, then it would have to be before Mark established himself in Alexandria (see below). Now most date 1 Corinthians from the mid 50s, say 55 A.D.[477] Colossians, however, is one of the "prison epistles" which he wrote at sometime during his first imprisonment, either in Jerusalem or Rome, between 58 and 62 A.D. when he was released.

If Mark did found the church of Alexandria, as tradition argues, then Barnabas must have died fairly early. This would point to a martyrdom date closer to the early to mid fifties. Thus Barnabas was dragged to his death where he was burned at the stake somewhere around 55 A.D.

164

Barsabbas (Joseph Justus Barsabas)

In Acts 1:23 two men are put forward as possible replacements for Judas Iscariot. The first was "Joseph called Barsabbas (who was also called Justus)." We then read nothing else of him, or do we?

Beginning with Clement of Alexandria many have assumed that Barsabbas and Barnabas are one and the same.[478] This error is repeated by Eusebius[479] and echoed down to Van Braght who speaks of the "multiplicity of his names."[480] Where did this notion originate?

It could be that because Barnabas's given name was Joseph, like Barsabbas (Acts 4:36), Clement mistook them for the same person. There may also be some confusion with the Judas Barsabbas of Acts 15:22, who was a prophet (15:32). In any case, there is no reason to believe that Barnabas and Barsabbas were the same person. Joseph was a very common name, and aside from having this same given name there is nothing in Scripture or history to suggest that they were identical. There is, however, some indication that Justus Barsabbas was different, for we have some traditions regarding his life, if not his death.

It is apparent that Barsabbas was one of the seventy (cf. Acts 1:21). According to Hippolytus the only Justus to be among the seventy served as a bishop at Eleutheropolis,[481] which lay approximately twenty miles southwest of Jerusalem, and about ten miles west of Hebron. This same Justus also became, if tradition is to be believed, the third bishop of Jerusalem after James the Just and Simeon, the son of Cleopas.[482]

Beyond this we know nothing of Barsabbas save Papias's matter of fact statement that he was forced to drink poison but suffered no harm (cf. Mark 16).[483] If tradition is of any value, this was not uncommon among the early church. We read many accounts of Christians being forced to drink poison, but when the poison was found to take no effect, the Christians were subjected to other forms of execution. We might then infer that Barsabbas died a martyr's death, but Papias's failure to mention this cast doubt on that. Certainly given the political situation in Jerusalem at that time makes this is a strong possibility, but only a possibility for where history is silent, so must we be silent.

Carpus

Carpus was one of the seventy and is described by some as the bishop pf Troas,[484] but by others as the bishop of Berytus in Thracia.[485] Given that his only appearance in the Bible is when Paul asks Timothy to "bring the cloak which I left at Troas with Carpus" (2 Timothy 4:13) it seems apparent that Carpus was overseer there in Troas, on the coastal city of modern day Turkey. We do not know any specifics about his death save that he died a martyr in Troas, quite probably during the Neronian persecutions.[486]

Dionysius

Dionysius the Areopagite was presumably a convert of the apostle Paul (Acts 17:34). He is listed as among the seventy by some martyrologists[487] but not by Hippolytus.[488] If he was a convert of Paul, then he most likely was not among the seventy, unless the seventy were, for a time, replenished with successors; which I doubt. We have no information on him except that he was among those who died a martyr, probably during Trajan's reign.[489]

Epaphas

Epaphas was a prisoner along with Paul during his first imprisonment (Colossians 1:7; 4:12; Philemon 1:23). Like Paul, and many others, he probably escaped his first trial, but following the fire in Rome, he was eventually arrested again and and slain for his faith in Christ.[490]

Ignatius Theophorus

Ignatius, though not mentioned in the Bible, was an acquaintance of Onesimus and allegedly tutored under John along with Polycarp. Legend claims that he was the child called by Jesus in Matthew 18:2.[491] This is probably pure legend, but his association with the apostles, though not mentioned therein, has long been held, and given his position and proximity to them, it is almost certain.

Eusebius says that Ignatius became the bishop of Antioch, Syria[492] probably around 66 or 67 A.D. His surname, Theophorus means "the Bearer of God." Among his famous quotations was that "the life of man is a continual death, unless it be that Christ lives in us."[493] He survived the first two persecutions under Nero and Domitian, but under Trajan's reign, about 111 A.D., Ignatius was arrested and brought to Rome as a sort of trophy for the emperor; perhaps because he was among the last of the apostolic fathers who had actually seen and heard the apostles. Ignatius's famous epistles, which survive to this day, were all written during his imprisonment journey to Rome. When he arrived, all Rome had heard of the circus and that Ignatius, one of a hundful who remained alive that had witnessed and spoken to the apostles, was to be fed to wild beasts. Calmly entering the arena, Ignatius's words from his epistles were reflected in his death, as well as his life. "As the world hates the Christians, so God loves them."[494]

Jean-Leon Gerome – The Christian Martyr's Last Prayer – 1860

Lions were said to have devoured his so that even his bones were knawed in half.[495] His martyrdom served as a rally to believers during the time of Trajan. Martyrdom was now looked to as something almost to be desired, as emulating Christ.

It was this faithfulness and eagerness to die for what is right that would profoundly change the empire, and the world.

Indich (or Fudich, the Ethiopian Eunuch)

Acts 8 relates the story of the Ethiopian Eunuch to whom Philip taught the gospel. Here is the story in full:

> "An angel of the Lord spoke to Philip saying, 'Get up and go south to the road that descends from Jerusalem to Gaza.' (This is a desert *road*.) So he got up and went; and there was an Ethiopian eunuch, a court official of Candace, queen of the Ethiopians, who was in charge of all her treasure; and he had come to Jerusalem to worship, and he was returning and sitting in his chariot, and was reading the prophet Isaiah. Then the Spirit said to Philip, Go up and join this chariot. Philip ran up and heard him reading Isaiah the prophet, and said, Do you understand what you are reading? And he said, Well, how could I, unless someone guides me? And he invited Philip to come up and sit with him. Now the passage of Scripture which he was reading was this: 'He was led as a sheep to slaughter; and as a lamb before its shearer is silent, so He does not open his mouth. In humiliation His judgment was taken away; who will relate His generation? For His life is removed from the earth.' The eunuch answered Philip and said, 'Please *tell me*, of whom does the prophet say this? Of himself or of someone else?' Then Philip opened his mouth, and beginning from this Scripture he preached Jesus to him. As they went along the road they came to some water; and the eunuch said, 'Look! Water! What prevents me from being baptized?' [And Philip said, 'If you believe with all your heart, you may.' And he answered and said, 'I believe that Jesus Christ is the Son of God.'] And he ordered the chariot to stop; and they both went down into the water, Philip as well as the eunuch, and he baptized him. When they came up out of the water, the Spirit of the Lord snatched Philip away; and the eunuch no longer saw him, but went on his way rejoicing" (Acts 8:26-39)."

Many questions have been asked about this encounter, such as why an Ethiopian would even be reading the Scriptures, but Ethiopia actually has a long tradition, true or not, that their kings and queens are descendants of King Solomon through the Queen of Sheba, who ruled over Ethiopia as well as southern Arabia.[496] It is therefore no surprise that an Ethiopian Eunuch would have been a Jewish proselyte. Nor is it a surprise that the Lord had desired the Great Commission to commence at once, and reach out into all the world.

Tradition calls this eunuch Indich or Fudich.[497] He is alleged to have been the founder of the church of Ethiopia,[498] which seems logical. As a man of some prominence he would certainly have had authority to found a church with Candice's permission. Moreover, upon her death Indich would probably have become a free man due to his prominent position. It is then, we are told, that he began to preach the gospel in Arabia Felix (Saudi Arabia) and one of the many tiny islands off the coast of Ethiopia in the Red Sea, called Caprobano or Ceylon. Today it called the Dahlak Archipelago in the country of Eritrea. There he was martyred in circa 110 A.D.[499]

John Mark

With the exception of Luke, perhaps there is no companion of the apostles better known than Mark. Universally held to be the author of the gospel which bears his name, Papias said of him that "Mark having become the interpreter of Peter, wrote down accurately whatsoever he remember. It was not, however, in exact order that he related the sayings of deeds of Christ. For he neither heard the Lord nor accompanied Him. But afterwards, as I said, he accompanied Peter, who accommodated his instructions."[500] Clement of Alexandria said that "being a the companion of Peter, he would leave in writing a record of the teaching which had been delivered to them verbally."[501] Interestingly enough, the tradition found in the *Acts of Barnabas* states that Mark had a copy of the gospel of Matthew, before having written his own gospel.[502] Clement was, of course, a bishop of Alexandria which is supposed to have been founded by Mark.

The *Teachings of the Apostles* calls him "Mark from Alexandria the Great"[503] and says that "Alexandria the Great, and Thebais, and the whole of Inner Egypt, and all the country of Pelusium, and extending as far as the borders of the Indians [or rather Ethiopia - see endnote], received the apostles' ordination to the priesthood from Mark the evangelist, who was ruler and guide there in the church which he had built, in which, he also ministered."[504]

The question is how did Mark get to Alexandria? He is last heard of in Acts as departing with his cousin Barnabas (cf. Colossians 4:10) for the island of Cyprus (Acts 15:39). He had traveled with Paul on his first journey, but apparently left for some reason at Pamphylia, in southern Turkey. This angered Paul which was the reason that he and Barnabas split, for Barnabas refused to leave his cousin behind. Nevertheless, all was apparently forgiven as Mark is mentioned three times by Paul in his epistles, including a letter to Timothy when he specifically requested that Mark come to see him, "for he is useful to me for service" (2 Timothy 4:11). He is also mentioned affectionately as "son" by Simon Peter in 1 Peter 5:13.

According to the *Acts of Barnabas* Mark fled Cyprus after the martyrdom of Barnabas and "we found an Egyptian ship; and having embarked in it, we landed at Alexandria. And there I remained, teaching the brethren that came the word of the Lord"[505] When was this? As stated under Barnabas, I believe this must have taken place just before 55 A.D. Nicephorous said "he journeyed to Africa, filling Libya, Marmorica, Ammonica, and Pentapolis with the doctrine of the holy Gospel."[506]

Thus the universal testimony of the ancients was that Mark spent some time in Egypt spreading the gospel in the nearby regions, but it is equally clear that he was in Rome at some point thereafter. He is described as a fellow prisoner of Paul in Philemon 1:24 during Paul's first imprisonment and Paul had requested his presence as well during his second imprisonment (2 Timothy 4:11). Peter's epistle is also said to have been written after the fire in Rome and the beginning of the persecutions (1 Peter 5:13). Thus we may conclude that Mark had been reunited with Paul sometime during his first imprisonment (58-62 A.D.). We also know that he was in Rome shortly after the persecutions of Nero erupted (cf. 2 Timothy 4:11; 1 Peter 5:13).

What then can we make this? If Hippolytus is to be believed then Mark was at one time a bishop of Apollonia, Illyria,[507] in modern day Albania, northwest of Greece. When would this have happened? It seems that Mark spent many years in Egypt and the surrounding region, after which he rejoined Paul and was taken prisoner to Rome. After their first acquittal it may be that Mark journeyed to the Aegean sea with Paul, and then separated to minister in Illyria whereas Paul went on to Spain. However, when the fire in Rome erupted, Mark returned to Rome at Paul's request, meeting with Peter and Paul before their martyrdom. It is here, however, that Mark's history becomes confused in the traditions.

Mark Dragged through the Street with Hooks – 1742

All ancient traditions place Mark's death in Alexandria, but at different times and with slightly differing accounts. One account says that Mark was fastened with hooks and dragged through the streets until he died.[508] Another ancient tradition says that he was dragged out to a place called "Bucolus" where they had hoped to burn him alive, but he had died en route.

171

They decided to burn the body, but heavy rains prevented them from so doing.[509] Finally, another tradition records that he was dragged with hooks to "Bucolus" where he was burned alive.[510] From these traditions it is most likely that he was dragged through the streets to the place of execution. There he was tied to a stake for burning, but whether he was still alive when they lit the fires cannot be said.

The greater problem is the date of his death. The *Babylon Namebook* says that he died in the eight year of Nero, but Dorotheus places his death in the times of Trajan (between 112 and 117 A.D.). Clearly the Neronian date must be rejected. First, the eighth year of Nero would 62 A.D. when we know he was with Paul. We also know that Paul was released, and so must have Mark. Moreover, Eusebius claims that Mark surrendered his bishopry of Alexandria for a time, after ten years.[511] However, it is not clear if Eusebius saw this Mark of Alexandria as the same as Mark the Evangelist and gospel author. For one thing, he claimed that Mark was "appointed" as a replacement for the first bishop after fifteen years, and then retired after ten years. Assuming the Alexandrian church was founded in 55 A.D. this would mean he became bishop around 70 A.D. and retired around 80 A.D.[512] Certainly this would fit better with the view that Mark of Alexandria died under Trajan. So the question is whether or not Mark of Alexandria was Mark the Evangelist or whether or not their traditions have become conflated.

One possibility is that Mark did indeed found the church of Alexandria, for it seems universal from antiquity that he did, but that this Mark, bishop of Alexandria, is another Mark with whom the famed evangelist has been mistaken. One thing is clear, this Mark of Alexandria was most probably the one dragged through the streets with hooks during the reign of Trajan. His death has traditionally been observed as April 21,[513] but the year is confused (possibly because of confusion with the evangelist). Mark was young enough that he may well have lived unto the time of Trajan, as did John who was older than him. Consequently, I will tentatively say the following.

It was Mark who founded the church of Alexandria around 55 A.D. and appointed the first bishop or overseer while he evangelized the surrounding areas. Leaving the church in the care of this Eumenes,[514] Mark returned to meet Peter and Paul. He was later imprisoned with Paul during his first imprisonment. Following their acquittal Mark probably journeyed with Paul to the Aegean areas where he left to evangelize the Illyrium. There he served for a while in Apollonia. He then returned to Rome at Paul's request following the fires of Rome. He met with both Peter and Paul before their execution, but appears to have escaped death himself, eventually returning to Alexandria which he made his home. He served for a time as overseer (or bishop) after Eumenes died, but stepped down to devote himself to other duties. He met his death in the times of Trajan, being dragged through the streets with hooks, and being burned at the stake.

Jude, the Brother of James

Under Judas Thaddæus I presented my case that he and Jude were not the same person. This Jude is the brother of James the Just, but not Judas Thaddæus (see chapter 11 for my defense of this). Consequently, it becomes obvious that the traditions of Judas Thaddæus were conflated with those of Jude. By separating the conflicting traditions it became obvious which should apply to Judas Thaddæus and which should apply to Jude. Unfortunately, there is only a little that can be definitively said of Jude. Let us, therefore, look first at what can be gleaned from the epistle of Jude.

Jude, the brother of James, does not call himself Jesus's brother (Jude 1). Nor does he call himself an apostle, but rather beseeches his readers to "remember the words that were spoken beforehand by the apostles of our Lord Jesus Christ" (v. 17). Most scholars place the date for Jude's writing in the late 60s. Some, however, believe that this reference to "remember ... beforehand" indicate an even later date, around 80 A.D.[515] Clearly it implies that most of the apostles had already died. If we exclude John, then the last of the apostles to die had died around 74 A.D. Jude may have been written after this time.

This calls into question Jude's age. He was probably James's younger brother, and if this be so then he may be the same Jude (or Judas) whom Eusebius calls the last Jewish bishop of Jerusalem.[516] The problem with this is that it was Hadrian who expelled all Jews from Jerusalem around 132 A.D. However, Eusebius's list does not fit chronologically. He list fifteen bishops from Christ until Hadrian, but the second bishop he names, Simeon, son of Cleopas, he claims did not die until he was 120 years old![517] How then could thirteen bishops have followed him?

One thing that seems clear is that the Judas of whom Hippolytus speaks is not the apostle, despite what Hippolytus thinks. He claims that Jude died in Berytus (Beruit), Lebanon of a natural death.[518] A Syrian tradition, which also conflates Jude with Judas Thaddæus, says that Jude fell ill and died the fourteenth of the month Iyar"[519] (the beginning of May). We know that these traditions do not belong to Thaddæus (see chapter 11) and therefore rightly belong to Jude. Thus it seems that Jude died an old man in Lebannon. This fits the facts, for it seems reasonable that Jude left Jerusalem before its conquest by Rome in 70 A.D. Jude 17 implies a remoteness from the apostles which further indicates that some time had passed. It is likely that Jude died sometime after this, quite possible decades later, at peace.

Junias – See Andronicus

Justus (Joseph Barsabas) – See Barsabas

Linus

Linus is mentioned only in 2 Timothy as one of Paul's companions who was in Rome with him (4:21). All the ancient fathers claim that he was the *first* overseer (bishop) of Rome, although later church fathers make him out to be Peter's successor.

Irenaeus said, "the blessed apostles, then, having founded and built up the Church, committed into the hands of Linus the office of the episcopate. Of this Linus, Paul makes mention in the Epistles to Timothy."[520] Hegesippus also called him the first overseer of Rome.[521] Ignatius said that Linus was tutored by Paul[522] and Hippolytus counted him as one of the seventy.[523]

The real curiousity is in the "when" of his bishopry. All historians from the third to fourth century onward have tried to list Linus as the successor of Peter, and hence begin his bishopry in the mid 60s. However, the fourth century *Catalogus*

Liberianus says that Linus became overseer (bishop) in 56 A.D. and ended in 67 A.D.[524] Later papist seem to have "corrected" this since they hold that Peter was the first bishop of Rome. Nonetheless, this and the early apostolic fathers seems adequate proof that Linus served as the overseer of the Church while Peter and Paul, who were apostles and not bishops, yet lived. Moreover, it answers some curious questions.

There are some later traditions, or "legends" so the Catholics say,[525] that Linus died a martyr under Nero. Given the brutal persecution of Christians at that time and Linus's leadership role in the church it is hard to believe he would have escaped such a persecution. Catholics, however, must place Linus as the successor to Peter and hence delay his papacy until after Peter's death (despite the testimony of the apostolic fathers and the *Catalogus Liberianus*). They must also reject his martyrdom for this very reason, but the best evidence from the most ancient sources do not support this revision. The early witnesses describe Linus as overseer (or bishop) from 56 A.D. Perhaps Aquila did not want to be overseer himself, or perhaps he still did some traveling with Paul and could not commit to the office. In any case Linus served in Rome in a prominent role until the time of Nero when he may well have died along with thousands of his fellow believers, and the two great apostles, Peter and Paul.

Luke

Luke was both a physician (Colossians 4:14) and a historian who wrote the gospel of Luke and the book of Acts. He was a traveling companion of Paul who was with Paul up until the very end. Indeed, at the end of Paul's life he lamented that "only Luke is with me" (2 Timothy 4:11). Tradition says he was from Antioch and met Paul in that city.[526] The history of Luke, therefore, follows that of Paul up until his death.

After Paul's death it appears, so says the *Teaching of the Apostles*, that Luke started his own ministry in Macedonia.[527] It also says, "Byzantium, and all the country of Thrace, and of the parts about it as far as the great river, the boundary which separates from the barbarians, received the apostles' ordination to the priesthood from Luke the apostle, who himself built a church there, and ministered there in his office of Ruler and Guide which he held there."[528]   However, this same tradition gives Luke the title of an apostle and claims that Priscilla and Aquila accompanied Luke until his death.[529]   This is almost certainly incorrect, for most accounts have that Priscilla and Aquila dying under Nero's persecution (see notes under "Aquila"). We must therefore reject this part of the tradition, but that he did minister in the area of Macedonia, Greece, and Thrace seems supported by the accounts of Luke's martyrdom.

According to the *Babylon Namebook* Luke was preaching in Greece when Domitian began his persecution and passed an edict throughout the whole empire against Christians. At age eighty-four, in 93 A.D., Luke was hung by the neck upon an olive tree until dead.[530]

Nicanor

Nicanor was one of the seven deacons who, along with Stephen, was elected to care for the church duties so that the apostles could concentrate upon evangelism (Acts 6:5). According to Acts 8:1 the very day that Stephen died "a great persecution began against the church." If Dorotheus is to be believed then there were two thousand Christians slain that day, including Nicanor.[531]   That Nicanor died in this persecution is also attested by Hippolytus.[532]

Onesimus

Onesimus was an escaped slave who met Paul and became a convert (Philemon 10). Since being an escaped slave was punishable by crucifixion, and because Philemon had himself become a convert of Paul, the apostle sent a letter to Philemon urging him to take back Onesimus "no longer as a slave, but more than a slave, a beloved brother" (v. 16).

Ignatius, who knew the apostles, said that Onesimus became an overseer at Ephesus.[533]   He remained there, ministering the gospel until the time of Trajan when he was arrested and sent to Rome where he was stoned to death in 111 A.D.[534]

Onesiphorus

Onesiphorus is mentioned as a friend of Paul who was not ashamed to be seen with the prisoner when he was awaiting his execution (2 Timothy 1:16). Hippolytus called him a bishop, overseer, of Corone,[535] or Colophon, not far from Ephesus in Asia. Apparently his affection for Paul in chains did not escape the eyes of Rome. Sometime after returning to Asia he was arrested by the governor who had him scourged and then tied to wild horses which were unleashed. Thereupon he was dragged to death.[536]

Parmenas

Parmenas was another of the seven deacons (Acts 6:5). Of him we know almost nothing except that he is alleged to have been overseer in a city called Soli,[537] whose location today we can only guess. It is further said that he died a martyr, although the time and manner of his death also remain a mystery.[538]

Philip the Evangelist

Philip the Evangelist was one of the seven deacons (Acts 6:5; 15:2, 4, 6, 22-23; 16:4). Many believe he is the one who converted the Ethiopian Eunuch, rather than the apostle Philip.[539] Conversely there are many who believe that the apostle Philip is one and the same as Philip the Evangelist. However, I have demonstrated that in chapter six that I believe these to be two different individuals. It is, in part, because the apostle Philip died fairly early in north Africa that the fame of Philip the Evangelist grew and later authors began to confuse them. It would seem that Philip the Evangelist was actually more famous than Philip the Apostle!

What is clear from the eariest of sources is that Philip settled in Hierapolis of Asia with his four prophetess daughters (Acts 21:9).[540] Unlike the apostle, who "gave his daughters in marriage,"[541] at least three of the four daughters of Philip the Evangelist are said to have died virgins, and been buried with their father in Hierapolis.[542]

Hippolytus said that "Philip preached in Phrygia, and was crucified in Hierapolis with his head downward in the time of Domitian,"[543] but the apocryphal *Acts of Philip* says that he died in the time of Trajan.[544] The manner of death is very close to Hippolytus's description. It says the prefect "ordered Philip to be hanged, and his ankles to be pierced, and to bring also iron hooks, and his heels also to be driven through, and to be hanged head downwards."[545]

Although the description of crucifixion in the *Acts of Philip* is probably accurate, the date given by Hippolytus makes more sense. Philip was present with the apostles from the beginning. Even if he was only twenty years old at the time, this would mean he was born no later than 14 A.D. The persecutions of Trajan began around 111 A.D. or thereabouts. Obviously Philip would have been close to a hundred (or more) years of age. While this is possible, Hippolytus seems more credible than the apocryphal *Acts of Philip* which is filled with embellishments and factual errors. I, therefore, conclude that Philip died in Hierapolis, about the same time John was taken to Rome by Domitian, and was crucified upside down in the manner so described.

Priscilla (or Prisca) – See Aquila

Prochorus

Prochorus was another of the seven deacons of Acts 6:5. He is counted as one of the seventy and called an overseer of the church in Nicomedia, Bithynia[546] which is about fifty miles east of modern day Istabul, Turkey. Curiously though, Hippolytus says that he "was the first that departed, believing together with his daughters."[547] Perhaps he meant that Prochorus was among the first to leave for foreign missions.

Prochorus is also said to be a nephew of Stephen and a companion of the apostle John.[548] He is said to have died under the persecutions of Nero in Antioch.[549]

Rufus

Rufus is mentioned in Romans 16:13 as being at Rome. It is probable that this Rufus is the same son of Simon of Cyrene

(Mark 15:21), as his mother was dear to Paul (Romans 16:13). Polycarp mentions Rufus, and a certain Zosimus, along with Ignatius and Paul as leaders of the church in Asia.[550] Hippolytus calls him one of the seventy and the overseer of Thebes, Greece near Corinth.[551]

Of particular interest is the fact that Rufus and Zosimus were spoken of so highly by Polycarp in a letter addressed to Philippi, which is the same city where the two men are said to have been martyred. If the date for Polycarp's epistle is correct, then these two men had died martyrs just a year or two before. Thus Polycarp appealed to them as inspiration for the Philippians during the persecutions of Trajan. So it seems that Rufus and Zosimus were beheaded in 109 A.D. under the persecution of Trajan.[552]

Silas

Silas was a prophet (Acts 15:32) with whom Paul traveled in his second journey. He had been chosen by the apostles to accompany Paul along with a Judas Barsabbas (Acts 15:22). He is last heard of in Acts 18:5, indicating that he did not accompany Paul on his third missionary journey. However, he does appear in the epistles.

2 Corinthians 1:19 makes it clear that Silas and Silvanus are one and the same (cf. Acts 17:15). Apparently Silas is a surname or nickname for Silvanus. He is also mentioned in both epistles to the Thessalonians, alongside with Timothy and Paul himself (1 Thessalonians 1:1; 2 Thessalonians 2:1). He furthermore was a "faithful brother" of Peter (1 Peter 5:12). Hippolytus calls him an overseer of Corinth[553] where he first preached gospel alongside Paul, but under the name Silvanus, Hippolytus also seems to call him the overseer of Thessalonica.[554] Might these statements by Hippolytus be mere assumption based upon the epistles of Paul? We cannot say.

As to his end it is said that Silas was scourged and suffered many other tortures before finally meeting his death, which was apparently either at the very end of Nero's persecutions of shortly thereafter.[555]

Simeon Cleopas

As with Jude and others, Simon the brother of James the Just (Mark 6:3) was been conflated with Simon the Zealot (see chapter 12). However, it is much easier to separate the two traditions since this Simon (or Simeon), appears to have lived in Jerusalem for his entire life.[556]

Simeon is universally considered to be the second overseer of Jerusalem after the death of James the Just.[557] He apparently spent the first part of his bishopry in exile, so to speak, as Jerusalem soon after came under seige by Rome. After the fall of Jerusalem, however, he was allowed to return to the occupied city where he lived a long and fruitful life until the reign of Trajan. This Trajan sought not only to erradicate Christians, but also Jews and specifically the entire lineage of King David. As a member of all three, Simeon was a prime target by Atticus, the Roman procurator.

Hegesippus said:

> "Simon, son of Clopas ... was tortured for many days in giving his witness, so that all, even the governor, were astounded at how he endured it all at 120 years of age; and he was sentenced to crucifixion."[558]

His martyrdom is dated to 109 A.D.[559]

Stephen

The record of Stephen is found in Acts 6 and 7 and nothing need be added to this record. His name is included here for the sake of completeness.

Timon

Timon was another of the seven deacons (Acts 6:5) and one of the seventy. According to the *Acts of Barnabas*, largely considered historical, he joined Barnabas and Mark in Cyprus where he was taken ill. Soon after recovering they began to distribute Matthew's gospel. When Barnabas was martyred, he fled Cyprus along with Mark and went to Alexandria.[560] From there he appears to have moved to Nabatæa, which was a country then engulfing all of the Arabian peninsula, most of Jordan, and southern Syria of today. There he appears to have become the overseer of Bostra, in southern Syria, east of Israel.[561]   According to Dorotheus, he was burned alive, becoming one of the six deacons known to have died a martyr[562] (only the fate of Nicolas fate is unknown).[563]

Timothy

Timothy was like a son to Paul (1 Timothy 1:18; 2 Timothy 1:2). He accompanied Paul on his second and third missionary journeys and when he was sitting in jail awaiting his execution Paul wrote three epistles, two of which he addressed to Timothy. Several of his letters list Timothy as co-author (in spirit, but not in actuality - cf. 2 Corinthians 1:1; Philippians 1:1; Colossians 1:1; 1 Thessalonians 1:1; 2 Thessalonians 1:1). On his death bed, he asked Timothy to come visit him before his execution (2 Timothy 4:9).

It was when Paul departed for Macedonia during his third missionary trip that he asked Timothy to go to Ephesus and instruct the church (1 Timothy 1:3). There is no doubt that Timothy served there in Ephesus for many years. It also seems that Timothy spent some time in prison for the faith (Hebrew 13:23), although it is uncertain when this took place.

Tradition claims that Timothy served as overseer at Ephesus for fifteen years,[564] but give conflictings dates for his death. Some date it to the time of Nero, but if he spent fifteen years at Ephesus, then his death could be no earlier than than 73 A.D. Others date his death to the time of Domitian.[565] Given Timothy's young age he was certainly still alive and active in the 90s and as a leader of the church would have been a primary target for Domitian. On the other hand, all ancients say that Timothy was stoned to death for preaching against idolatry. This seems a mob act, and thus it is possible that attempts to tie his death to one of the Roman persecutions may be in error. If he did die in a persecution then his death was probably 98 A.D. as Van Braght believed, but if it was a mob act motivated out of idolatry then the fifteen year date for his service in Ephesus may point to a death around 75 A.D. In either case, all we cab say is that he was stoned to death by pagans.[566]

Trophimus

Trophimus is mentioned three times in the Bible (Acts 20:4; 21:29; 2 Timothy 4:20). He is considered to be among the seventy and is said to have been beheaded alongside Paul.[567]

Zosimus – See Rufus

Appendix A
—
The Ante-Nicene Sources

Although I have quoted various sources from ancient to modern, the ante-Nicene fathers are the most important in historical research because they were the ones who lived closest to the apostles. The "apostolic fathers" are the ones who knew one or more of the apostles, and the "sub-apostolic age" is that generation immediately following who were tutored under the apostles' disciples, making them only one or two generations removed. These would be the people we would expect to have the most accurate information about the lives of the apostles.

Ante-Nicene actually means "before Nicea" which was the famous church council called by Emperor Constantine in 325 A.D. Eusebius, who knew the emperor, is often considered the first true Church historian. Like the ante-Nicene fathers he is important because he had access to documents and writings which no longer exist. Eusebius is thus a link to lost documents more ancient than himself.

Of course most of the church fathers do not write about history. Consequently, they say only a little about the apostles personal lives and histories. This complicates matters because it leaves us having to rely upon works of historical fiction or traditions. These writings (which are also ante-Nicene) embellish stories about the apostles but are sometimes based on historical incidents. Deciphering what is fiction from what is history is not always easy. This is why the works of ancient historians and church fathers must serve as a guide to help us determine and trace the historical elements. These traditions must be weighed carefully, but can be valuable when used properly.

Below I have listed brief comments and biographies on all the ante-Nicene sources up to, and including, the Nicene historian Eusebius. Although I do quote post-Nicene fathers as well, I do not include them here in this Appendix. Rather this is reserved for the ante-Nicene sources so that the reader may determine on his own what value should be placed upon their opinions.

Ante-Nicene and Nicene Church Fathers and Historians

First Century Historian

Josephus (37-100 A.D.) : The famed Jewish historian was once a general in the Jewish revolt but upon capture agreed to write a history of the Jewish War and its failures for Rome. He then became a famous historian, writing on the history of the Jewish people. His works provide non-Christian confirmation of several parts of the New Testament.

The Apostolic Fathers

Clement of Rome (d. 101 A.D.) : Clement of Rome was listed as the third overseer of the church in Rome according to the earliest sources.[568] He presumably resided in that office from approximately 91 to 101 A.D.[569] although the famed *Catalogus Liberianus* places his episcopate twenty-five years earlier.[570] He is sometimes believed to have been the same Clement mentioned in Philippians 4:3. He almost certainly knew or had met one or more of the apostles and was well acquainted with some of their associates.

Ignatius (circa 30-111 A.D.) : One of the earliest and most famous apostolic fathers, Ignatius Theophorus is alleged to have pupiled under John along with Polycarp. He is also a famous martyr, having died in Rome, being fed to lions.

Polycarp (69-155 A.D.) : Polycarp was a disciple of the apostle John, and a companion of Papias. He considered one of the three most important "apostolic fathers" along with Clement and Ignatius. He died a martyr in Smyrna, Turkey.

Papias (70-155 A.D.) : Papias was the bishop Hierapolis. It is believed he knew Philip the Evangelist personally. He also heard John the Apostle and was a friend of John's disciple, Polycarp.

The Sub-Apostolic Age

Dionysius (d. 171 A.D.) : Dionysius was an overseer at the Church in Corinth.

Hegesippus (110-180 A.D.) : He is considered the earliest Christian "chronologer," a sort of historian specializing in the chronology of the apostles and earlier apostolic fathers.

Irenaeus (120-202 A.D.) : Irenaeus was the student and disciple of Polycarp, who was in turn the disciple of the apostle John himself. Irenaeus was then a second generation disciple removed from one of the apostles. He was the bishop of Lyons in Gaul (modern France) where he worked to refute heresies which were growing rapidly in the Christian Church.

Polycrates (130-196 A.D.) : Polycrates served as the Bishop of Ephesus and was probably an associate of both Polycarp and Irenaeus.

Later Ante-Nicene Fathers

Clement of Alexandria (150-211 A.D.) : Clement was the bishop of Alexandria Egypt. His writings were influenced by Greek philosophy, but he has more to say of church history than most of the church fathers, making him a valuable source of information.

Tertullian (145-220 A.D.) : A pagan educated at Rome, Tertullian became a convert to the Christian faith in 185 A.D. and a presbyter only five years later. A great apologist, he wrote extensively and most of his writings are extant.

Gaius (or Caius) of Rome (circa 200 A.D.) : An early presbyter of the church in Rome whose only extant writing dates to 200 A.D. He died a martyr.[571]

Hippolytus (170-236 A.D.) : Hippolytus was himself a disciple of Irenaeus. The bishop of Portus, in Italy, Hippolytus was not afraid to refute heresies in the church. In 217 he was elected bishop of Rome, but a Callistus was also elected, creating a rift in the church. He is accepted by the Catholics as one of their great church fathers, and yet he is also listed an antipope, or false pope. He also suffered martyrdom (along side Callistus) in the persecutions of Maximinus.

Cyprian (190-258 A.D.) : Cyprian was the bishop of Carthage. He survived the persecutions of Decius, only to die under the later persecutions of Valerian.

Nicene Fathers

Lactantius (240-330 A.D.) : Lactantius was a famous Christian apologist and rhetorician who came to befriend the newly Christian emperor Constantine. He later became the tutor for Constantine's oldest son. He is considered an ante-Nicene Church Father even though he lived to see the council of Nicaea.

Dorotheus (255-362 A.D.) : The bishop of Tyre was the teacher of Eusebius. He was exiled under Diocletian, but returned under Constantine. Most of his works are ante-Nicene and he is believed to have written at least one volume on the history of the seventy disciples (Luke 10:1).

Eusebius (263-339 A.D.) : Considered the father of Church history, he wrote the first full church history from the time of the apostles up to the time of Constantine.

Apocryphal Works and Traditions

Acts and Martyrdom of the Holy Apostle Andrew : This is an apocryphal work which has been variously dated from as early as 80 A.D. to as late as the forth century.[572] Pope Gelasius I (492-496 A.D.) deemed the work heretical for some of the teachings contained therein.

Acts of the Holy Apostle Thomas : Often considered to reflect false (Gnostic) teachings, the apocryphal story nevertheless contains ancient traditions of Thomas. In one form or another it appears to be traceable back to as early as the first century, and certainly the second.

Acts of Barnabas : This book is considered one of the few apocryphal "acts" to be grounded in history, rather than embellishments. The manuscript dates to the fifth century, but its original composition is presumed to be ancient on account of the *Acts* historical reliability and geographic accuracy.

Acts of Peter : Believed to date to the middle of the second century, this is one of the earliest pieces of historical fiction concerning Peter. It relates traditions much older than its composition which are found in other apocryphal works. It is considered heretical by pope Gelasius I (492-496 A.D.).

The Apostolic Constitutions : At one time dated to the third century,[573] later scholia and scribes said it was found in the "most ancient" manuscripts which no longer exist.[574] Essentially it is compilation of different works from the first two centuries of Christianity, telling the teachings, doctrines, and history of the apostles.

Teaching of the Apostles : Also called the *Didascalia Apostolorum*, this is an ancient Syrian document dating to around 230 A.D.[575] Like the *Apostolic Constitutions* it is a collection of teachings, doctrines, and history of the apostles.

Acts of the Apostles and The History of Philip : This book is written in Syriac, meaning it is from the region near Mesopotamia. It's exact date is unknown but dates to either the second or third century.

Acts of the Holy Apostle and Evangelist John the Theologian (aka Acts of John) : Although the date of this apocryphal book is unknown, it is quoted by Eusebius and many others, indicating that it had been an accepted published work for some time. It is thus ante-Nicene and possibly as early as the second century.

Acts of the Holy Apostles Peter and Paul : Dating no later than the third century, for it is quoted by Origen, this apocryphal book recounts some of the same traditions as *The Acts of Peter* but with minor differences and additions; especially the introduction of Paul into the story.

Acts of Andrew and Matthias : Another apocryphal work which has been declared heretical, but carries some traditions which may be ancient or medieval. Some date it to as early as the second century, but others make it much later, even early medieval.[576] There is debate as to whether or not it is Matthew or Matthias, for the earliest manuscript contains Matthias, whereas later ones have Matthew.[577]

Martyrdom of the Holy and Glorious Apostle Bartholomew : This apocryphal story has been alleged to have been translated into Greek by Julius Africanus (160-240 A.D.), but most reject this. Nonetheless, the legends of his translating the work imply an original composition date close to his time. Others believe that this is merely the original source for the *Pseudo-Abdias* version of the story.

Acts of the Holy Apostle Thaddæus : This is a third century document relating the traditions and legends of Thaddæus.

Teaching of Addæus the Apostle : Another Syriac document dating to the third century or earlier.

Acts of Philip : Our copy is incomplete and its date is unknown, although some suggest it is a late third century text. In either case some of the traditions found therein are known to be ancient. The book is considered heretical by pope Gelasius I (492-496 A.D.).

Acts of Saint Philip the Apostle When He Went to Upper Hellas :
Another apocryphal work of an unknown date, but believed to be
ante-Nicene in nature.

Consummation of Thomas the Apostle : An apocryphal work upon
Thomas. It's date is unknown, but ante-Nicene.

Book of John Concerning the Falling Asleep of Mary (**aka**
Assumption of Mary) : This text, originally written in Greek, is said to
date *no later* than the fourth century. It is apocryphal, of course, but
claims to have been written by John, who was entrusted with the care of
Jesus's mother (John 19:26-27).

Acts of Abdias : The so-called *Acts of Abdias*, or *Pseudo-Abdias*, is a
medieval collection of ancient traditions and stories about the apostles.
It is included because many of the traditions are clearly borrowed from
ancient sources, some of which we have in our possession (such as
those listed here).

Acts and Martyrdom of St. Matthew the Apostle : This is a late
tradition which dates to the early middle ages, about the sixth century.
It is included only because of the lack of older material on Matthew.

Appendix B

—

Charts and Graphs

Sometimes it is hard for people living in the modern world to follow the Biblical geography since nations have risen and fallen so many times in the past. Many of the countries of the apostles' times no longer exist, and those which have survived occupy different territories, having vastly different boundaries. In some cases, the modern day country does not even touch the borders of the ancient one from which its name is drawn.

Additionally, it is hard to remember the fate of all these men. Therefore, I have provided below three section with a few charts and graphs to assist the reader. The first section is a summary of the apostles and their companions, briefly outlining my own conclusions. The second section shows the manner in which the apostles divided their ministries after the Council of Jerusalem. The last section discusses the countries which were evangelized by the disciples, including both modern and ancient countries.

The Apostles and Their Disciples

The apostles and their disciples left an imprint upon history which is indebted to their founder, Jesus Christ. Like our founder and God, many of these men died a fate not unlike our Lord's. Such was the dedication to His service and the terrible price that had to be paid to follow Him. In the west today service to God has become all too easy with little or no price to pay. One can only wonder how dedicated we would be if we were given a choice of offering sacrifices to non-existent gods or facing cruel death. How many of us would falter and waver? To be sure, there were a number of lapsed believers back in antiquity, even as there would be today. Most of these lapsed believers later repented and rejoined the church, although not without controversy. Some did not want to forgive them. Others took them back with open arms. This is, however, beyond the scope of this book. Rather here is a summary of my general conclusions (some of them tentative) upon the life and death of the apostles and their followers.

189

The Apostles

Apostle	Ministry (modern day name)	Death
James the Greater	Judea	Executed in 44 A.D.
Philip	Tunisia, Northern Africa	Stoned in 54 A.D.
James the Less	Overseer of Jerusalem	Thrown from temple parapet and stoned, on Passover 62 or 63 A.D.
Simon Peter	The greater Roman Empire including Italy	Crucified upside down in Rome in 65 A.D.
Paul	Throughout the Roman Empire	Beheaded near Rome under Nero in 65 A.D.
Matthias	Judea	Martyred in 69 or 70 A.D.
Matthew	Egypt and Ethiopia	Assassinated in 70 A.D.
Thomas	Moved east into modern day Iran, Turkmenistan, Afghanistan, Pakistan, Kashmir, and India	Martyred in Chennai, India around 70 A.D.
Andrew	Turkey, Greece, and all countries by the Black Sea	Crucified in 70 A.D.
Bartholomew	Syria, Turkey, Armenia, Azerbaijan, Iran, and India	Martyred in Mumbai, India around 70 A.D.
Judas Thaddæus	Moved across the Middle East from Syria to Iran	Crucified in 72 A.D.
Simon the Zealot	Moved across North Africa and then traveled to Britain	Crucified in England around 74 A.D.
John	Several countries in modern day Turkey	Only apostle to die a natural death in Ephesus in 101 or possibly 106 A.D.

Thus all the apostles, save John, died a martyrs death at the hands of those who hated the Lord. From Rome to India to Britain, they paid the ultimate price for love of God. To paraphrase Ignatius, "As the world hates Christians, so we love them." As God gave His own life for us, so the apostles gave their lives for the very men who tortured and slew them. Even Paul, who once killed us, became one of us and died as one of us. These are the lessons that our generation should learn, for there is coming a time soon when true persecution will return the west. As history has always allowed a respite for the gospel to grow, so we have had a respite in the west, but that time may soon be coming to end.

Even as the apostles gave their lives, their disciples did not fail to escape the same fate. Below is a list of my conclusions upon the disciples.

The Disciples

Disciple	Ministry (modern day name)	Death
Barnabas	Syria, Turkey, and Cyprus	Burned alive in Cyprus around 55 A.D.
Epaphas	Unknown	Slain under Nero around 65 A.D.
Trophimus	Unknown	Beheaded alongside Paul.
Andronicus	Hungary, Croatia, Bosnia, and Serbia	Slain under Nero between 65 and 68 A.D.
Aquila	Italy, Turkey, Greece, and Macedonia	Slain under Nero between 65 and 68 A.D.
Aristarchus	Greece, Italy, and possibly Macedonia	Fed to lions between 65 and 68 A.D.
Carpus	Turkey and possibly Bulgaria or even Romania	Slain under Nero between 65 and 68 A.D.
Prochorus	Turkey	Slain under Nero.
Priscilla (Prisca)	Italy, Turkey, Greece, and Macedonia	Slain under Nero between 65 and 68 A.D.
Linus	Italy	Unknown. Possibly a martyr under Nero.
Onesiphorus	Turkey	Dragged to death under Nero.
Silas	Turkey, Greece, and Macedonia	Scourged and martyred under Nero's reign.
Timothy	Turkey, Greece, and Macedonia.	Stoned to death.
Jude	Judea, Samaria, Galilee, and Lebanon	Probably died of natural causes at a ripe old age.
Justus Barsabbas	Judea	Unknown
Timon	Cyprus, Egypt, Jordan, and Syria	Burned alive.
Luke	Macedonia, Greece, and possibly Bulgaria	Hung on an olive tree around 93 A.D.
Antipas	Turkey	Sealed in a bronze idol and cooked alive about 95 A.D.
Philip the Evangelist	Turkey	Crucified upside down, probably under Domitian.
John Mark	Turkey, Italy, Cyprus, and Egypt, with the possibly of Albania and Greece	Possibly dragged and burned in Alexandria in Trajan's time.
Rufus	Italy, Greece	Beheaded in 109 A.D. under Trajan.
Simeon Cleopas	Judea	Tortured and martyred about 109 A.D.
Indich (aka Fudich)	Ethiopia, Saudi Arabia, and Eritrea	Martyred circa 110 A.D.
Dionysius	Unknown	Martyred, possibly under Trajan circa 111 A.D.
Onesimus	Turkey	Stoned around 111 A.D.

191

It was only *after* I had done my research on the apostles and reached my conclusions that I noticed a curiosity. Eusebius insinuates that the apostles' mission fields were chosen by lot,[578] and the missionary lands were thus divided. Logically they would have divided the mission field evenly among the eleven surviving apostles (James the Greater had already died). This appears to have been exactly what the apostles did. The chart below shows how the known earth was divided among the apostles who were send out in fulfillment of the Great Commission.

The Four Quarters of the Earth Divided

Northern Africa	Europe/Asia Minor	Palestine	The Eastern World
Matthew	Peter	James the Greater	Thomas
Philip	John	James the Less	Bartholomew
Simon the Zealot	Andrew	Matthias	Judas Thaddæus

Please bear in mind that this is a conclusion I arrived at only after I determined that Philip, Simon, and Judas were conflated in the traditions. This therefore had no bearing upon my conclusions, but is the result of my research and further evidence of those conclusions.

The Countries Evangelized

Countries change often, or perhaps I should say borders change often. Countries rise and fall, but the people who once populated the land leave descendants who will always remember their past. Consider Mauritania, evangelized by Simon the Zealot. The country still exist today, but its borders do not even overlap the ancient borders of the country which Simon visited. Rather the country of Mauritania which Simon passed through is now occupied by Algeria and Morocco. Modern day Mauritania is to the south of those counties.

Also bear in mind that the people of countries are usually proud of their heritage. Even a country whose history is filled with strife and barbarity will feel pride at having overthrown the dictators or tyrants of their land, or long for the days when they had freedom. So also they love their patron saints. Naturally, people would prefer to take a patron saint from someone who actually visited their country. This is one reason that traditions of patron saints are important, but not infallible, for sometimes a country may not have been evangelized until a century or more after the apostles. It is then that traditions become legends, such as Thomas visiting Peking, China. Since no apostle ever made it as far as China, the Kushans of China, when they invaded India, learned of Thomas and brought back his memory with them. Later Chinese then claimed that Thomas had been to their land, although he had only been as far as India.

Here then are various charts showing the apostles and their companions (but only the ones discussed in chapter fifteen) and the countries they have evangelized. I have divided this into two charts. The first chart list the countries evangelized as they existed in antiquity. As such it is the most accurate. The second chart list the modern day country and what disciple may have witnessed within its modern day borders. This is not usually difficult, but without knowing the exact cities which the apostles' evangelized in some of these countries, there is only a probability or possibility of evangelisim in some cases, due to changing borders.

Apostles by Ancient Country Chart

Country	Probable/Certain	Possible
Achaia	*Paul*, *Peter*, *Andrew*, *John*, Mark, Luke, Barnabas, Silas, Timothy, Aristarchus, Aquila, Priscilla, and Rufus	Philip the Evangelist
Armenia	*Judas Thaddæus*, *Bartholomew*	*Andrew*, *Thomas*
Africa	*Simon the Zealot*	
Arabia	*Judas Thaddæus*, *Bartholomew*, Indich (Fudich)	
Asia	*Peter*, *Paul*, *Andrew*, *John*, Timothy, Philip the Evangelist, Carpus, Onesimus, Onesiphorus, Silas	Luke
Bactria	*Thomas*	
Bithynia	*Peter*, *Andrew*, Prochorus	
Britannica	*Simon the Zealot*	

193

Apostles by Ancient Country Chart cont.

Country	Probable/Certain	Possible
Carmania	*Thomas*	
Carthage	*Philip, Simon the Zealot*	
Cappadocia	*Peter, Andrew*	
Cilicia	*Paul*, Silas	
Egypt	*Matthew, Simon the Zealot,* Mark, Timon	
Ethiopia	*Matthew*, Indich (Fudich)	
Galatia	*Paul, Peter, Andrew,* Barnabas, John Mark, and Silas	
Hispania		*Paul*
Hyrcania	*Thomas*	
Illyria	Mark,	*Paul*
Italia	*Paul, Peter, John,* Mark, Luke, Aquila, Priscilla, Linus, Rufus, Aristarchus, Epaphas, Onesimus, and Clement	
Pannonia	Andronicus	
Persia	*Thomas, Judas Thaddæus*	*Bartholomew*
Pontus	*Peter, Andrew*, Aquila	*John* and Priscilla (Prisca)
Lycia	*Paul*, Barnabas, John Mark	
Macedonia	*Paul, Andrew,* Luke, Timothy, and Aristarchus	*Peter* and Mark
Malta	*Paul* and Luke	Andronicus, Junias, and Mark
Mauritania	*Simon the Zealot*	
Media	*Thomas, Judas Thaddæus*	*Bartholomew*
Mesopotamia	*Thomas, Judas Thaddæus, Bartholomew*	
Nabatæa	Timon	*Paul*
Osroene	*Thomas, Judas Thaddæus, Bartholomew*	
Scythia	*Andrew*	Philip the Evangelist
Sicilia	*Paul* and Luke	Andronicus, Junias, and Mark
Syria	Almost all of the apostles, and most of their companions	
Thessalia	*Andrew*	
Thracia	*Andrew*, Luke, Carpus	*Paul*, Mark

Apostles by Modern Country Chart

Country	Probable/Certain	Possible
Afghanistan	*Thomas*	
Albania	Mark	*Paul, Peter*
Algeria	*Simon the Zealot*	*The Apostle Philip*
Armenia	*Judas Thaddæus, Bartholomew*	*Andrew, Thomas*
Azerbaijan	*Judas Thaddæus, Bartholomew*	*Thomas*
Bosnia	Andronicus	
Britain	*Simon the Zealot*	
Bulgaria	*Andrew*, Luke	Carpus, Philip the Evangelist
Croatia	Andronicus	
Cyprus	*Paul*, Barnabas, Mark, Timon	
Egypt	*Matthew, Simon the Zealot*, Mark, Timon	
Eritrea	Indich (Fudich)	*Matthew*
Ethiopia	*Matthew*, Indich (Fudich)	
Georgia	*Andrew*	
Greece	*Paul, Peter, Andrew, John,* Luke, Aristarchus, Silas, and Rufus	
Hungary	Andronicus	
India	*Thomas, Bartholomew*	
Iran	*Thomas, Judas Thaddæus*	*Bartholomew*
Iraq	*Thomas, Judas Thaddæus, and Bartholomew*	
Israel	All of them!	
Italy	*Paul, Peter, John,* Mark, Luke, Aquila, Priscilla, Linus, Rufus, Aristarchus, Epaphas, Onesimus, and Clement	
Jordan	Timon	Many of the apostles may have passed through part of Jordan.
Kosovo		Mark
Lebannon	Most of the apostles, and Simeon Cleopas	
Libya	*Simon the Zealot*, Mark	*Matthew*
Macedonia	*Paul, Andrew,* Luke, and Timothy	*Peter*, Andronicus

Apostles by Modern Country Chart cont.

Country	Probable/Certain	Possible
Malta	*Paul*, Luke	Andronicus, Junias, and Mark
Mauritania	*Simon the Zealot**	
Moldavia		*Andrew*, Philip the Evangelist
Morocco	*Simon the Zealot*	
Oman		*Bartholomew*
Pakistan	*Thomas*	
Portugal		*Paul*
Romania	*Andrew*	Philip the Evangelist, Carpus
Russia	*Andrew*	
Saudi Arabia	*Judas Thaddæus*, Indich (Fudich)	*Bartholomew*
Serbia	Andronicus	
Sicily	*Paul*, Luke	
Spain		*Paul*
Sudan	*Matthew*, Indich (Fudich)	
Syria	Almost all of the apostles, and most of their companions	
Tunisia	*Philip, Simon the Zealot*	
Turkey	*Paul, Peter, John, Andrew*, Aquila, Timothy, Philip the Evangelist, Silas, Carpus, Prochorus, Onesimus, Onesiphorus, and Luke	
Turkmenistan	*Thomas*	
Ukraine	*Andrew*	
U. A. E.	*Bartholomew*	

* See notes below.

Here is a list of modern day counties with a more specific description of the possibilities of certain apostles or disciples ministering within their borders.

Afghanistan
Thomas passed through Afghanistan en route to India. The most likely route he would have taken would have been to enter Afghanistan in the northwest after visiting Hyrcania (in Turkmenistan) and then skirt down south to avoid a direct climb over the Hindu-Kush mountains. He skirted the mountains, stopping to evangelize in the eastern part of ancient Persia and Carmania, which would correspond the southwestern

part of Afghanistan. Then he would have moved east below the mountains in the Kandahar region and began to move northeast toward Taxila, India in modern day Pakistan.

Albania

Albania lays in what was the western region of ancient Macedonia. Paul and many of his companions evangelized Macedonia, but as far we know for certain only John Mark established a ministry in the western part of Macedonia, at Apollonia, Illyria. The ruins of that city are located in the Fier region of Albania.

Algeria

The very northern part of Algeria was a part of the Roman country called "Africa," from which the continent now gets its name. Simon the Zealot certainly passed through the northern part of Algeria and spread the gospel. It is also possible, but by no means certain, that Philip had visited the most northeastern part of what is now Algeria when he was evangelizing Carthage.

Armenia

Armenia of today is just a small part of what was the ancient kingdom of Armenia. Caught between the Roman empire in the west, the Parthian empire in the east, and the Scythians of the north, Armenia remarkably survived throughout history in one form or another. To this day they recognize Judas Thaddæus and Bartholomew as the apostles who first evangelized Armenia.

It is also probable that Thomas at least passed through the Kingdom of Armenia before moving eastward, and Andrew probably passed through Armenia as he returned from Scythia in the north. However it is not certain if their journeys took them through the modern day county.

Azerbaijan

Azerbaijan occupies the eastern portion of what was once the kingdom of Armenia. Consequently we can say that Judas Thaddæus and Bartholomew ministered in Azerbaijan. Thomas may also have been there, although it is less likely that Andrew ventured that far east.

Britain

Although legends have arisen over Joseph of Arimathea and even Peter, the truth is that only Simon the Zealot may have visited Britain. There is fairly good evidence that Simon did so, and even that he died a martyr there in the southern part of Britain during the Roman war.

Bulgaria

Bulgaria corresponds relatively close to the northern part of ancient Thrace and the southern most part of Moesia. It is likely that Andrew passed through Bulgaria en route to Scythia. Luke may also have visited Bulgaria, although this is less certain. Finally, Carpus is said to have been a bishop in a city called Berytus in Thracia, but we do not know where this city once lay so we cannot know if it was Bulgaria.

Cyprus

Paul and Barnabas first passed through Cyprus on their initial missionary journey. After Paul left for his second missionary journey Barnabas and John Mark again visited Cyprus where they were joined by Timon. It is also there in Cyprus where Barnabas was martyred.

Egypt

Both Matthew and Simon the Zealot were probably the first to enter Egypt. Simon eventually moved on westward across northern Africa while Matthew established his permanent mission here and in the surrounding countries. He was soon joined by John Mark and Timon who had fled from Cyprus. Mark is credited with establishing the church in Alexandria, and living there for many years after returning from his journey's with Paul and Peter. It is also possible, but less likely, that Philip passed through Egypt en route to Carthage, although he probably took the sea route.

On a different note, Paul said that he traveled to Arabia after his conversion (Galatians 1:17). However, the portion of Arabia to which Paul most likely traveled was the Arabian, or Sinai, Peninsula. This part of ancient Arabia was actually a part of a country then called Nabatæa, but is today occupied by Egypt and Israel. Thus is it possible that Paul resided in the part of Sinai which is today Egypt, but this cannot be known for certain since Paul does not tell us what city he resided within.

Eritrea

Eritrea is a small country which lay between Ethiopia and the Red Sea. It is not certain whether or not Matthew ventured to this particular part of ancient Ethiopia, but we may assume that he at least passed through it at some point. More likely, however, is that Indich (or Fudich) evangelized this area and most probably was martyred on one of the islands of the Dahlak Archipelago.

Ethiopia

Indich (or Fudich) is alleged to be the name of the Ethiopian Eunuch converted by Philip. It is he who first brought the gospel to Ethiopia when he returned from Judea. Many decades later he was joined by Matthew who was martyred here.

France

Although late traditions attribute Peter and Philip as evangelists in ancient Gaul these are almost certainly legends grasping at a link to the apostles, for Gaul was never mentioned as a missionary destination by anyone until the third century, and that document probably infers that it was Peter's disciples, not him, who later evangelized Gaul. The first tradition to personally place Peter or Philip in Gaul is early medieval. Thus some of Peter's disciples moved up north of Italy and evangelized Gaul, but none of the apostles appear to have made it this far.

Georgia

Located north of Armenia between the Black Sea and Caspian sea, the modern day country may have been visited by those who evangelized Armenia, but the only one we can say for sure passed through this region would have been Andrew becyase most of Georgia lay in the southern reaches of Scythia. Andrew would certainly have passed through Georgia if he returned to Asia Minor by land, rather than sea.

Greece

Greece was evangelized by Paul, Peter, and Andrew. John was also there when he was imprisoned at Patmos. Additionally, Barnabas, Mark, Silas, Aquila, Priscilla, Rufus, Luke, and presumably even Philip the Evangelist all did missionary work in Greece as well. Greece was thus the apostles' most visited country outside of Israel and Turkey.

India

Thomas was the first to minister to India. He first entered the northern Punjab region where he apparently witnessed the gospel and then moving down to the nearest sea port, he sailed down to Kerala where he established a permanent home and mission. He was martyred in Chennai, India.

Bartholomew also evangelized India in the central region, which was a separate country from Kerala at the time. There he gave them a copy of Matthew's gospel and ministered until his own martyrdom near modern day Mumbai (Bombay).

Iran

Iran encompasses most of ancient Persia, Hyrcania, and Media, as well as small portions of Carmania, Mesopotamia, and even up to the edge of the kingdom of Armenia. If we ignore the apostles who ventured into Armenia and Osroene (because Iran barely overlaps a small portion of those kingdoms), then we are left with Persia, Media, and Hyrcania, all of which were evangelized by Thomas. In addition, Judas Thaddæus conducted missionary journeys into part of modern day Iran. It is also possible, and even likely, that Bartholomew ventured into the western portion of Iran and/or the sea ports of the Persian Gulf that were located in Iran.

Iraq
Iraq covers ancient Mesopotamia and part of Persia. Thomas, Judas Thaddæus, and Bartholomew all ministered in what is today Iraq.

Israel
All the apostles came from Israel and ministered in Israel. It was from Israel that Jesus was born and it was from the Jews that salvation was promised. To the Jews the gospel was first presented, and to the Jews the gospel shall one day be accepted. Israel is the home of Jesus and of the apostles. They have no patron saint for all the saints came from there, and most importantly, the Messiah, Jesus Christ our Lord came from Israel.

Italy
The Bible explicitly says that Paul ministered to Italy. Although some do not wish to admit it, both the Bible and history are equally clear that Peter visited Italy at least before his death, if not before. Aside from these two men only John went to Rome, and that as a prisoner before Domitian. However, a great many of the apostles' companions served in Italy. It is most likely that Aquila and Priscilla were the first to establish a mission in Rome. Linus, of course, is held to be the first overseer of that church. Clement was a later overseer. Mark and Luke were also in Rome at various times. The companions of the apostles who died a martyr in Rome are numerous. These include Rufus, Aristarchus, Epaphas, and Onesimus.

Jordan
Jordan borders Syria, Iraq, and Saudi Arabia. It most closely corresponds to the ancient kingdom of Nabatæa. Because it also borders Israel it is possible that many of the apostles visited a portion of Jordan, but the only one that we can definitively say ministered in Jordan is Timon, who moved up from Egypt through Nabatæa and into Syria.

Kashmir
Kashmir is a disputed province between India and Pakistan in which the ancient city of Taxila resided. It is here where Thomas ministered to the northern kingdom of ancient India.

Kosovo

Kosovo lay just north of Macedonia. Although it is possible that several apostles passed through or visited this country, it is by no means certain that any of them entered this land with the exception of John Mark who evangelized nearby Albania.

Lebanon

Lebanon is a country which is a part of the Promised Land. In Jesus's time it was a part of ancient Syria. It is on the shores of the Mediterranean, just north of Israel. There is little doubt that almost all, if not all, of the apostles had been here at one time or another. However, of particular interest is the specific mention of Simeon, the son of Cleopas, who died in Beirut, Lebanon at an advanced age.

Libya

The north African country which borders Egypt was evangelized by Simon the Zealot and John Mark. It is also possible that Matthew's ministry reached as far as Libya but this cannot be proven.

Macedonia

Just north of Greece, it is possible that most any of the apostles who visited Greece also visited Macedonia, but the only ones we can be certain about are Paul, Andrew, Luke, and Timothy, as well as the probability of Andronicus.

Malta

Malta is a small island off the coast of Sicily where Paul was shipwrecked. Luke was also with Paul, so we can say that Paul and all those who were prisoners with him at the time were in Malta. We know that Andronicus, Junias, and John Mark are all called "fellow prisoners" with Paul (Romans 1:11; 15:24; Philemon 1:24), presumably during his first imprisonment and thus may too have been there.

Mauritania

The modern country takes its name from the ancient country of the same name but its boundaries have changed to such an extent that none of modern day Mauritania even touches the land of ancient Mauritania. Nevertheless, since ancient Mauritania is a part of the country's heritage it is fair to say that Simon the Zealot did indeed evangelize the country, or at least is ancient ancestral lands.

Moldavia

Moldavia is a small country between Romania and the Ukraine. In antiquity it was a part of Scythia and thus was probably visited by

Andrew. Additionally, the possibility that Philip the Evangelist may have gone to Scythia, although by no means certain, makes his visitation possible as well.

Morocco
Morocco lays in the western portion of ancient Mauritania and was for a time the home of Simon the Zealot's missionary activities. It is doubtless from a Moroccan port that Simon set sail for Britain.

Oman
Oman is on the south-eastern tip of the Arabian Felix, extending up to the Gulf of Oman. Although it is unlikely that any missionary activity was extensively done in this region, Bartholomew is said to have witnessed the gospel in Arabia en route to India. The northern sea port of Oman in the Gulf of Oman is one of the possible ports in which Bartholomew may have landed. Consequently, his visitation remains a possibility.

Pakistan
Pakistan lay southeast of the Hindu-Kush mountains and was a part of ancient Indo-Parthia, later conquered by the Kushan empire. It is actually here where the northern part of Thomas's ministry rested. For a few years, in the early 50s Thomas taught and preached in the kingdom of Gundaphoros in the Punjab region of modern day Pakistan.

Romania
Romania is north of Bulgaria in eastern Europe and covers the northern tip of ancient Thracia, the larger eastern portion of ancient Moesia, Dacia, and part of Scythia. There is no doubt that Andrew passed through Romania and probably ministered here. Additionally, if the stories of Philip the Evangelist traveling to Scythia are true, then he too would have passed through this region. Finally, Carpus is said by some to have been a bishop in Berytus, Thracia, but it is not known if this city was a part of the region now occupied by Romania.

Russia
The southern most part of Russia, bordering the Black Sea, is almost certainly the part of Scythia in which Andrew once ministered. It is for this reason that Andrew is considered the parton saint of the Russian Orthodox church.

Saudi Arabia
Ancient Arabia Felix is the name given to the then largely nomadic lands now occupied predominantly by Saudi Arabia. These lands were made up of exiles and nomads with city-states and no centralized

governments. Many considered it a dangerous land of anarchy and bandits. This is why the land was virtually untouched until Mohammad united all the various waring tribes into what would become the Arabian empires of history. Nonetheless, there is a strong possibility that this land was not neglected by some of the early disciples. It is probable that the northern most part of Arabia Felix was a part of Judas Thaddæus's ministry. It is also possible that Saudi Arabia was one of the stopping points for Bartholomew en route to India. Finally, it is likely that Indich (Fudich) ministered in the south-western portion of modern day Saudi Arabia.

Sicily
Sicily was a port at which the prison ship stopped while carrying Paul and his fellow prisoners (cf. Acts 28:12). It is therefore certain that Paul visited Sicily as well as Luke. Other probablities are Andronicus, Junias, and John Mark based on their being "fellow prisoners" with Paul (Romans 1:11; 15:24; Philemon 1:24)

Spain
Paul expressed a desire to visit Spain (or Hispania) in Romans 15:24. It is very likely that Paul fulfilled that desire shortly before his return to Rome and subsequent martyrdom. Late and conflated traditions of Peter and/or James visiting Spain are to be rejected.

Sudan
The Sudan lays between ancient Egypt and Ethiopia. It would have been part of the missionary grounds for Mattthew and Indich (or Fudich).

Syria
Syria is north of Israel and the home of Antioch where all of the apostles, except James the Greater, resided for a time after being driven away from Jerusalem. Antioch was the staging ground for the Apostle Paul's journeys and the base of some of the other apostles' ministries in their earlier days. Additionally, Timon was a bishop in this region, and other companions such as Mark and Barnabas served here for a time. Aside from Israel there is arguably no country which has a richer history of the apostles.

Tunesia
Tunesia lays in central northern Africa on the coast of the Mediterranean Sea. It is also the home of ancient Carthage where the apostle Philip most likely served and died. Simon the Zealot also passed through this region, establishing churches as he went.

Turkey

Except for Israel and Syria there is no modern day country which has had a richer tradition than Turkey. The modern day country encompasses the ancient countries of Cilicia, Galatia, Pontus, Bithynia, Lycia, Asia, and Cappadocia. The regions of Phrygia, Pisidia, Pamphylia, and Lycaonia are also in Turkey, overlapping these countries.

We know that Paul established churches in Lycia and Galatia, and was from Tarsus, which is in Cilicia. We also know that he worked with churches, which he may or may not have founded, in Asia. Peter is also said to have worked in all of these countries with the possible exceptions of Cilicia and Lycia. Two other apostles also worked in Asia Minor, or Turkey. These were Andrew and John. Andrew worked in Pontus, Bithynia, Galatia, and probably Asia. John worked primarily in the country called Asia.

In addition to these apostles many of their companions probably worked here, but the only ones we can know for sure are Barnabas, John Mark, Timothy, Silas, Philip the Evangelist, Carpus, Onesimus, Onesiphorus, Prochorus, Aquila and Priscilla (Prisca). Timothy traveled with Paul during one of his journeys, as did Silas, Barnabas, and John Mark. Prochorus is believed to have been a bishop in Bithynia and Carpus, Onesimus, and Onesiphorus all served in Asia. Philip the Evangelist lived in Hierapolis. Finally Aquila was a native of Pontus.

Turkmenistan

Turkmenistan overlaps the ancient Parthian country called Hycania which the apostle Thomas passed through and evangelized briefly on his journey to India.

Ukraine

The Ukraine lays just north of the Black Sea in ancient Scythia. Andrew would have ministered there at one time.

United Arab Emirate

The U.A.E. occupies the tip of old Arabian Felix that leads from the Persian Gulf out into the Gulf of Oman. It is very possible that Bartholomew stopped at the sea port therein en route to India and did some ministering there at that time.

1   Tertullian, "Apology," *Ante-Nicene Fathers Vol. 3*   Alexander Roberts & James Donaldson, eds., Charles Scribner (New York, NY) 1886 pg. 54
2   Ibid. pg. 55
3   Cornelius Tacitus, *The Annals: The Reigns of Tiberius, Claudius, and Nero* XV.44 Oxford University (Oxford, England) 2008
4 Bruce Metzger, *The Text of the New Testament : Its Transmission, Corruption, and Restoration* Oxford University (Oxford, England) 1964   pg. 217
5 Alexander Mar Thoma Metropolitan, *The Mar Thoma Church : Heritage and Mission* Puthethu Offset (Thiruvalla, Kerala, India) 1985 pg. 11
6   Erwin Lueker, ed., *Lutheran Cyclopedia* Concordia Press (St. Louis, MI) 1975 pg. 406
7 Eusebius, *Eusebius, The Church History* 5.10   Paul Maier, trans. Kregel Publishers (Grand Rapids, Mich.) 1999 pg. 185
8 C. Bernard Ruffin, *The Twelve : The Lives of the Apostles After Calvary* One Sunday Visitor (Huntington, IN) 1970 pg. 76
9   Irenaeus, "Against Heresies," 3:3, *Ante-Nicene Fathers Vol. I* Alexander Roberts & James Donaldson, eds., Charles Scribner (New York, NY) 1886 pg. 416
10 Because Greek has no "sh," the Greek sigma ("s") replaces it, and all proper male Greek names must end in a sigma ("s"), thus Joshua (or Jeshua) becomes Jesus.
11 Ruffin, op. cit. pg. 18
12   J.N.D. Kelly, *The Oxford Dictionary of Popes* Oxford University Press (Oxford, England) 1986 pg. 7
13 Ibid.
14   Clement of Rome, "The First Epistle of Clement," 1 Clement 5:4, *Ante-Nicene Fathers Vol. I* op. cit. pg. 6
15   Cleveland Coxe, *Ante-Nicene Fathers Vol. 8* Alexander Roberts & James Donaldson, eds., Charles Scribner (New York, NY) 1886 pg. 765
16 Dionysius of Corinth, "Letter to the Roman Church," III, Ibid. pg. 765
17 Cf. Coxe, *Ante-Nicene Fathers Vol. I* op. cit. pg. 309
18   Irenaeus, "Against Heresies," 3:2, *Ante-Nicene Fathers Vol. I* op. cit. pg. 415
19 Ibid. pg. 416
20   Clement of Alexandria, "Miscellanies," 7.11.63-64 *Ante-Nicene Fathers Vol. 2* Alexander Roberts & James Donaldson, eds., Charles Scribner (New York, NY) 1886 pg. 541
21 Clement of Alexandria, "Miscellanies," 3.6.52 Ibid. pg. 390
22   Hippolytus, "On the Twelve Apostles," *Ante-Nicene Fathers Vol. 8* Alexander Roberts & James Donaldson, eds., Charles Scribner (New York, NY) 1886 pp. 254-256
23 Ruffin, op. cit. pg. 53
24 The full text of *the Acts of Peter* may be found at
http://www.earlychristianwritings.com/text/actspeter.html
25 Ibid.
26 Ibid.
27 Ibid.

28 Asterius Urbanus, *Ante-Nicene Fathers Vol. 7* Alexander Roberts & James Donaldson, eds., Charles Scribner (New York, NY) 1886 pg. 337

29 Gaius of Rome, "Dialogue with Proclus," *Eusebius, The Church History* 2.25 Paul Maier, trans. Kregel Publishers (Grand Rapids, Mich.) 1999 pg. 86

30 Tertullian, "Scorpiace," *Ante-Nicene Fathers Vol. 2* Alexander Roberts & James Donaldson, eds., Charles Scribner (New York, NY) 1886 pg. 648

31 Tertullian, "On Prescription Against Heretics," *Ante-Nicene Fathers Vol. 2* op. cit. pg. 260

32 "The Teachings of the Apostles," *Ante-Nicene Fathers Vol. 8* op. cit. pg. 671

33 Cyprian, "Epistles of Cyprian," *Ante-Nicene Fathers Vol. 5* Alexander Roberts & James Donaldson, eds., Charles Scribner (New York, NY) 1886 pg. 377 & 394

34 Lactantius, "On the Manner in Which the Persecutors Died," *Ante-Nicene Fathers Vol. 7* op. cit. pg. 302

35 Eusebius, *Eusebius, The Church History* 2.13-15 Paul Maier, trans. Kregel Publishers (Grand Rapids, Mich.) 1999 pp. 72-72

36 Ibid. pp. 85, 93, 118-119

37 James Montgomery Boice, *The Gospel of John Vol. 2* Zondervan Press (Grand Rapids, Mich) 1975 pg. 307

38 B.F Wescott, *The Gospel According to St. John* Wm. B Eerdmans (Grand Rapids, Mich.) 1954 pg. 141

39 The Apostolic Constitutions 6.ix, *Ante-Nicene Fathers Vol. 7* op. cit. pg. 453

40 "The Acts of the Holy Apostles Peter and Paul," *Ante-Nicene Fathers Vol. 8* op. cit. pp. 477-486

41 Ibid.

42 "The Teachings of the Apostles," *Ante-Nicene Fathers Vol. 8* op. cit. pg. 671

43 Ruffin, op. cit. pg. 51

44 Coxe, *Ante-Nicene Fathers Vol. 8* op. cit.

45 "The Teachings of the Apostles," *Ante-Nicene Fathers Vol. 8* op. cit. pg. 671

46 Cited in Ruffin, op. cit. pg. 51

47 Ruffin, op. cit. pg. 50

48 Dionysius of Corinth, "Letter to the Roman Church," III, *Ante-Nicene Fathers Vol. 8* op. cit. pg. 765

49 Georges Roux, *Ancient Iraq* Penguin Books (New York, NY) 1992 ed. pg. 413

50 Ibid.

51 Ibid.

52 Ibid. pg. 416

53 Ibid.

54 Ibid. pg. 414

55 Cf. Merrill Tenney, *New Testament Survey* W. B. Eerdmans (Grand Rapids, Mich.) 1985 pg. 347 & Robert Gundry, *A Survey of the New Testament* Zondervan Publishers (Grand Rapids, Mich.) 1994 pg. 437

56 Van Braght, op. cit. pg. 98

57 Cf. Tertullian, "Scorpiace," *Ante-Nicene Fathers Vol. 2* op. cit. pg. 648

58   Joseph Alexander, *Commentary on the Acts of the Apostles in One Volume* Zondervan Publishers (Grand Rapids, Mich.) 1956 pg. 37

59   John Foxe, *Foxe's Book of Martyrs* Clarion Classics (Grand Rapids, Mich.) 1926 (abridged ed.)

60   Thieleman J. van Braght, *Martyrs' Mirror* Herald Press (Scottdale, PN) 1950 ed. (1660 orig.)

61   Justin Martyr, "The First Apology of Justin," *Ante-Nicene Fathers Vol. 1* op. cit. pg. 171

62   Note on Eusebius 2:13, op. cit. pg. 72

63   Coxe, *Ante-Nicene Fathers Vol. 1* op. cit. pg. 171

64   Irenaeus, "Against Heresies," 3:2, *Ante-Nicene Fathers Vol. 1* op. cit. pg. 415

65   Dionysius of Corinth, quoted in *Eusebius, The Church History* 2.25 Paul Maier, trans. Kregel Publishers (Grand Rapids, Mich.) 1999 pg. 86

66   Gaius of Rome, "Dialogue with Proclus," *Eusebius, The Church History* 2.25 Paul Maier, trans. Kregel Publishers (Grand Rapids, Mich.) 1999 pg. 86

67   Coxe, *Ante-Nicene Fathers Vol. 5* op. cit. pg. 47

68   Ruffin, op. cit. pp. 51-52

69   *The Acts of Peter*, op. cit.

70   Ruffin, op. cit. pg. 52

71   Cyprian, "Epistles of Cyprian," *Ante-Nicene Fathers Vol. 5* op. cit. pg. 377 & 394

72   Irenaeus, "Against Heresies," 3:3, *Ante-Nicene Fathers Vol. 1* op. cit. pg. 416

73   Ruffin, op. cit. pg. 20

74   Clement of Alexandria, "Miscellanies," 3.6.52 *Ante-Nicene Fathers Vol. 2* op. cit. pg. 390

75   Clement of Alexandria, "Miscellanies," 7.11.63-64 *Ante-Nicene Fathers Vol. 2* op. cit. pg. 541

76   Ruffin, op. cit. pg. 57

77   Dionysius of Corinth, "Letter to the Roman Church," III *Ante-Nicene Fathers Vol. 8* op. cit. pg. 765

78   Clement of Rome, "The First Epistle of Clement," 1 Clement 5:4, *Ante-Nicene Fathers Vol. 1* op. cit. pg. 6

79   Ruffin, op. cit. pg. 57

80   Tacitus, *Annals*, op. cit. 15.44

81   Ruffin, op. cit. pg. 55

82   Merrill Unger, *Unger's Bible Dictionary* Moody Press (Chicago, Ill.) 1957 pg. 851

83   The Latin words for "where are you going" are *"quo vadis"* from whence the famous book and movies drew their name.

84   *The Acts of Peter* op. cit.

85   Robert Gundry, *A Survey of the New Testament* Zondervan Publishers (Grand Rapids, Mich.) 1994 pg. 437

86   Ruffin, op. cit. pg. 57

87   James Ussher, *Annals of the World* Master Books (Green Forest, AR) 2003 pg. 872

88   *The Acts of Peter* op. cit.

89   Cf. Tertullian, "Scorpiace," *Ante-Nicene Fathers Vol. 2* op. cit. pg. 648

90 Cf. David Criswell, *Controversies in the Gospels* Fortress Adonai Press (Dallas, TX) 2012

91 Cf. Sutonius, *Lives of the Twelve Caesars* VI Rains (Great Britain) 1957 pp. 198-207

92 Cf. Sutonius, op. cit. & Tacitus, op. cit.

93 Philip Schaff, *History of the Christian Church* Vol. 1 Hendrickson Publishers (Peabody, Mass.) 1996 ed. pg. 417

94 Ruffin, op. cit. pg. 72

95 Ibid. pg. 76

96 Ussher, op. cit. pg. 843

97 John Foxe, *Acts and Monuments of the Church* Vol. 1 Religious Tract Society (London, England) 1853 reprint pg. 95

98 Unger, op. cit. pg. 25

99 Clement of Alexandria, "Hypotyposes," *Ante-Nicene Fathers Vol. 2* op. cit. pg. 579

100 Some have tried to dispute this, but the facts are overwhelming. For additional discussion see my *Controversies in Acts and the Epistles* and *Controversies in Revelation*.

101 Irenaeus, "Against Heresies," 3:4, *Ante-Nicene Fathers Vol. 1* op. cit. pg. 416

102 Tertullian, "On Prescription Against Heretics," *Ante-Nicene Fathers Vol. 2* op. cit. pg. 260

103 Hippolytus, "On the Twelve Apostles," *Ante-Nicene Fathers Vol. 8* op. cit. pp. 254-256

104 "The Teachings of the Apostles," *Ante-Nicene Fathers Vol. 8* op. cit. pg. 670

105 Ibid. pg. 671

106 Clement of Alexandria, "Who is the Rich Man?" *Ante-Nicene Fathers Vol. 2* op. cit. pp. 603-604

107 Eusebius, 3.1 op. cit. pg. 93

108 Eusebius, 3.18 op. cit. pg. 93

109 "Acts of the Holy Apostle and Evangelist John the Theologian," *Ante-Nicene Fathers Vol. 8* op. cit. pg. 560-564

110 "The Acts of Philip," *Ante-Nicene Fathers Vol. 8* op. cit. pg. 497-503

111 "Book of John Concerning the Falling Asleep of Mary," *Ante-Nicene Fathers Vol. 8* op. cit. pg. 587-591

112 John Foxe, *Foxe's Book of Martyrs* Clarion Classics (Grand Rapids, Mich.) 1926 (abridged ed.) pg. 5

113 Ruffin, op. cit. pg. 94

114 Ibid.

115 See David Criswell, *Controversies in Revelation* Fortress Adonai (Dallas, TX) 2012 for a full debate.

116 Ruffin, op. cit. pg. 94

117 Tertullian, "On Prescription Against Heretics," *Ante-Nicene Fathers Vol. 2* op. cit. pg. 260

118 Clement of Alexandria, "Who is the Rich Man?" *Ante-Nicene Fathers Vol. 2* op. cit. pp. 603-604

119 Irenaeus, "Against Heresies," 3:4, *Ante-Nicene Fathers Vol. 1* op. cit. pg. 416

120 "Acts of the Holy Apostle and Evangelist John the Theologian," *Ante-Nicene Fathers Vol. 8* op. cit. pg. 560-564

121 Tertullian, "On Prescription Against Heretics," *Ante-Nicene Fathers Vol. 2* op. cit. pg. 260

122 "Acts of the Holy Apostle and Evangelist John the Theologian," *Ante-Nicene Fathers Vol. 8* op. cit. pg. 560-564

123 Hippolytus, "On the Twelve Apostles," *Ante-Nicene Fathers Vol. 8* op. cit. pp. 254-256

124 Augustine, *Ancient Christian Commentary on Scripture New Testament IV B John 11-21* John Elowsky, ed., InterVarsity Press (Downers Grove, Ill.) 2006 pg. 395

125 Tertullian, *Ancient Christian Commentary Vol. IV B* Ibid. pg. 395

126 Theodore of Mapsuestia, *Ancient Christian Commentary Vol. IV B* Ibid. pg. 395

127 John Foxe, *Foxe's Book of Martyrs* Clarion Classics (Grand Rapids, Mich.) 1926 (abridged ed.) pg. 5

128 Van Braght, op. cit. pg. 88

129 Eusebius, *Church History* 3.1 op. cit. pg. 93

130 Ruffin, op. cit. pg. 67

131 Coxe, *Ante-Nicene Fathers Vol. 8* op. cit. pg. 356

132 "The Acts and Martyrdom of the Apostle Andrew," *Ante-Nicene Fathers Vol. 8* op. cit. pp. 511-516

133 Ibid.

134 Ibid.

135 Hippolytus, "On the Twelve Apostles," *Ante-Nicene Fathers Vol. 8* op. cit. pp. 254-256

136 Gregory Woolfenden, *Daily Liturgical Prayer* Ashgate Publishing (Surrey, United Kingdom) 2004 pg. 2

137 "The Teachings of the Apostles," *Ante-Nicene Fathers Vol. 8* op. cit. pg. 671

138 Ibid.

139 Coxe, *Ante-Nicene Fathers Vol. 8* op. cit. pg. 356

140 Coxe, notes on "The Acts of Andrew and Matthias," *Ante-Nicene Fathers Vol. 8* op. cit. pp. 517

141 "The Acts of Andrew and Matthias," *Ante-Nicene Fathers Vol. 8* op. cit. pp. 517-525

142 Ruffin, op. cit. pg. 70

143 Ibid. pg. 67

144 Ibid. pg. 68

145 Van Braght, op. cit. pg. 88

146 Unger, *Bible Dictionary* op. cit. pg. 52

147 "The Acts and Martyrdom of the Apostle Andrew," *Ante-Nicene Fathers Vol. 8* op. cit. pg. 516

148 Van Braght, op. cit. pg. 88

149 Unger, *Bible Dictionary* op. cit. pg. 52

150 David Criswell, *Controversies in the Gospels* Fortress Adonai (Dallas, TX) 2012 pg. 115

151 Ruffin, op. cit. pg. 69

152 Van Braght, op. cit. pg. 88

153 Foxe, *Acts and Monuments Vol. I* op. cit. pg. 96
154 Ibid. pg. 97
155 Ibid.
156 Van Braght, op. cit. pg. 105
157 Ruffin, op. cit. pg. 103
158 Cf. Ibid. pp. 103-104
159 Ibid. pg. 104
160 Van Braght, op. cit. pg. 105
161 Papias, quoted by Eusebius, *The Church History*, 3.39 op. cit. pg. 127
162 Polycrates, quoted by Eusebius, *The Church History*, 3.31 op. cit. pg. 119
163 Clement of Alexandria, "Miscellanies," 3.6.52 *Ante-Nicene Fathers Vol. 2* op. cit. pg. 390
164 Hippolytus, "On the Twelve Apostles," *Ante-Nicene Fathers Vol. 8* op. cit. pp. 254-256
165 Gaius, quoted by Eusebius, *The Church History*, 3.31 op. cit. pg. 120
166 Ruffin, op. cit. pg. 109
167 "The Acts of Philip," *Ante-Nicene Fathers Vol. 8* op. cit. pg. 497
168 Ibid.
169 Ibid
170 Ibid. pg. 497-503
171 Ibid.
172 Ibid.
173 Ibid.
174 "The Acts of Saint Philip the Apostle When He Went to Upper Hellas" *Ante-Nicene Fathers Vol. 8* op. cit. pg. 497-503
175 "The History of Philip," *Apocryphal Acts of the Apostles Vol. 1*, J. B. Lightfoot, D.D, trans. Williams & Norgate (London, England) 1871
176 Ruffin, op. cit. pp. 104-105
177 http://www.thebereancall.org/content/who-was-philip-evangelist
178 Polycrates, quoted by Eusebius, *The Church History*, 3.31 op. cit. pg. 119
179 Clement of Alexandria, "Miscellanies," 3.6.52 *Ante-Nicene Fathers Vol. 2* op. cit. pg. 390
180 Foxe, *Acts and Monuments Vol. I* op. cit. pg. 97
181 Ruffin, op. cit. pg. 110
182 "The Acts of Philip," *Ante-Nicene Fathers Vol. 8* op. cit. pg. 497
183 Van Braght, op. cit. pg. 74
184 Ruffin, op. cit. pg. 109
185 Van Braght, op. cit. pg. 74
186 "The Acts of Philip," *Ante-Nicene Fathers Vol. 8* op. cit. pg. 497-503
187 Papias, quoted by Eusebius, *The Church History*, 3.39 op. cit. pg. 127
188 "The Acts of Saint Philip the Apostle When He Went to Upper Hellas" *Ante-Nicene Fathers Vol. 8* op. cit. pg. 497-503
189 Van Braght, op. cit. pg. 74
190 "The History of Philip," *Apocryphal Acts of the Apostles Vol. 1*, J. B. Lightfoot, D.D, trans. Williams & Norgate (London, England) 1871
191 Foxe, *Acts and Monuments Vol. I* op. cit. pg. 97
192 Hippolytus, "On the Twelve Apostles," *Ante-Nicene Fathers Vol. 8* op. cit. pp. 254-256
193 Eusebius, *The Church History*, 1.13 op. cit. pg. 49

194 Eusebius, *The Church History*, 5.10 op. cit. pg. 185

195 Hippolytus, "On the Twelve Apostles," *Ante-Nicene Fathers Vol. 8* op. cit. pp. 254-256

196 Gregory Woolfenden, *Daily Liturgical Prayer* Ashgate Publishing (Surrey, United Kingdom) 2004 pg. 2

197 "The Teachings of the Apostles," *Ante-Nicene Fathers Vol. 8* op. cit. pg. 671

198 Eusebius, *The Church History*, 3.1 op. cit. pg. 93

199 Eusebius, *The Church History*, 1.13 Ibid. pg. 48

200 Eusebius, *The Church History*, 1.13 Ibid. pg. 48

201 "Acts of the Holy Apostle Thomas," *Ante-Nicene Fathers Vol. 8* op. cit. pp. 535-549

202 Ibid.

203 "Consummation of Thomas the Apostle," *Ante-Nicene Fathers Vol. 8* op. cit. pp. 550-552

204 Ibid.

205 Ruffin, op. cit. pg. 134 There is considerable debate as to whether or not Jerome truly wrote the martyrology, but the debate is irrelevant, for the martyrology carries ancient traditions with it, which all that concerns us.

206 Van Braght, op. cit. pg. 90

207 Foxe, *Acts and Monuments Vol. I* op. cit. pg. 95

208 Van Braght, op. cit. pg. 90

209 J.M. Farquhar & G. Garitte, *The Apostle Thomas in India* Syrian Church Series (Kerala, India) 1972 pg. iv

210 Van Braght, op. cit. pg. 90

211 Foxe, *Acts and Monuments Vol. I* op. cit. pg. 95

212 Ruffin, op. cit. pg. 125

213 Ibid. pg. 130

214 Ibid. pg. 125

215 Paul Meier, *Eusebius, The Church History*, op. cit. pg. 50 See also my *Controversies in the Gospels* for evidence on the 33 A.D. crucifixion date.

216 Hippolytus, "On the Twelve Apostles," *Ante-Nicene Fathers Vol. 8* op. cit. pp. 254-256

217 This has variously been called Margia, Magia, and Magi. It is logical that Magia referred to the land of the Magi, which was Persia. Later readings have Margia, which is a deviant spelling of Magia.

218 Ruffin, op. cit. pg. 128

219 Ibid. pg. 129

220 John E. Hill, *Through the Jade Gate to Rome* BookSurge (Charleston, SC) 2009 pg. 29

221 Ruffin, op. cit. pg. 125

222 Ibid. pg. 129

223 Ibid.

224 Metropolitan, *The Mar Thoma Church : Heritage and Mission* op. cit. pg. 11

225 Ibid.

226 Ibid. pp. 12-13

227 Lueker, *Lutheran Cyclopedia* op. cit. pg. 406

228 Once again see my *Controversies in the Gospels* for evidence that Matthew was indeed the first gospel written, and that it was written before 49 A.D. when Thomas would have embarked on his journey.

229 Foxe, *Acts and Monuments Vol. I* op. cit. pg. 95

230 Ruffin, op. cit. pg. 131

231 Metropolitan, *The Mar Thoma Church : Heritage and Mission* op. cit. pg. 13

232 Van Braght, op. cit. pg. 90

233 See my forthcoming *Controversies in the Acts and Epistles* for a chronology of the books of Acts.

234 Ruffin, op. cit. pg. 130

235 Van Braght, op. cit. pg. 90

236 Assuming that Jerome truly wrote the martyrology to which his name is attached. Nevertheless, the martyrology is of importance because of its ancient traditions.

237 Ruffin, op. cit. pp. 133-134

238 "Consummation of Thomas the Apostle," *Ante-Nicene Fathers Vol. 8* op. cit. pp. 550-552

239 J.M. Farquhar & G. Garitte, *The Apostle Thomas in India* Syrian Church Series (Kerala, India) 1972 pg. iv

240 Mario Bussagli, *The Art of Gandhara* Livre de Poche (France) 1996 pg. 255

241 Metropolitan, *The Mar Thoma Church : Heritage and Mission* op. cit. pg. 13

242 Ruffin, op. cit. pg. 114-115

243 "Martyrdom of the Holy and Glorious Apostle Bartholomew," *Ante-Nicene Fathers Vol. 8* op. cit. pg. 553

244 Ibid. pp. 553-557

245 Ibid.

246 Ibid.

247 Hippolytus, "On the Twelve Apostles," *Ante-Nicene Fathers Vol. 5* op. cit. pp. 254-256

248 Eusebius, *Church History* 5.10 op. cit. pg. 185

249 Ruffin, op. cit. pg. 115

250 Ibid.

251 A.C. Perumalil, *The Apostles in India* St. Paul Press (Bangalore, India) 1952 pp. 11ff

252 "The Acts of Philip," *Ante-Nicene Fathers Vol. 8* op. cit. pg. 497

253 Ibid.

254 Ibid. pg. 497-503

255 Ibid.

256 Ibid.

257 Foxe, *Acts and Monuments Vol. I* op. cit. pg. 96

258 Van Braght, op. cit. pg. 88

259 http://www.rapidresponsereport.com/briefingpapers/APOSTLES.pdf

260 "The Acts of Philip," *Ante-Nicene Fathers Vol. 8* op. cit. pg. 497-503

261 Hippolytus, "On the Twelve Apostles," *Ante-Nicene Fathers Vol. 8* op. cit. pp. 254-256

262 Van Braght, op. cit. pg. 88

263 Ruffin, op. cit. pg. 119

264 Van Braght, op. cit. pg. 88

265 John Hananian, "The Armenian Apostolic Church in Iran," Lecture at Consolata Church, Teheran, 1969 as cited on Armenian Church website.

266 Van Braght, op. cit. pg. 88

267 Perumalil, *The Apostles in India* op. cit. pp. 11ff

268 Ruffin, op. cit. pg. 116

269 Hananian, op. cit.

270 Eusebius, *The Church History*, 5.10 op. cit. pg. 185

271 Perumalil, *The Apostles in India* op. cit.. 11ff

272 Ibid.

273 Ruffin, op. cit. pg. 116

274 "Martyrdom of the Holy and Glorious Apostle Bartholomew," *Ante-Nicene Fathers Vol. 8* op. cit. pg. 553

275 Ruffin, op. cit. pg. 116

276 Foxe, *Acts and Monuments Vol. I* op. cit. pg. 96

277 Perumalil, *The Apostles in India* op. cit. pp. 11ff

278 Ibid.

279 Ibid.

280 Ibid.

281 Ibid.

282 Ibid.

283 http://en.wikipedia.org/wiki/Satavahana

284 http://www.ibiblio.org/britishraj/Jackson2/appendix04.html

285 Perumalil, *The Apostles in India* op. cit. pp. 11ff

286 Ruffin, op. cit. pg. 119

287 Van Braght, op. cit. pg. 88

288 Frederick Zubige, M.D., *The Cross and the Shroud* Paragon House (New York, NY) 1988 pg. 14

289 Eusebius, *The Church History*, 5.10 op. cit. pg. 185

290 For a defense of this thesis see my *Controversies in the Gospels*.

291 Merrill Tenney, *New Testament Survey* W. B. Eerdmans (Grand Rapids, Mich.) 1985 pg. 149

292 Louis Barbieri, "Matthew," *The Bible Knowledge Commentary : New Testament* John F. Walvoord & Roy Zuck, eds., Victor Books (Wheaton, Ill.) 1986 pg. 15

293 Hippolytus, "On the Twelve Apostles," *Ante-Nicene Fathers Vol. 8* op. cit. pp. 254-256

294 C.I. Scofield, *First Scofield Reference Bible* A.C. Gaebelein (New York, NY) 1917

295 Merill Unger, *Unger's Bible Dictionary* Moody Press (Chicago, Ill.) 1957 pg. 706

296 Hippolytus, "On the Twelve Apostles," *Ante-Nicene Fathers Vol. 8* op. cit. pp. 254-256

297 E.g. Ruffin, op. cit. pg. 140

298 Clement of Alexandria, "Stromata," iv.9, *Ante-Nicene Fathers Vol. 2* op. cit. pg. 422

299 The *Acts of Abdias*, as cited by Ruffin, op. cit. pg. 141

300 http://www.friktech.com/rel/canon/acts.htm

301 "The Acts and Martyrdom of St. Matthew the Apostle," *Ante-Nicene Fathers Vol. 8* op. cit. pp. 528-534

302 Van Braght, op. cit. pg. 91

303 Ibid.

304 Foxe, *Foxe's Book of Martyrs* op. cit. pg. 3

305 Ruffin, op. cit. pg. 140

306 "The Acts and Martyrdom of St. Matthew the Apostle," *Ante-Nicene Fathers Vol. 8* op. cit. pp. 528-534

307 Hippolytus, "On the Twelve Apostles," *Ante-Nicene Fathers Vol. 8* op. cit. pp. 254-256

308 Clement of Alexandria, "Stromata," iv.9, *Ante-Nicene Fathers Vol. 2* op. cit. pg. 422

309 Coxe, *Ante-Nicene Fathers Vol. 8* op. cit. pg. 356

310 Tenney, op. cit. pg. 150

311 David Criswell, *Controversies in the Scriptures Vol. II* Fortress Adonai (Dallas, TX) 2010 pp. 140-142

312 The *Acts of Abdias*, as cited by Ruffin, op. cit. pg. 141

313 "The Acts and Martyrdom of St. Matthew the Apostle," *Ante-Nicene Fathers Vol. 8* op. cit. pp. 528-534

314 Van Braght, op. cit. pg. 91

315 Foxe, *Foxe's Book of Martyrs* op. cit. pg. 3

316 Ibid.

317 Criswell, *Controversies in the Gospels*, op. cit. pp. 8-9

318 The *Acts of Abdias*, as cited by Ruffin, op. cit. pg. 141

319 Van Braght, op. cit. pg. 91

320 Cf. Unger, op. cit. pp. 552-553

321 Philip Schaff, ed., *Nicene and Post-Nicene Fathers Second Series Vol. VI* Charles Scribner (New York, NY) 1892 pg. 337

322 Ruffin, op. cit. pg. 80

323 Foxe, *Foxe's Book of Martyrs* op. cit. pg. 3

324 I discuss the genealogies of Jesus in Controversies in the Gospels to a large degree. I will merely summarize my conclusion here that one of the two genealogies appears to be that of Joseph, and no Alphæus appears in either genealogy.

325 John Gill, "Commentary on the New Testament," John 19:25 E-Sword Software Commentary Series

326 Ibid.

327 Ruffin, op. cit. pg. 79

328 Josephus, "Antiquities of the Jews," 20.9.1, *The Complete Works of Josephus* Kregel Publishers (Grand Rapids, Mich) 1981 pg. 423

329 Hegesippus, "Memoirs," *Eusebius The Church History*, 2:23 op. cit. pp. 81-82

330 Hippolytus, "On the Twelve Apostles," *Ante-Nicene Fathers Vol. 8* op. cit. pp. 254-256

331 Ibid.

332 Clement of Alexandria, "Hypotyposes," *Ante-Nicene Fathers Vol. 2* op. cit. pg. 579

333 Ibid.

334 "The Teachings of the Apostles," *Ante-Nicene Fathers* *Vol. 8* op. cit. pg. 671

335 Ibid. pg. 670

336 The Apostolic Constitutions 5.viii, *Ante-Nicene Fathers* *Vol. 7* op. cit. pg. 442

337 Van Braght, op. cit. pg. 75

338 Ruffin, op. cit. pg. 149

339 Unger, op. cit. pg. 1086

340 D.A. Carson, "Matthew," *The Expositor's Bible Commentary* *Vol. 8* Frank Gaebelain, ed. Zondervan Publishers (Grand Rapids, Mich.) 1984 pg. 239

341 Joseph Thayer, *Thayer's Greek-English Lexicon* Baker Book House (Grand Rapids, Mich.) 1977 pg. 282

342 Unger, op. cit. pg. 1086

343 "The Teachings of the Apostles," *Ante-Nicene Fathers* *Vol. 8* op. cit. pg. 671

344 Hippolytus, "On the Twelve Apostles," *Ante-Nicene Fathers* *Vol. 8* op. cit. pp. 254-256

345 Ibid.

346 Eusebius, *The Church History*, 1.13 op. cit. pg. 48

347 "Concerning the King of Edessa," *Ante-Nicene Fathers* *Vol. 8* op. cit. pp. 651-653

348 Ibid.

349 "Acts of Abdias," as cited by Ruffin, op. cit. pp. 155-156

350 "The Acts of the Holy Apostle Thaddæus," *Ante-Nicene Fathers* *Vol. 8* op. cit. pp. 558-559

351 "The Acts of the Holy Apostle Thaddæus," *Ante-Nicene Fathers* *Vol. 8* op. cit. pp. 558-559

352 "Teaching of Addæus the Apostle," *Ante-Nicene Fathers* *Vol. 8* op. cit. pp. 657-665

353 "Extracts concerning Abgar the king and Addæus the Apostle," *Ante-Nicene Fathers* *Vol. 8* op. cit. pp. 655-656

354 Dorotheus, as cited by Foxe, *Acts and Monuments* *Vol. I* op. cit. pg. 95

355 Van Braght, op. cit. pg. 91

356 Richard Young, *Intermediate New Testament Greek* Broadman & Holdman Publishers (Nashville, TN) 1994 pp. 25-26

357 Or seventy-two, "The Teachings of the Apostles," *Ante-Nicene Fathers* *Vol. 8* op. cit. pg. 671

358 Hippolytus, "On the Twelve Apostles," *Ante-Nicene Fathers* *Vol. 8* op. cit. pp. 254-256

359 "Concerning the King of Edessa," *Ante-Nicene Fathers* *Vol. 8* op. cit. pg. 653

360 Coxe, "Concerning the King of Edessa," *Ante-Nicene Fathers* *Vol. 8* op. cit. pg. 653

361 Ibid.

362 Eusebius, *The Church History*, 2.1 op. cit. pp. 58-59

363 Hippolytus, "On the Twelve Apostles," *Ante-Nicene Fathers* *Vol. 8* op. cit. pp. 254-256

364 "Teaching of Addæus the Apostle," *Ante-Nicene Fathers* *Vol. 8* op. cit. pp. 657-665

365   This is the date commemorated in the Nestorian churches of the east.
http://www.syriac.talktalk.net/chron_tab1.html
366   Dorotheus, as cited by Foxe, *Acts and Monuments Vol. I* op. cit. pg. 95
367   "Teaching of Addæus the Apostle," *Ante-Nicene Fathers Vol. 8* op. cit.
pp. 657-665
368   http://www.nestorian.org/kings_of_edessa.html
369   "Teaching of Addæus the Apostle," *Ante-Nicene Fathers Vol. 8* op. cit.
pp. 657-665
370   "The Acts of the Holy Apostle Thaddæus," *Ante-Nicene Fathers Vol. 8* op.
cit. pp. 558-559
371   Van Braght, op. cit. pp. 91-92
372   History records that the Parthians of this time viewed Christianity as a
"western" or "foreign" religion at odds with they religions. This is indicated in
"Teaching of Addæus the Apostle."
373   Foxe, *Acts and Monuments Vol. I* op. cit. pg. 95
374   Hippolytus, "On the Twelve Apostles," *Ante-Nicene Fathers Vol. 8* op. cit.
pp. 254-256
375   Dorotheus, as cited by *Acts and Monuments Vol. I* op. cit. pg. 97 Cf.
Foxe, *Foxe's Book of Martyrs* op. cit. pg. 5
376   Eusebius, 3:32 op. cit. pg. 121
377   "Acts of Abdias," as cited by Ruffin, op. cit. pp. 155-156
378   Ruffin, op. cit. pg. 146
379   Isidore of Seville, as cited by Van Braght, op. cit. pg. 91
380   Van Braght, op. cit. pg. 91
381   Ibid.
382   Ibid.
383   Nicephorus of Constantinople, as cited by Van Braght, op. cit. pg. 91
384   Ruffin, op. cit. pg. 146
385   Ibid. pg. 145
386   G. H. R. Horsley, *New Documents Illustrating Early Christianity: a Review
of the Greek Inscriptions and Papyri* William B. Eerdmans (Grand Rapids,
Mich.) 1987 pg. 138
387   Dorotheus, as cited by *Acts and Monuments Vol. I* op. cit. pg. 97 Cf.
Foxe, *Foxe's Book of Martyrs* op. cit pg. 5
388   Ruffin, op. cit. pg. 148
389   Hegesippus, as cited by Eusebius, 3:32 op. cit. pg. 121
390   Kenneth Morgan, ed., *Oxford Illustrated History of Britain* Oxford
University Press (Oxford, England) 1984 pg. 19
391   Hippolytus, "On the Twelve Apostles," *Ante-Nicene Fathers Vol. 8* op. cit.
pp. 254-256
392   Eusebius, 4.5, op. cit. pg. 137
393   Ibid.
394   Cited in Van Braght, op. cit. pp. 92-93
395   Coxe, notes on "The Acts of Andrew and Matthias," *Ante-Nicene Fathers
Vol. 8* op. cit. pp. 517
396   "The Acts of Andrew and Matthias," *Ante-Nicene Fathers Vol. 8* op. cit.
pp. 517-525
397   http://www.friktech.com/rel/canon/acts.htm

398 "The Acts and Martyrdom of St. Matthew the Apostle," *Ante-Nicene Fathers Vol. 8* op. cit. pp. 528-534

399 Van Braght, op. cit. pp. 92-93

400 Foxe, *Acts and Monuments Vol. I* op. cit. pg. 97

401 McBirnie as cited by Ruffin, op. cit. pg. 184

402 Van Braght, op. cit. pg. 93

403 Eusebius, 4.5, op. cit. pg. 137

404 David Wenham, "Appendix," *A Theology of the New Testament* George Eldon Ladd, William B. Eedrmans (Grand Rapids, Mich.) 1974 pg. 704

405 Chaim Potok, *Wanderings* Fawcett Publishers (New York, NY) 1978 pg. 297

406 Cf. Wenham, op. cit.

407 1 Clement 5:5-6, Clement of Rome, *The Apostolic Fathers*, J.B. Lightfoot & J.R. Harmer, eds., Baker Books (Grand Rapids, Mich.) 1984 pg. 59

408 Irenaeus, "Against Heresies," 3:4, *Ante-Nicene Fathers Vol. 1* op. cit. pg. 416

409 Irenaeus, "Against Heresies," 3:2, Ibid. pg. 415

410 Dionysius of Corinth, "Letter to the Roman Church," III, *Ante-Nicene Fathers Vol. 8* op. cit. pg. 765

411 Tertullian, "Scorpiace," *Ante-Nicene Fathers Vol. 2* op. cit. pg. 648

412 Tertullian, "On Prescription Against Heretics," *Ante-Nicene Fathers Vol. 2* op. cit. pg. 260

413 Hippolytus, "On the Twelve Apostles," *Ante-Nicene Fathers Vol. 8* op. cit. pp. 254-256

414 Eusebius, 2.22, op. cit. pg. 80

415 Eusebius, 2.25, op. cit. pg. 85

416 *The Acts of Peter*, op. cit.

417 The Acts of the Holy Apostles Peter and Paul, *Ante-Nicene Fathers Vol. 8* op. cit. pp. 477-486

418 *Pseudo-Abdias*, as cited by Foxe, op. cit. pg. 103

419 Ibid. pg. 104

420 Foxe, op. cit. pg. 104

421 Richard Longenecker, "Acts of the Apostles," *The Expositor's Bible Commentary Vol. 9* Frank Gaebelain, ed. Zondervan Publishers (Grand Rapids, Mich.) 1984 pg. 572

422 H.H. Scullard, *From the Gracchi to Nero* Routledge (New York, NY) 1959 pg. 304

423 Ibid. pp. 306-307

424 Cf. Unger, op. cit. pg. 837

425 Scullard, op. cit. pg. 352

426 Marta Sordi, *The Christian and the Roman Empire* University of Oklohama (Oklahoma City, OK) 1986 pg. 31

427 Cf. Suetonius, op. cit.

428 Sorti, op. cit. pg. 29

429 Cf. *Acts of Peter*, op. cit. & Sorti, op. cit. pg. 27

430 1 Clement 5:5-6, Clement of Rome, *The Apostolic Fathers* op. cit. pg. 59

431 Hippolytus, "On the Twelve Apostles," *Ante-Nicene Fathers Vol. 8* op. cit. pp. 254-256

432 Unger, op. cit. pg.

433 "The Acts of the Holy Apostles Peter and Paul," *Ante-Nicene Fathers Vol. 8* op. cit. pp. 477-486

434 Unger, op. cit. pp. 837-838

435 See Sorti, op. cit. pg. 34 on summary trials and executions.

436 This silly argument does not even make sense. There was no such thing as an edict restricted to a specific city, or Christians would merely have left Rome and been safe.

437 Cornelius Tacitus, *The Annals: The Reigns of Tiberius, Claudius, and Nero* XV.44 Oxford University (Oxford, England) 2008

438 1 Clement 5:5, Clement of Rome, *The Apostolic Fathers* op. cit. pg. 59

439 Dionysius of Corinth, "Letter to the Roman Church," III, *Ante-Nicene Fathers Vol. 8* op. cit. pg. 765

440 Foxe, op. cit. pg. 104

441 *Pseudo-Abdias*, as cited by Foxe, op. cit. pg. 103

442 Foxe, op. cit. pg. 104

443 Hippolytus, "On the Twelve Apostles," *Ante-Nicene Fathers Vol. 8* op. cit. pp. 254-256

444 Note that the dates of Nero's reign have sometimes been erroneously misdated. It is not uncommon to hear ancient historians placing Nero's death in 70 A.D., so we cannot assume that Hippolytus's 35 year ministry proves anything in regard to an exact chronology to Nero's reign.

445 Foxe, op. cit. pg. 104

446 *Pseudo-Abdias*, as cited by Foxe, op. cit. pg. 103

447 Foxe, op. cit. pg. 104

448 Ussher, op. cit. pg. 872

449 Foxe, op. cit. pg. 104

450 Dionysius of Corinth, "Letter to the Roman Church," III, *Ante-Nicene Fathers Vol. 8* op. cit. pg. 765

451 Ibid.

452 Ussher, op. cit. pg. 872

453 Suetonius, *Lives of the Twelve Caesars* VI.28 Rains Publishers (New York, NY) 1957 pg. 195

454 Suetonius, VI.31 op. cit. pg. 197

455 Cf. Notes on Clement of Rome.

456 1 Clement 5:5, Clement of Rome, *The Apostolic Fathers* op. cit. pg. 59

457 Hippolytus, "On the Twelve Apostles," *Ante-Nicene Fathers Vol. 8* op. cit. pp. 254-256

458 Ibid.

459 Van Braght, op. cit. pg. 86

460 Hippolytus, "On the Twelve Apostles," *Ante-Nicene Fathers Vol. 8* op. cit. pp. 254-256

461 The Apostolic Constitutions 6.viii, *Ante-Nicene Fathers Vol. 7* op. cit. pg. 453

462 "Regonitions of Clement," *Ante-Nicene Fathers Vol. 7* op. cit. pg. 98, also see "The Clementine Homilies," op. cit. pp. 232, 300-302

463 "Regonitions of Clement," *Ante-Nicene Fathers Vol. 7* op. cit. pp. 157, 162-163, 176-182, 190-191,

464 "The Teachings of the Apostles," *Ante-Nicene Fathers Vol. 8* op. cit. pg. 671

465 Van Braght, op. cit. pg. 86
466 Ibid.
467 Ibid. pg. 85
468 Hippolytus, "On the Twelve Apostles," *Ante-Nicene Fathers Vol. 8* op. cit. pp. 254-256
469 Van Braght, op. cit. pg. 85
470 "Regonitions of Clement," *Ante-Nicene Fathers Vol. 7* op. cit. pp. 78-80
471 Clement of Alexandria, "Hypotyposes," *Ante-Nicene Fathers Vol. 2* op. cit. pg. 579
472 It claims that Mark was baptized by Paul at Iconium, but John appears to have already been a convert in Acts 12:12, and Paul took Mark with him in 12:25. Would Mark really never have been baptized until Acts 14 when they arrived at Iconium?
473 "The Acts of Barnabas," *Ante-Nicene Fathers Vol. 8* op. cit. pg. 493-486
474 Ibid.
475 Van Braght, op. cit. pg. 76
476 Foxe, *Foxe's Book of Martyrs* op. cit. pg. 5
477 Cf. Merrill Tenney, *New Testament Survey* W. B. Eerdmans (Grand Rapids, Mich.) 1985
478 Clement of Alexandria, "Hypotyposes," *Ante-Nicene Fathers Vol. 2* op. cit. pg. 579
479 Cf. Clement of Alexandria, cited by Eusebius, 2.1 op. cit. pg. 58; Van Braght, op. cit. pg. 75
480 Ibid.
481 Hippolytus, "On the Twelve Apostles," *Ante-Nicene Fathers Vol. 8* op. cit. pp. 254-256
482 Eusebius, 4.5, op. cit. pg. 137
483 Papias, "Fragments of Papias," *Ante-Nicene Fathers Vol. 1* op. cit. pg. 154
484 Van Braght, op. cit. pg. 94
485 Hippolytus, "On the Twelve Apostles," *Ante-Nicene Fathers Vol. 8* op. cit. pp. 254-256
486 Van Braght, op. cit. pg. 94
487 Ibid.
488 Hippolytus, "On the Twelve Apostles," *Ante-Nicene Fathers Vol. 8* op. cit. pp. 254-256
489 Van Braght, op. cit. pg. 107
490 Ibid. pg. 86
491 Coxe, *Ante-Nicene Fathers Vol. 1* op. cit. pg. 45
492 Eusebius, 3.36 op. cit. pg. 123
493 Ignatius, *The Apostolic Fathers* Baker Books (Grand Rapids, Mich.) 1984 pp. 137-162
494 Ibid.
495 Van Braght, op. cit. pg. 107
496 See my *Controversies in the Acts and Epistles* and *Controversies in the Old Testament Vol. II* for more on this tradition.
497 Ussher, op. cit. pg. 327
498 Van Braght, op. cit. pg. 105
499 Ibid.

500 Papias, "Fragments of Papias," *Ante-Nicene Fathers Vol. 1* op. cit. pp. 154-155

501 Clement of Alexandria, "Hypotyposes," *Ante-Nicene Fathers Vol. 2* op. cit. pp. 579-580

502 "The Acts of Barnabas," *Ante-Nicene Fathers Vol. 8* op. cit. pg. 493-486

503 "The Teachings of the Apostles," *Ante-Nicene Fathers Vol. 8* op. cit. pg. 670

504 Ibid. pg. 671 (Note that India here is conflated with Ethiopia due to the fact that Ethiopia was called "Cush" in antiquity whereas India was bordered by the Hindu-Kush mountains and part of India was occupied by the Kushans after 55 A.D.)

505 "The Acts of Barnabas," *Ante-Nicene Fathers Vol. 8* op. cit. pg. 493-486

506 Nicephorus of Constantinople, as cited by Van Braght, op. cit. pg. 77

507 Hippolytus, "On the Twelve Apostles," *Ante-Nicene Fathers Vol. 8* op. cit. pp. 254-256

508 Van Braght, op. cit. pg. 78

509 The *Babylon Namebook*, as cited by Van Braght, op. cit. pg. 78

510 Dorotheus, as cited by Foxe, *Acts and Monuments* op. cit. pg. 95

511 Eusebius, 4.11 op. cit. pg. 143

512 Ibid.

513 Van Braght, op. cit. pg. 78

514 Eusebius, 4.11 op. cit. pg. 143 (Note that Eumenes actually means "Good Menes." Menes is held to be the name of the first king of Egypt, thus this bishop was probably a native of Egypt).

515 Tenney, op. cit. pg. 370

516 Eusebius, 4.5, op. cit. pg. 137

517 Eusebius, 3:32 op. cit. pg. 121

518 Hippolytus, "On the Twelve Apostles," *Ante-Nicene Fathers Vol. 8* op. cit. pp. 254-256

519 "Teaching of Addæus the Apostle," *Ante-Nicene Fathers Vol. 8* op. cit. pp. 657-665

520 Irenaeus, "Against Heresies," 3:3, *Ante-Nicene Fathers Vol. 1* op. cit. pg. 416

521 Hegesippus, as cited in J.N.D. Kelly, *The Oxford Dictionary of Popes* Oxford University Press (Oxford, England) 1986 pg. 6

522 Ignatius, "Epistle to the Trallians," *Ante-Nicene Fathers Vol. 1* op. cit. pg. 69 Also cf. Ignatius, "Epistle to Mary at Neapolis," pg. 122

523 Hippolytus, "On the Twelve Apostles," *Ante-Nicene Fathers Vol. 8* op. cit. pp. 254-256

524 *Catalogus Liberianus*, It may be found online at: www.tertullian.org/fathers/chronography_of_354_13_bishops_of_rome.htm

525 J.N.D. Kelly, *The Oxford Dictionary of Popes* Oxford University Press (Oxford, England) 1986 pg. 7

526 The *Babylon Namebook*, as cited by Van Braght, op. cit. pg. 95

527 "The Teachings of the Apostles," *Ante-Nicene Fathers Vol. 8* op. cit. pg. 670

528 Ibid. pg. 671

529 Ibid.

530 The *Babylon Namebook*, as cited by Van Braght, op. cit. pg. 95

531 Dorotheus, as cited by Foxe, *Acts and Monuments* op. cit. pg. 95

532 Hippolytus, "On the Twelve Apostles," *Ante-Nicene Fathers Vol. 8* op. cit. pp. 254-256

533 Ignatius, "Epistle to the Ephesians," *Ante-Nicene Fathers Vol. 1* op. cit. pp. 49-52, 101, 112,

534 Van Braght, op. cit. pg. 107

535 Hippolytus, "On the Twelve Apostles," *Ante-Nicene Fathers Vol. 8* op. cit. pp. 254-256

536 Van Braght, op. cit. pg. 87

537 Hippolytus, "On the Twelve Apostles," *Ante-Nicene Fathers Vol. 8* op. cit. pp. 254-256

538 Dorotheus, as cited by Foxe, *Acts and Monuments* op. cit. pg. 95

539 http://www.thebereancall.org/content/who-was-philip-evangelist

540 Polycrates & Papias, quoted by Eusebius, *The Church History*, 3.31 op. cit. pg. 119 & 3.39 pg. 127

541 Clement of Alexandria, "Miscellanies," 3.6.52 SSS

542 Polycrates, quoted by Eusebius, *The Church History*, 3.31 op. cit. pg. 119

543 Hippolytus, "On the Twelve Apostles," *Ante-Nicene Fathers Vol. 8* op. cit. pp. 254-256

544 "The Acts of Philip," *Ante-Nicene Fathers Vol. 8* op. cit. pg. 497

545 Ibid. pg. 497-503

546 Hippolytus, "On the Twelve Apostles," *Ante-Nicene Fathers Vol. 8* op. cit. pp. 254-256

547 Ibid.

548 Van Braght, op. cit. pg. 93

549 Ibid.

550 Polycarp, "The Epistle of Polycarp," *Ante-Nicene Fathers Vol. 1* op. cit. pg. 35

551 Hippolytus, "On the Twelve Apostles," *Ante-Nicene Fathers Vol. 8* op. cit. pp. 254-256

552 Van Braght, op. cit. pg. 105

553 Hippolytus, "On the Twelve Apostles," *Ante-Nicene Fathers Vol. 8* op. cit. pp. 254-256

554 Ibid.

555 Van Braght, op. cit. pg. 86

556 Although Dorotheus does not conflate Simeon with Simon the Zealot intentionally, he nevertheless appears to conflate traditions accidentally, claiming that he died in Egypt, rather than Jerusalem. This cannot be for Atticus was the procurator of Jerusalem, not Egypt. In all other respects, he is correct. Foxe, *Acts and Monuments Vol. I* op. cit. pg. 95

557 Eusebius, 4.5, op. cit. pg. 137

558 Hegesippus, *Memoirs,* as cited by Eusebius, 3:32 op. cit. pg. 121

559 Van Braght, op. cit. pg. 105

560 "The Acts of Barnabas," *Ante-Nicene Fathers Vol. 8* op. cit. pg. 493-486

561 Hippolytus, "On the Twelve Apostles," *Ante-Nicene Fathers Vol. 8* op. cit. pp. 254-256

562 Dorotheus, as cited by Foxe, *Acts and Monuments* op. cit. pg. 95

563 Interestingly enough Nicholas is alleged to be the founder of the Christian cult called the Nicolaitans (Revelation 2:6, 15) [cf. Hippolytus, Refutation of All

Heresies, VII.xxiv *Ante-Nicene Fathers Vol. 5* op. cit. pg. 115], but this is strictly denied by Clement of Alexandria and other early fathers who insist that the Nicolaitans took his name and perverted his words for their own purposes [Clement of Alexandria, op. cit. pg. 385]. His fate is, therefore, as unknown as his history.

564 Van Braght, op. cit. pg. 98

565 Ibid.

566 Ibid.

567 Hippolytus, "On the Twelve Apostles," *Ante-Nicene Fathers Vol. 8* op. cit. pp. 254-256   Also see Van Braght, op. cit. pg. 94

568 J.N.D. Kelly, *The Oxford Dictionary of Popes* Oxford University Press (Oxford, England) 1986 pg. 7

569 Ibid.

570 *Catalogus Liberianus*, op. cit. In order to adjust for Linus's rule (see notes in Chapter 15 : Linus), it is probable that Clement's episcopate was shortened and moved to a slightly later date. See note 524.

571 Asterius Urbanus, *Ante-Nicene Fathers Vol. 7* op. cit. pg. 337

572 Coxe, *Ante-Nicene Fathers Vol. 8* op. cit. pg. 356

573 James Montgomery Boice, *The Gospel of John Vol. 2* Zondervan Press (Grand Rapids, Mich) 1975 pg. 307

574 B.F Wescott, *The Gospel According to St. John* Wm. B Eerdmans (Grand Rapids, Mich.) 1954 pg. 141

575 Gregory Woolfenden, *Daily Liturgical Prayer* Ashgate Publishing (Surrey, United Kingdom) 2004 pg. 2

576 Coxe, *Ante-Nicene Fathers Vol. 8* op. cit. pg. 356

577 Coxe, notes on "The Acts of Andrew and Matthias," *Ante-Nicene Fathers Vol. 8* op. cit. pp. 517

578 Eusebius, 3.1 op. cit. pg. 93

Made in the USA
Lexington, KY
04 September 2015